T0261023

Deep Learning Cookbook
Practical Recipes to Get Started Quickly

Douwe Osinga

Beijing · Boston · Farnham · Sebastopol · Tokyo

Deep Learning Cookbook

by Douwe Osinga

Published by O'Reilly Media, Inc., 1005 Gravenstein Highway North, Sebastopol, CA 95472.

O'Reilly books may be purchased for educational, business, or sales promotional use. Online editions are also available for most titles (*http://oreilly.com/safari*). For more information, contact our corporate/institutional sales department: 800-998-9938 or *corporate@oreilly.com*.

Editors: Rachel Roumeliotis and Jeff Bleiel	**Indexer:** WordCo Indexing Services, Inc.
Production Editor: Colleen Cole	**Interior Designer:** David Futato
Copyeditor: Rachel Head	**Cover Designer:** Randy Comer
Proofreader: Charles Roumeliotis	**Illustrator:** Rebecca Demarest

June 2018:   First Edition

Revision History for the First Edition

2018-05-23:   First Release

See *http://oreilly.com/catalog/errata.csp?isbn=9781491995846* for release details.

978-1-491-99584-6

[LSI]

Table of Contents

Preface

A Brief History of Deep Learning

The roots of the current deep learning boom go surprisingly far back, to the 1950s. While vague ideas of "intelligent machines" can be found further back in fiction and speculation, the 1950s and '60s saw the introduction of the first "artificial neural networks," based on a dramatically simplified model of biological neurons. Amongst these models, the Perceptron system articulated by Frank Rosenblatt garnered particular interest (and hype). Connected to a simple "camera" circuit, it could learn to distinguish different types of objects. Although the first version ran as software on an IBM computer, subsequent versions were done in pure hardware.

Interest in the multilayer perceptron (MLP) model continued through the '60s. This changed when, in 1969, Marvin Minksy and Seymour Papert published their book *Perceptrons* (MIT Press). The book contained a proof showing that linear perceptrons could not classify the behavior of a nonlinear function (XOR). Despite the limitations of the proof (nonlinear perceptron models existed at the time of the book's publication, and are even noted by the authors), its publication heralded the plummeting of funding for neural network models. Research would not recover until the 1980s, with the rise of a new generation of researchers.

The increase in computing power together with the development of the back-propagation technique (known in various forms since the '60s, but not applied in general until the '80s) prompted a resurgence of interest in neural networks. Not only did computers have the power to train larger networks, but we also had the techniques to train deeper networks efficiently. The first convolutional neural networks combined these insights with a model of visual recognition from mammalian brains, yielding for the first time networks that could efficiently recognize complex images such as handwritten digits and faces. Convolutional networks do this by applying the same "subnetwork" to different locations of the image and aggregating the results of these into higher-level features. In Chapter 12 we look at how this works in more detail.

In the '90s and early 2000s interest in neural networks declined again as more "understandable" models like support vector machines (SVMs) and decision trees became popular. SVMs proved to be excellent classifiers for many data sources of the time, especially when coupled with human-engineered features. In computer vision, "feature engineering" became popular. This involves building feature detectors for small elements in a picture and combining them by hand into something that recognizes more complex forms. It later turned out that deep learning nets learn to recognize very similar features and learn to combine them in a very similar way. In Chapter 12 we explore some of the inner workings of these networks and visualize what they learn.

With the advent of general-purpose programming on graphics processing units (GPUs) in the late 2000s, neural network architectures were able to make great strides over the competition. GPUs contain thousands of small processors that can do trillions of operations per second in parallel. Originally developed for computer gaming, where this is needed to render complex 3D scenes in real time, it turned out that the same hardware can be used to train neural networks in parallel, achieving speed improvements of a factor of 10 or higher.

The other thing that happened was that the internet made very large training sets available. Where researchers had been training classifiers with thousands of images before, now they had access to tens if not hundreds of millions of images. Combined with larger networks, neural networks had their chance to shine. This dominance has only continued in the succeeding years, with improved techniques and applications of neural networks to areas outside of image recognition, including translation, speech recognition, and image synthesis.

Why Now?

While the boom in computational power and better techniques led to an increase in interest in neural networks, we have also seen huge strides in *usability*. In particular, deep learning frameworks like TensorFlow, Theano, and Torch allow nonexperts to construct complex neural networks to solve their own machine learning problems. This has turned a task that used to require months or years of handcoding and head-on-table-banging effort (writing efficient GPU kernels is hard!) into something that anyone can do in an afternoon (or really a few days in practice). Increased usability has greatly increased the number of researchers who can work on deep learning problems. Frameworks like Keras with an even higher level of abstraction make it possible for anyone with a working knowledge of Python and some tools to run some interesting experiments, as this book will show.

A second important factor for "why now" is that large datasets have become available for everybody. Yes, Facebook and Google might still have the upper hand with access to billions of pictures, user comments, and what have you, but datasets with millions of items can be had from a variety of sources. In Chapter 1 we'll look at a variety of options, and throughout the book the example code for each chapter will usually show in the first recipe how to get the needed training data.

At the same time, private companies have started to produce and collect orders of magnitude more data, which has made the whole area of deep learning suddenly commercially very interesting. A model that can tell the difference between a cat and a dog is all very well, but a model that increases sales by 15% by taking all historic sales data into account can be the difference between life and death for a company.

What Do You Need to Know?

These days there is a wide choice of platforms, technologies, and programming languages for deep learning. In this book all the examples are in Python and most of the code relies on the excellent Keras framework. The example code is available on GitHub as a set of Python notebooks, one per chapter. So, having a working knowledge of the following will help:

Python
  Python 3 is preferred, but Python 2.7 should also work. We use a variety of helper libraries that all can easily be installed using pip. The code is generally straightforward so even a relative novice should be able to follow the action.

Keras
  The heavy lifting for machine learning is done almost completely by Keras. Keras is an abstraction over either TensorFlow or Theano, both deep learning frameworks. Keras makes it easy to define neural networks in a very readable way. All code is tested against TensorFlow but should also work with Theano.

NumPy, SciPy, scikit-learn
  These useful and extensive libraries are casually used in many recipes. Most of the time it should be clear what is happening from the context, but a quick read-up on them won't hurt.

Jupyter Notebook
  Notebooks are a very nice way to share code; they allow for a mixture of code, output of code, and comments, all viewable in the browser.

Each chapter has a corresponding notebook that contains working code. The code in the book often leaves out details like imports, so it is a good idea to get the code from Git and launch a local notebook. First check out the code and enter the new directory:

```
git clone https://github.com/DOsinga/deep_learning_cookbook.git
cd deep_learning_cookbook
```

Then set up a virtual environment for the project:

```
python3 -m venv venv3
source venv3/bin/activate
```

And install the dependencies:

```
pip install -r requirements.txt
```

If you have a GPU and want to use that, you'll need to uninstall `tensorflow` and install `tensorflow-gpu` instead, which you can easily do using pip:

```
pip uninstall tensorflow
pip install tensorflow-gpu
```

You'll also need to have a compatible GPU library setup, which can be a bit of a hassle.

Finally, bring up the IPython notebook server:

```
jupyter notebook
```

If everything worked, this should automatically open a web browser with an overview of the notebooks, one for each chapter. Feel free to play with the code; you can use Git to easily undo any changes you've made if you want to go back to the baseline:

```
git checkout <notebook_to_reset>.ipynb
```

The first section of every chapter lists the notebooks relevant for that chapter and the notebooks are numbered according to the chapters, so it should in general be easy to find your way around. In the notebook folder, you'll also find three other directories:

Data
Contains data needed by the various notebooks—mostly samples of open datasets or things that would be too cumbersome to generate yourself.

Generated
Used to store intermediate data.

Zoo
Contains a subdirectory for each chapter that holds saved models for that chapter. If you don't have the time to actually train the models, you can still run the models by loading them from here.

How This Book Is Structured

Chapter 1 provides in-depth information about how neural networks function, where to get data from, and how to preprocess that data to make it easier to consume. Chapter 2 is about getting stuck and what to do about it. Neural nets are notoriously hard to debug and the tips and tricks in this chapter on how to make them behave will come in handy when going through the more project-oriented recipes in the rest of the book. If you are impatient, you can skip this chapter and go back to it later when you do get stuck.

Chapters 3 through 15 are grouped around media, starting with text processing, followed by image processing, and finally music processing in Chapter 15. Each chapter describes one project split into various recipes. Typically a chapter will start with a data acquisition recipe, followed by a few recipes that build toward the goal of the chapter and a recipe on data visualization.

Chapter 16 is about using models in production. Running experiments in notebooks is great, but ultimately we want to share our results with actual users and get our models run on real servers or mobile devices. This chapter goes through the options.

Conventions Used in This Book

The following typographical conventions are used in this book:

Italic
    Indicates new terms, URLs, email addresses, filenames, and file extensions.

`Constant width`
    Used for program listings, as well as within paragraphs to refer to program elements such as variable or function names, databases, data types, environment variables, statements, and keywords.

`Constant width italic`
    Shows text that should be replaced with user-supplied values or by values determined by context.

This element signifies a tip or suggestion.

This element signifies a general note.

Accompanying Code

Each chapter in this book comes with one or more Python notebooks that contain the example code referred to in the chapters themselves. You can read the chapters without running the code, but it is more fun to work with the notebooks as you read. The code can be found at *https://github.com/DOsinga/deep_learning_cookbook*.

To get the example code for the recipes up and running, execute the following commands in a shell:

```
git clone https://github.com/DOsinga/deep_learning_cookbook.git
cd deep_learning_cookbook
python3 -m venv venv3
source venv3/bin/activate
pip install -r requirements.txt
jupyter notebook
```

This book is here to help you get your job done. All code in the accompanying notebooks is licensed under the permissive Apache License 2.0.

We appreciate, but do not require, attribution. An attribution usually includes the title, author, publisher, and ISBN. For example: "*Deep Learning Cookbook* by Douwe Osinga (O'Reilly). Copyright 2018 Douwe Osinga, 978-1-491-99584-6."

O'Reilly Safari

Safari (formerly Safari Books Online) is a membership-based training and reference platform for enterprise, government, educators, and individuals.

Members have access to thousands of books, training videos, Learning Paths, interactive tutorials, and curated playlists from over 250 publishers, including O'Reilly Media, Harvard Business Review, Prentice Hall Professional, Addison-Wesley Professional, Microsoft Press, Sams, Que, Peachpit Press, Adobe, Focal Press, Cisco Press, John Wiley & Sons, Syngress, Morgan Kaufmann, IBM Redbooks, Packt, Adobe Press, FT Press, Apress, Manning, New Riders, McGraw-Hill, Jones & Bartlett, and Course Technology, among others.

For more information, please visit *http://oreilly.com/safari*.

How to Contact Us

Please address comments and questions concerning this book to the publisher:

O'Reilly Media, Inc.
1005 Gravenstein Highway North
Sebastopol, CA 95472
800-998-9938 (in the United States or Canada)
707-829-0515 (international or local)
707-829-0104 (fax)

We have a web page for this book, where we list errata, examples, and any additional information. You can access this page at *http://bit.ly/deep-learning-cookbook*.

To comment or ask technical questions about this book, send email to *bookquestions@oreilly.com*.

For more information about our books, courses, conferences, and news, see our website at *http://www.oreilly.com*.

Find us on Facebook: *http://facebook.com/oreilly*

Follow us on Twitter: *http://twitter.com/oreillymedia*

Watch us on YouTube: *http://www.youtube.com/oreillymedia*

Acknowledgments

From academics sharing new ideas by (pre)publishing papers on *https://arxiv.org*, to hackers coding up those ideas on GitHub to public and private institutions publishing datasets for anybody to use, the world of machine learning is full of people and organizations that welcome newcomers and make it as easy to get started as it is. Open data, open source, and open access publishing—this book wouldn't be here without machine learning's culture of sharing.

What is true for the ideas presented in this book is even more true for the code in this book. Writing a machine learning model from scratch is hard, so almost all the models in the notebooks are based on code from somewhere else. This is the best way to get things done—find a model that does something similar to what you want and change it step by step, verifying at each step that things still work.

A special thanks goes out to my friend and coauthor for this book, Russell Power. Apart from helping to write this Preface, Chapter 6, and Chapter 7, he has been instrumental in checking the technical soundness of the book and the accompanying code. Moreover, he's been an invaluable asset as a sounding board for many ideas, some of which made it into the book.

Then there is my lovely wife, who was the first line of defense when it came to proof-reading chapters as they came into being. She has an uncanny ability to spot mistakes in a text that is neither in her native language nor about a subject she's previously been an expert on.

The *requirements.in* file lists the open source packages that are used in this book. A heartfelt thank you goes out to all the contributors to all of these projects. This goes doubly for Keras, since almost all the code is based on that framework and often borrows from its examples.

Example code and ideas from these packages and many blog posts contributed to this book. In particular:

Chapter 2, Getting Unstuck
> This chapter takes ideas from Slav Ivanov's blog post "37 Reasons Why Your Neural Network Is Not Working" (*http://bit.ly/2IDxljz*).

Chapter 3, Calculating Text Similarity Using Word Embeddings
> Thanks to Google for publishing its Word2vec model.
>
> Radim Řehůřek's Gensim powers this chapter, and some of the code is based on examples from this great project.

Chapter 5, Generating Text in the Style of an Example Text
> This chapter draws heavily on the great blog post "The Unreasonable Effectiveness of Recurrent Neural Networks" (*http://karpathy.github.io/2015/05/21/rnn-effectiveness/*) by Andrej Karpathy. That blog post rekindled my interest in neural networks.
>
> The visualization was inspired by Motoki Wu's "Visualizations of Recurrent Neural Networks" (*http://bit.ly/2s8uAvg*).

Chapter 6, Question Matching
> This chapter was somewhat inspired by the Quora Question Pairs challenge on Kaggle (*https://www.kaggle.com/c/quora-question-pairs*).

Chapter 8, Sequence-to-Sequence Mapping
> The example code is copied from one of the Keras examples, but applied on a slightly different dataset.

Chapter 11, Detecting Multiple Images
> This chapter is based on Yann Henon's *keras_frcnn* (*https://github.com/yhenon/keras-frcnn*).

Chapter 12, Image Style

This borrows from "How Convolutional Neural Networks See the World" (*http://bit.ly/2s4ORCf*) and of course Google's DeepDream (*https://github.com/google/deepdream/blob/master/dream.ipynb*).

Chapter 13, Generating Images with Autoencoders

Code and ideas are based on Nicholas Normandin's Conditional Variational Autoencoder (*http://nnormandin.com/science/2017/07/01/cvae.html*).

Chapter 14, Generating Icons Using Deep Nets

Autoencoder training code for Keras is based on Qin Yongliang's DCGAN-Keras (*https://github.com/ctmakro/DCGAN-Keras/blob/master/lets_gan.py*).

Chapter 15, Music and Deep Learning

This was inspired by Heitor Guimarães's *gtzan.keras* (*https://github.com/Hguimaraes/gtzan.keras*).

Tools and Techniques

In this chapter we'll take a look at common tools and techniques for deep learning. It's a good chapter to read through once to get an idea of what's what and to come back to when you need it.

We'll start out with an overview of the different types of neural networks that are covered in this book. Most of the recipes later in the book focus on getting things done and only briefly discuss how deep neural networks are architected.

We'll then discuss where to get data from. Tech giants like Facebook and Google have access to tremendous amounts of data to do their deep learning research, but there's enough data out there for us to do interesting stuff too. The recipes in this book take their data from a wide range of sources.

The next part is about preprocessing of data. This is a very important area that is often overlooked. Even if you have the right network setup and you have great data, you still need to make sure that the data you have is presented in the best way to the network. You want to make it as easy as possible for the network to learn the things it needs to learn and not get distracted by other irrelevant bits in the data.

1.1 Types of Neural Networks

Throughout this chapter and indeed the book we will talk about *networks* and *models*. Network is short for neural network and refers to a stack of connected *layers*. You feed data in on one side and transformed data comes out on the other side. Each layer implements a mathematical operation on the data flowing through it and has a set of variables that can be modified that determine the exact behavior of the layer. *Data* here refers to a *tensor*, a vector with multiple dimensions (typically two or three).

A full discussion of the different types of layers and the math behind their operations is beyond the scope of this book. The simplest type of layer, the *fully connected* layer, takes its input as a matrix, multiplies that matrix with another matrix called the *weights*, and adds a third matrix called the *bias*. Each layer is followed by an *activation* function, a mathematical function that maps the output of one layer to the input of the next layer. For example, a simple activation function called ReLU passes on all positive values, but sets negative values to zero.

Technically the term *network* refers to the architecture, the way in which the various layers are connected to each other, while a *model* is a network plus all the variables that determine the runtime behavior. Training a model modifies those variables to make the predictions fit the expected output better. In practice, though, the two terms are often used interchangeably.

The terms "deep learning" and "neural networks" in reality encompass a wide variety of models. Most of these networks will share some elements (for example, almost all classification networks will use a particular form of *loss function*). While the space of models is diverse, we can group most of them into some broad categories. Some models will use pieces from multiple categories: for example, many image classification networks have a fully connected section "head" to perform the final classification.

Fully Connected Networks

Fully connected networks were the first type of network to be researched, and dominated interest until the late 1980s. In a fully connected network, each output unit is calculated as a weighted sum of all of the inputs. The term "fully connected" arises from this behavior: every output is connected to every input. We can write this as a formula:

$$y_i = \Sigma_j W_{ij} x_j$$

For brevity, most papers represent a fully connected network using matrix notation. In this case we are multiplying a vector of inputs with a weight matrix W to get a vector of outputs:

$$y = Wx$$

As matrix multiplication is a linear operation, a network that only contained matrix multiplies would be limited to learning linear mappings. In order to make our networks more expressive, we follow the matrix multiply with a nonlinear activation function. This can be any differentiable function, but a few are very common. The hyperbolic tangent, or *tanh*, function was until recently the dominant type of activation function, and can still be found in some models:

$$tanh(x) = \frac{e^x - e^{-x}}{e^x + e^{-x}}$$

The difficulty with the tanh function is that it is very "flat" when an input is far from zero. This results in a small gradient, which means that a network can take a very long time to change behavior. Recently, other activation functions have become popular. One of the most common is the rectified linear unit, or *ReLU*, activation function:

$$relu(x) = \begin{cases} 0 & \text{if x} < 0 \\ x & \text{if x} \geq 0 \end{cases}$$

Finally, many networks use a *sigmoid* activation function in the last layer of the network. This function always outputs a value between 0 and 1. This allows the outputs to be treated as probabilities:

$$sigmoid(x) = \frac{1}{1 + e^{-x}}$$

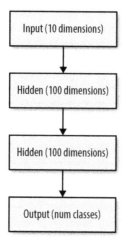

A matrix multiplication followed by the activation function is referred to as a *layer* of the network. In some networks the complete network can have over 100 layers, though fully connected networks tend to be limited to a handful. If we are solving a classification problem ("What type of cat is in this picture?"), the last layer of the network is called a *classification layer*. It will always have the same number of outputs as we have classes to choose from.

Layers in the middle of the network are called *hidden layers*, and the individual outputs from a hidden layer are sometimes referred to as *hidden units*. The term "hidden" comes from the fact that these units are not directly visible from the outside as inputs or outputs for our model. The number of outputs in these layers depends on the model:

Input (10 dimensions)

↓

Hidden (100 dimensions)

↓

Hidden (100 dimensions)

↓

Output (num classes)

While there are some rules of thumb about how to choose the number and size of hidden layers, there is no general policy for choosing the best setup other than trial and error.

Convolutional Networks

Early research used fully connected networks to try to solve a wide variety of problems. But when our input is images, fully connected networks can be a poor choice. Images are very large: a single 256×256-pixel image (a common resolution for classification) has 256×256×3 inputs (3 colors for each pixel). If this model has a single hidden layer with 1,000 hidden units, then this layer will have almost 200 million parameters (learnable values)! Since image models require quite a few layers to perform well at classification, if we implemented them just using fully connected layers we would end up with billions of parameters.

With so many parameters, it would be almost impossible for us to avoid *overfitting* our model (overfitting is described in detail in the next chapter; it refers to when a network fails to generalize, but just memorizes outcomes). *Convolutional neural networks* (CNNs) provide a way for us to train superhuman image classifiers using far fewer parameters. They do this by mimicking how animals and humans see:

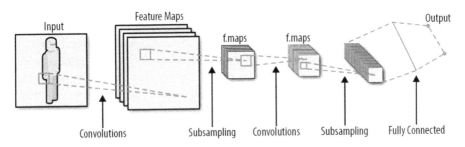

The fundamental operation in a CNN is a *convolution*. Instead of applying a function to an entire input image, a convolution scans across a small window of the image at a time. At each location it applies a *kernel* (typically a matrix multiplication followed by an activation function, just like in a fully connected network). Individual kernels are often referred to as *filters*. The result of applying the kernel to the entire image is a new, possibly smaller image. For example, a common filter shape is (3, 3). If we were to apply 32 of these filters to our input image, we would need 3 * 3 * 3 (input colors) * 32 = 864 parameters—that's a big savings over a fully connected network!

Subsampling

This operation saves on the number of parameters, but now we have a different problem. Each layer in the network can only "look" at a 3×3 layer of the image at a time: if this is the case, how can we possibly recognize objects that take up the entire image?

To handle this, a typical convolution network uses *subsampling* to reduce the size of the image as it passes through the network. Two common mechanisms are used for subsampling:

Strided convolutions

In a strided convolution, we simply skip one or more pixels while sliding our convolution filter across the image. This results in a smaller size image. For example, if our input image was 256×256, and we skip every other pixel, then our output image will be 128×128 (we are ignoring the issue of padding at the edges of the image for simplicity). This type of strided downsampling is commonly found in generator networks (see "Adversarial Networks and Autoencoders" on page 9).

Pooling

Instead of skipping over pixels during convolution, many networks use *pooling layers* to shrink their inputs. A pooling layer is actually another form of convolution, but instead of multiplying our input by a matrix, we apply a pooling operator. Typically pooling uses the *max* or *average* operator. Max pooling takes the largest value from each *channel* (color) over the region it is scanning. Average pooling instead averages all of the values over the region. (It can be thought of as a simple type of blurring of the input.)

One way to think about subsampling is as a way to increase the abstraction level of what the network is doing. On the lowest level, our convolutions detect small, local features. There are many features that are not very deep. With each pooling step, we increase the abstraction level; the number of features is reduced, but the depth of each feature increases. This process is continued until we end up with very few features with a high level of abstraction that can be used for prediction.

Prediction

After stacking a number of convolutional and pooling layers together, CNNs use one or two fully connected layers at the head of the network to output a prediction.

Recurrent Networks

Recurrent neural networks (RNNs) are similar in concept to CNNs but are structurally very different. Recurrent networks are frequently applied when we have a sequential input. These inputs are commonly found when working with text or voice processing. Instead of processing a single example completely (as we might use a CNN for an image), with sequential problems we can process only a portion of the problem at a time. For example, let's consider building a network that writes Shakespearean plays for us. Our input would naturally be the existing plays by Shakespeare:

```
Lear. Attend the lords of France and Burgundy, Gloucester.
Glou. I shall, my liege.
```

What we want the network to learn to do is to predict the next word of the play for us. To do so, it needs to "remember" the text that it has seen so far. Recurrent networks give us a mechanism to do this. They also allow us to build models that naturally work across inputs of varying lengths (sentences or chunks of speech, for example). The most basic form of an RNN looks like this:

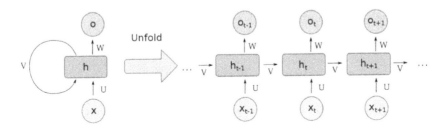

Conceptually, you can think of this RNN as a very deep fully connected network that we have "unrolled." In this conceptual model, each layer of the network takes two inputs instead of the one we are used to:

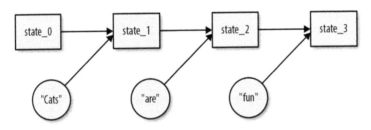

Recall that in our original fully connected network, we had a matrix multiplication operation like:

$$y = Wx$$

The simplest way to add our second input to this operation is to just concatenate it to our hidden state:

$$hidden_i = W\{hidden_{i-1}|x\}$$

where in this case the "|" stands for concatenate. As with our fully connected network, we can apply an activation function to the output of our matrix multiplication to obtain our new state:

$$hidden_i = f\big(W\{hidden_{i-1}|x\}\big)$$

With this interpretation of our RNN, we also can easily understand how it can be trained: we simply treat the RNN as we would an unrolled fully connected network and train it normally. This is referred to in literature as *backpropagation through time* (BPTT). If we have very long inputs, it is common to split them into smaller-sized pieces and train each piece independently. While this does not work for every problem, it is generally safe and is a widely used technique.

Vanishing gradients and LSTMs

Our naive RNN unfortunately tends to perform more poorly than we would like for long input sequences. This is because its structure makes it likely to encounter the "vanishing gradients" problem. Vanishing gradients result from the fact that our unrolled network is very deep. Each time we go through an activation function, there's a chance it will result in a small gradient getting passed through (for instance, ReLU activation functions have a zero gradient for any input < 0). Once this happens for a single unit, no more training can be passed down further through the network via that unit. This results in an ever-sparser training signal as we go down. The observed result is extremely slow or nonexistent learning of the network.

To combat this, researchers developed an alternative mechanism for building RNNs. The basic model of unrolling our state over time is kept, but instead of doing a simple matrix multiply followed by the activation function, we have a more complex way of passing our state forward (source: Wikipedia (*https://bit.ly/2HJL86P*)):

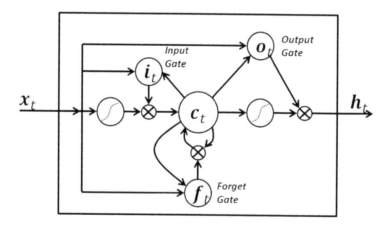

A *long short-term memory network* (LSTM) replaces our single matrix multiplication with four, and introduces the idea of *gates* that are multiplied with a vector. The key behavior that enables an LSTM to learn more effectively than vanilla RNNs is that there is always a path from the final prediction to any layer that preserves gradients. The details of how it accomplishes this are beyond the scope of this chapter, but several excellent tutorials (*http://colah.github.io/posts/2015-08-Understanding-LSTMs/*) exist on the web.

Adversarial Networks and Autoencoders

Adversarial networks and autoencoders do not introduce new structural components, like the networks we've talked about so far. Instead, they use the structure most appropriate to the problem: an adversarial network or autoencoder for images will use convolutions, for example. Where they differ is in how they are trained. Most normal networks are trained to predict an output (is this a cat?) from an input (a picture):

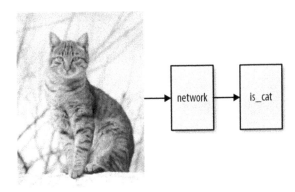

Autoencoders are instead trained to output back the image they are presented:

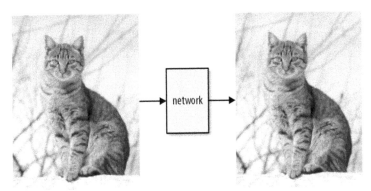

Why would we want to do this? If the hidden layers in the middle of our network contain a representation of the input image that has (significantly) less information than the original image yet from which the original image can be reconstructed, then this results in a form of compression: we can take any image and represent it just by the values from the hidden layer. One way to think about this is that we take the original image and use the network to project it into an abstract space. Each point in that space can then be converted back into an image.

Autoencoders have been successfully applied to small images, but the mechanism for training them does not scale up to larger problems. The space in the middle from which the images are drawn is in practice not "dense" enough, and many of the points don't actually represent coherent images.

We'll seen an example of an autoencoder network in Chapter 13.

Adversarial networks are a more recent model that can actually generate realistic images. They work by splitting the problem into two parts: a generator network and a discriminator network. The generator network takes a small random seed and produces a picture (or text). The discriminator network tries to determine if an input image is "real" or if it came from the generator network.

When we train our adversarial model, we train both of these networks at the same time:

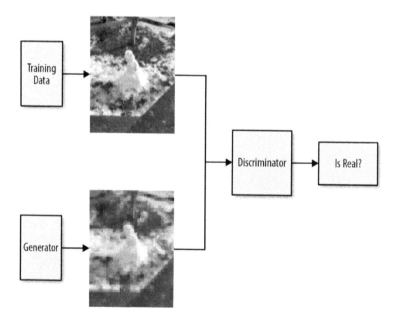

We sample some images from our generator network and feed them through our discriminator network. The generator network is rewarded for producing images that can fool the discriminator. The discriminator network also has to correctly recognize real images (it can't just always say an image is a fake). By making the networks compete against each other, this procedure can result in a generator network that produces high-quality natural images. Chapter 14 shows how we can use generative adversarial networks to generate icons.

Conclusion

There are a great many ways to architect a network, and the choice obviously is mostly driven by the purpose of the network. Designing a new type of network is firmly in the research realm, and even reimplementing a type of network described in a paper is hard. In practice the easiest thing to do is to find an example that does something in the direction of what you want and change it step by step until it really does what you want.

1.2 Acquiring Data

One of the key reasons why deep learning has taken off in recent years is the dramatic increase in the availability of data. Twenty years ago networks were trained with thousands of images; these days companies like Facebook and Google work with billions of images.

Having access to all the information from their users no doubt gives these and other internet giants a natural advantage in the deep learning field. However, there are many data sources easily accessible on the internet that, with a little massaging, can fit many training purposes. In this section, we'll discuss the most important ones. For each, we'll look into how to acquire the data, what popular libraries are available to help with parsing, and what typical use cases are. I'll also refer you to any recipes that use this data source.

Wikipedia

Not only does the English Wikipedia comprise more than 5 million articles, but Wikipedia is also available in hundreds of languages (*https://en.wikipedia.org/wiki/List_of_Wikipedias*), albeit with widely different levels of depth and quality. The basic wiki idea only supports links as a way to encode structure, but over time Wikipedia has gone beyond this.

Category pages link to pages that share a property or a subject, and since Wikipedia pages link back to their categories, we can effectively use them as tags. Categories can be very simple, like "Cats," but sometimes encode information in their names that effectively assigns (key, value) pairs to a page, like "Mammals described in 1758." The category hierarchy, like much on Wikipedia, is fairly ad hoc, though. Moreover, recursive categories can only be traced by walking up the tree.

Templates were originally designed as segments of wiki markup that are meant to be copied automatically ("transcluded") into a page. You add them by putting the template's name in `{{double braces}}`. This made it possible to keep the layout of different pages in sync—for example, all city pages have an info box with properties like population, location, and flag that are rendered consistently across pages.

These templates have parameters (like the population) and can be seen as a way to embed structured data into a Wikipedia page. In Chapter 4 we use this to extract a set of movies that we then use to train a movie recommender system.

Wikidata

Wikidata (*https://www.wikidata.org/*) is Wikipedia's structured data cousin. It is lesser known and also less complete, but even more ambitious. It is intended to provide a common source of data that can be used by anyone under a public domain license. As such, it makes for an excellent source of freely available data.

All Wikidata is stored as triplets of the form (subject, predicate, object). All subjects and predicates have their own entries in Wikidata that list all predicates that exist for them. Objects can be Wikidata entries or literals such as strings, numbers, or dates. This structure takes inspiration from early ideas around the semantic web.

Wikidata has its own query language that looks like SQL with some interesting extensions. For example:

```
SELECT ?item ?itemLabel ?pic
WHERE
{
        ?item wdt:P31 wd:Q146 .
        OPTIONAL {
                ?item wdt:P18 ?pic
        }
        SERVICE wikibase:label {
          bd:serviceParam wikibase:language "[AUTO_LANGUAGE],en"
        }
}
```

will select a series of cats and their pictures. Anything that starts with a question mark is a variable. wdt:P31, or property 31, means "is an instance of," and wd:Q146 is the class of house cats. So the fourth line stores in item anything that is an instance of cats. The OPTIONAL { .. } clause then tries to look up pictures for the item and the last magic line tries to find a label for the item using the auto-language feature or, failing that, English.

In Chapter 10 we use a combination of Wikidata and Wikipedia to acquire canonical images for categories to use as a basis for a reverse image search engine.

OpenStreetMap

OpenStreetMap (*https://www.openstreetmap.org/*) is like Wikipedia, but for maps. Whereas with Wikipedia the idea is that if everybody in the world put down everything they knew in a wiki, we'd have the best encyclopedia possible, OpenStreetMap (OSM) is based on the idea that if everybody put the roads they knew in a wiki, we'd have the best mapping system possible. Remarkably, both of these ideas have worked out quite well.

While the coverage of OSM is rather uneven, ranging from areas that are barely covered to places where it rivals or exceeds what can be found on Google Maps, the sheer amount of data and the fact that it is all freely available makes it a great resource for all types of projects that are of a geographical nature.

OSM is downloadable for free in a binary format or a huge XML file. The whole world is tens of gigabytes, but there are a number of locations on the internet where we can find OSM dumps per country or region if we want to start smaller.

The binary and XML formats both have the same structure: a map is made out of a series of *nodes* that each have a *latitude* and a *longitude*, followed by a series of *ways* that combine previously defined nodes into larger structures. Finally, there are *relations* that combine anything that was seen before (nodes, ways, or relations) into superstructures.

Nodes are used to represents points on the maps, including individual features, as well as to define the shapes of ways. Ways are used for simple shapes, like buildings and road segments. Finally, relations are used for anything that contains more than one shape or very big things like coastlines or borders.

Later in the book, we'll look at a model that takes in satellite images and rendered maps and tries to learn to recognize roads automatically. The actual data used for those recipes is not specifically from OSM, but it is the sort of thing that OSM is used for in deep learning. The "Images to OSM" project (*https://github.com/jremillard/images-to-osm*), for example, shows how to train a network to learn to extract shapes of sports fields from satellite images to improve OSM itself.

Twitter

As a social network Twitter might have trouble competing with the much bigger Facebook, but as a source for text to train deep learning models, it is much better. Twitter's API is nicely rounded and allows for all kinds of apps. To the budding machine learning hacker though, the streaming API is possibly the most interesting.

The so-called Firehose API offered by Twitter streams all tweets directly to a client. As one can imagine, this is a rather large amount of data. On top of that, Twitter charges serious money for this. It is less known that the free Twitter API offers a sampled version of the Firehose API. This API returns only 1% of all tweets, but that is plenty for many text processing applications.

Tweets are limited in size and come with a set of interesting metainformation like the author, a timestamp, sometimes a location, and of course tags, images, and URLs. In Chapter 7 we look at using this API to build a classifier to predict emojis based on a bit of text. We tap into the streaming API and keep only the tweets that contain exactly one emoji. It takes a few hours to get a decent training set, but if you have access to a computer with a stable internet connection, letting it run for a few days shouldn't be an issue.

Twitter is a popular source of data for experiments in sentiment analysis, which arguably predicting emojis is a variation of, but models aimed at language detection, location disambiguation, and named entity recognition have all been trained successfully on Twitter data too.

Project Gutenberg

Long before Google Books—in fact, long before Google and even the World Wide Web, back in 1971, Project Gutenberg (*http://www.gutenberg.org/*) launched with the aim to digitize all books. It contains the full text of over 50,000 works, not just novels, poetry, short stories, and drama, but also cookbooks, reference works, and issues of periodicals. Most of the works are in the public domain and they can all be freely downloaded from the website.

This is a massive amount of text in a convenient format, and if you don't mind that most of the texts are a little older (since they are no longer in copyright) it's a very good source of data for experiments in text processing. In Chapter 5 we use Project Gutenberg to get a copy of Shakespeare's collected works as a basis to generate more Shakespeare-like texts. All it takes is this one-liner if you have the Python library available:

```
shakespeare = strip_headers(load_etext(100))
```

The material available via Project Gutenberg is mostly in English, although a small amount of works are available in other languages. The project started out as pure ASCII but has since evolved to support a number of character encodings, so if you download a non-English text, you need to make sure that you have the right encoding —not everything in the world is UTF-8 yet. In Chapter 8 we extract all dialogue from a set of books retrieved from Project Gutenberg and then train a chatbot to mimic those conversations.

Flickr

Flickr (*https://www.flickr.com/*) is a photo sharing site that has been in operation since 2004. It originally started as a side project for a massively multiplayer online game called *Game Neverending*. When the game failed to become a business on its own, the company's founders realized that the photo sharing part of the company was taking off and so they executed what is called a *pivot*, completely changing the main focus of the company. Flickr was sold to Yahoo a year later.

Among the many, many photo sharing sites out there, Flickr stands out as a useful source of images for deep learning experiments for a few reasons.

One is that Flickr has been at this for a long time and has collected a set of billions of images. This might pale in comparison to the number of images that people upload to Facebook in a single month, but since users upload photos to Flickr that they are proud of for public consumption, Flickr images are on average of higher quality and of more general interest.

A second reason is licensing. Users on Flickr pick a license for their photos, and many pick some form of Creative Commons licensing (*https://creativecommons.org/*) that allows for reuse of some kind without asking permission. While you typically don't need this if you run a bunch of photos through your latest nifty algorithm and are only interested in the end results, it is quite essential if your project ultimately needs to republish the original or modified images. Flickr makes this possible.

The last and possibly most important advantage that Flickr has over most of its competitors is the API. Just like Twitter's, it is a well-thought-out, REST-style API that makes it easy to do anything you can do with the site in an automatic fashion. And just like with Twitter there are good Python bindings for the API, which makes it even easier to start experimenting. All you need is the right library and a Flickr API key.

The main features of the API relevant for this book are searching for images and fetching of images. The search is quite versatile and mimics most of the search options of the main website, although some advanced filters are unfortunately missing. Fetching images can be done for a large variety of sizes. It is often useful to get started more quickly with smaller versions of the images first and scale up later.

In Chapter 9 we use the Flickr API to fetch two sets of images, one with dogs and one with cats, and train a classifier to learn the difference between the two.

The Internet Archive

The Internet Archive (*https://archive.org/*) has a stated mission of providing "universal access to all knowledge." The project is probably most famous for its Wayback Machine, a web interface that lets users look at web pages over time. It contains over 300 billion captures dating all the way back to 2001 in what the project calls a three-dimensional web index.

But the Internet Archive is far bigger than the Wayback Machine and comprises a ragtag assortment of documents, media, and datasets covering everything from books out of copyright to NASA images to cover art for CDs to audio and video material.

These are all really worth browsing through and often inspire new projects on the spot.

One interesting example is a set of all Reddit comments up to 2015 with over 50 million entries. This started out as a project of a Reddit user who just patiently used the Reddit API to download all of them and then announced that on Reddit. When the question came up of where to host it, the Internet Archive turned out to be a good option (though the same data can be found on Google's BigQuery for even more immediate analysis).

An example we use in this book is the set of Stack Exchange questions (*https://archive.org/details/stackexchange*). Stack Exchange has always been licensed under a Creative Commons license, so nothing would stop us from downloading these sets ourselves, but getting them from the Internet Archive is so much easier. In this book we use this dataset to train a model to match questions with answers (see Chapter 6).

Crawling

If you need anything specific for your project, chances are that the data you are after is not accessible through a public API. And even if there is a public API, it might be rate limited to the point of being useless. Historic results for your favorite sports are hard to come by. Your local newspaper might have an online archive, but probably no API or data dump. Instagram has a nice API, but the recent changes to the terms of service make it hard to use it to acquire a large set of training data.

In these cases, you can always resort to scraping, or, if you want to sound more respectable, crawling. In the simplest scenario you just want to get a copy of a website on your local system and you have no prior knowledge about the structure of that website or the format of the URLs. In that case you just start with the root of the website, fetch the web content of it, extract all links from that web content, and do the same for each of those links until you find no more new links. This is how Google does it too, be it at a larger scale. Scrapy (*https://scrapy.org*) is a useful framework for this sort of thing.

Sometimes there is an obvious hierarchy, like a travel website with pages for countries, regions in those countries, cities in those regions, and finally attractions in those cities. In that case it might be more useful to write a more targeted scraper that successively works its way through the various layers of hierarchy until it has all the attractions.

Other times there is an internal API to take advantage of. Many content-oriented websites will load the overall layout and then use a JSON call back to the web server to get the actual data and insert this on the fly into the template. This makes it easy to support infinite scrolling and search. The JSON returned from the server is often easy to make sense of, as are the parameters passed to the server. The Chrome extension

Request Maker (*http://bit.ly/request-maker*) shows all requests that a page makes and is a good way to see if anything useful goes over the line.

Then there are the websites that don't want to be crawled. Google might have built an empire on scraping the world, but many of its services very cleverly detect signs of scraping and will block you and possibly anybody making requests from your IP address until you do a captcha. You can play with rate limiting and user agents, but at some point you might have to resort to scraping using a browser.

WebDriver, a framework developed for testing websites by instrumenting a browser, can be very helpful in these situations. The fetching of the pages is done with your choice of browser, so to the web server everything seems as real as it can get. You can then "click" on links using your control script to go to the next page and inspect the results. Consider sprinkling the code with delays to make it seem like a human is exploring the site and you should be good to go.

The code in Chapter 10 uses crawling techniques to fetch images from Wikipedia. There is a URL scheme to go from a Wikipedia ID to the corresponding image, but it doesn't always pan out. In that case we fetch the page that contains the image and follow the link graph until we get to the actual image.

Other Options

There are many ways to get data. The ProgrammableWeb (*https://www.programmable web.com/*) lists more than 18,000 public APIs (though some of those are in a state of disrepair). Here are three that are worth highlighting:

Common Crawl
> Crawling one site is doable if the site is not very big. But what if you want to crawl all of the major pages of the internet? The Common Crawl (*http://common crawl.org/*) runs a monthly crawl fetching around 2 billion web pages each time in an easy-to-process format. AWS has this as a public dataset, so if you happen to run on that platform that's an easy way to run jobs on the web at large.

Facebook
> Over the years the Facebook API has shifted subtly from being a really useful resource to build applications on top of Facebook's data to a resource to build applications that make Facebook's data better. While this is understandable from Facebook's perspective, as a data prospector one often wonders about the data it could make public. Still, the Facebook API is a useful resource—especially the Places API in situations where OSM is just too unevenly edited.

US government
> The US government on all levels publishes a huge amount of data, and all of it is freely accessible. For example, the census data (*https://www.census.gov*) has detailed information about the US population, while Data.gov (*https://*

www.data.gov/) has a portal with many different datasets all over the spectrum. On top of that, individual states and cities have their own resources worth looking at.

1.3 Preprocessing Data

Deep neural networks are remarkably good at finding patterns in data that can help in learning to predict the labels for the data. This also means that we have to be careful with the data we give them; any pattern in the data that is not relevant for our problem can make the network learn the wrong thing. By preprocessing data the right way we can make sure that we make things as easy as possible for our networks.

Getting a Balanced Training Set

An apocryphal story relates how the US Army once trained a neural network to discriminate between camouflaged tanks and plain forest—a useful skill when automatically analyzing satellite data. At first sight they did everything right. On one day they flew a plane over a forest with camouflaged tanks in it and took pictures, and on another day they did the same when there were no tanks, making sure to photograph scenes that were similar but not quite the same. They split the data up into training and test sets and let the network train.

The network trained well and started to get good results. However, when the researchers sent it out to be tested in the wild, people thought it was a joke. The predictions seemed utterly random. After some digging, it turned out that the input data had a problem. All the pictures containing tanks had been taken on a sunny day, while the pictures with just forest happened to have been taken on a cloudy day. So while the researchers thought their network had learned to discriminate between tanks and nontanks, they really had trained a network to observe the weather.

Preprocessing data is all about making sure the network picks up on the signals we want it to pick up on and is not distracted by things that don't matter. The first step here is to make sure that we actually have the right input data. Ideally the data should resemble as closely as possible the real-world situation.

Making sure that the signal in the data is the signal we are trying to learn seems obvious, but it is easy to get this wrong. Getting data is hard, and every source has its own peculiarities.

There are a few things we can do when we find our input data is tainted. The best thing is, of course, to rebalance the data. So in the tanks versus forest example, we would try to get pictures for both scenarios in all types of weather. (When you think about it, even if all the original pictures had been taken in sunny weather, the training set would still have been suboptimal—a balanced set would contain weather conditions of all types.)

A second option is to just throw out some data to make the set more balanced. Maybe there were some pictures of tanks taken on cloudy days after all, but not enough—so we could throw out some of the sunny pictures. This obviously cuts down the size of the training set, however, and might not be an option. (Data augmentation, discussed in "Preprocessing of Images" on page 22, could help.)

A third option is to try to fix the input data, say by using a photo filter that makes the weather conditions appear more similar. This is tricky though, and can easily lead to other or even more artifacts that the network might detect.

Creating Data Batches

Neural networks consume data in batches (sets of input/output pairs). It is important to make sure that these batches are properly randomized. Imagine we have a set of pictures, the first half all depicting cats and the second half dogs. Without shuffling, it would be impossible for the network to learn anything from this dataset: almost all batches would either contain only cats or only dogs. If we use Keras and if we have our data entirely in memory, this is easily accomplished using the `fit` method since it will do the shuffling for us:

```
char_cnn_model.fit(training_data, training_labels, epochs=20, batch_size=128)
```

This will randomly create batches with a size of 128 from the `training_data` and `training_labels` sets. Keras takes care of the proper randomizing. As long as we have our data in memory, this is usually the way to go.

> In some circumstances we might want to call `fit` with one batch at a time, in which case we do need to make sure things are properly shuffled. `numpy.random.shuffle` will do just fine, though we have to take care to shuffle the data and the labels in unison.

We don't always have all the data in memory, though. Sometimes the data would be too big or needs to be processed on the fly and isn't available in the ideal format. In those situations we use `fit_generator`:

```
char_cnn_model.fit_generator(
    data_generator(train_tweets, batch_size=BATCH_SIZE),
    epochs=20
)
```

Here, `data_generator` is a generator that yields batches of data. The generator has to make sure that the data is properly randomized. If the data is read from a file, shuffling is not really an option. If the file comes from an SSD and the records are all the same size, we can shuffle by seeking randomly inside of the file. If this is not the case and the file has some sort of sorting, we can increase randomness by having multiple file handles in the same file, all at different locations.

When setting up a generator that produces batches on the fly, we also need to pay attention to keep things properly randomized. For example, in Chapter 4 we build a movie recommender system by training on Wikipedia articles, using as the unit of training links from the movie page to some other page. The easiest way to generate these (FromPage, ToPage) pairs would be to randomly pick a FromPage and then randomly pick a ToPage from all the links found on FromPage.

This works, of course, but it will select links from pages with fewer links on them more often than it should. A FromPage with one link on it has the same chance of being picked in the first step as a page with a hundred links. In the second step, though, that one link is certain to be picked, while any of the links from the page with a hundred links has only a small chance of selection.

Training, Testing, and Validation Data

After we've set up our clean, normalized data and before the actual training phase, we need to split the data up in a training set, a test set, and possibly a validation set. As with many things, the reason we do this has to do with overfitting. Networks will almost always memorize a little bit of the training data rather than learn generalizations. By separating a small amount of the data into a test set that we don't use for training, we can measure to what extent this is happening; after each epoch we measure accuracy over both the training and the test set, and as long as the two numbers don't diverge too much, we're fine.

If we have our data in memory we can use `train_test_split` from `sklearn` to neatly split our data into training and test sets:

```
data_train, data_test, label_train, label_test = train_test_split(
    data, labels, test_size=0.33, random_state=42)
```

This will create a test set containing 33% of the data. The `random_state` variable is used for the random seed, which guarantees that if we run the same program twice, we get the same results.

When feeding our network using a generator, we need to do the splitting ourselves. One general though not very efficient approach would be to use something like:

```
def train_or_test(gen, train=True):
    for i, x in enumerate(gen):
        if (i % 4 == 0) != train:
            yield x
```

When `train` is `False` this yields every fourth element coming from the generator `gen`. When it is `True` it yields the rest.

Sometimes a third set is split off from the training data, called the *validation set*. There is some confusion in the naming here; when there are only two sets the test set is sometimes also called the validation set (or holdout set). In a scenario where we have training, validation, and test sets, the validation set is used to measure performance while tuning the model. The test set is meant to be used only when all tuning is done and no more changes are going to be made to the code.

The reason to keep this third set is to stop us from manually overfitting. A complex neural network can have a very large number of tuning options or hyperparameters. Finding the right values for these hyperparameters is an optimization problem that can also suffer from overfitting. We keep adjusting those parameters until the performance on the validation set no longer increases. By having a test set that was not used during tuning, we can make sure that we didn't inadvertently optimize our hyper parameters for the validation set.

Preprocessing of Text

A lot of neural networking problems involve text processing. Preprocessing the input texts in these situations involves mapping the input text to a vector or matrix that we can feed into a network.

Typically, the first step is to break up the text into units. There are two common ways to do this: on a character or a word basis.

Breaking up a text into a stream of single characters is straightforward and gives us a predictable number of different tokens. If all our text is in one phoneme-based script, the number of different tokens is quite restricted.

Breaking up a text into words is a more complicated tokenizing strategy, especially in scripts that don't indicate the beginning and ending of words. Moreover, there is no obvious upper limit to the number of different tokens that we'll end up with. A number of text processing toolkits have a "tokenize" function that usually also allows for the removal of accents and optionally converts all tokens to lowercase.

A process called *stemming*, where we convert each word to its root form (by dropping any grammar-related modifications), can help, especially for languages that are more grammar-heavy than English. In Chapter 8 we'll encounter a subword tokenizing strategy that breaks up complicated words into subtokens thereby guaranteeing a specific upper limit on the number of different tokens.

Once we have our text split up into tokens, we need to vectorize it. The simplest way of doing this is called *one-hot encoding*. Here, we assign to each unique token an integer i from 0 to the number of tokens and then represent each token as a vector containing only 0s, except for the ith entry, which contains a 1. In Python code this would be:

```
idx_to_token = list(set(tokens))
token_to_idx = {token: idx for idx, token in enumerate(idx_to_token)}
one_hot = lambda token: [1 if i == token_to_idx[token] else 0
```

```
                          for i in range(len(idx_to_token))]
    encoded = np.asarray([one_hot(token) for token in tokens])
```

This should leave us with a large two-dimensional array ready for consumption.

One-hot encoding works when we process text at a character level. It also works for word-level processing, though for texts with large vocabularies it can get unwieldy. There are two popular encoding strategies that work around this.

The first one is to treat a document as a "bag of words." Here, we don't care about the order of the words, just whether a certain word is present. We can then represent a document as a vector with an entry for each unique token. In the simplest scheme we just put a 1 if the word is present in that document and a 0 if not.

Since the top 100 most frequently occurring words in English make up about half of all texts, they are not very useful for text classifying tasks; almost all documents will contain them, so having those in our vectors doesn't really help much. A common strategy is to just drop them from our bag of words so the network can focus on the words that do make a difference.

Term frequency–inverse document frequency, or tf–idf, is a more sophisticated version of this. Instead of storing a 1 if a token is present in a document, we store the relative frequency of the term in the document compared to how often the term occurs throughout the entire corpus of documents. The intuition here is that it is more meaningful for a less common token to appear in a document than a token that appears all the time. Scikit-learn comes with methods to calculate this automatically.

A second way to handle word-level encoding is by way of embeddings. Chapter 3 is all about embeddings and offers a good way to understand how they work. With embeddings we associate a vector of a certain size—typically with a length of 50 to 300—with each token. When we feed in a document represented as a sequence of token IDs, an embedding layer will automatically look up the corresponding embedding vectors and output a two-dimensional array.

The embedding layer will learn the right weights for each term, just like any layer in a neural network. This often takes a lot of learning, both in terms of processing and the required amount of data. A nice aspect of embeddings, though, is that there are pretrained sets available for download and we can seed our embedding layer with these. Chapter 7 has a good example of this approach.

Preprocessing of Images

Deep neural networks have turned out to be very effective when it comes to working with images, for anything from detecting cats in videos to applying the style of different artists to selfies. As with text, though, it is essential to properly preprocess the input images.

The first step is normalization. Many networks only operate on a specific size, so the first step is to resize/crop the images to that target size. Both center cropping and direct resizing are often used, though sometimes a combination works better in order to preserve more of the image while keeping resize distortion somewhat in check.

To normalize the colors, for each pixel we usually subtract the mean value and divide by the standard deviation. This makes sure that all values on average center around 0 and that the nearly 70% of all values are within the comfortable [–1, 1] range. A new development here is the use of *batch normalization*; rather than normalizing all data beforehand, this subtracts the mean of the batch and divides by the standard deviation. This leads to better results and can just be made part of the network.

Data augmentation is a strategy to increase the amount of training data by adding variations of our training images. If we add to our training data versions of our images flipped horizontally, in a way we double our training data—a mirrored cat is still a cat. Looking at this in another way, what we are doing is telling our network that flips can be ignored. If all our cat pictures have the cat looking in one direction, our network might learn that that is part of catness; adding flips undoes that.

Keras has a handy `ImageDataGenerator` class that you can configure to produce all kinds of image variations, including rotations, translations, color adjustments, and magnification. You can then use that as a data generator for the `fit_generator` method on your model:

```
datagen = ImageDataGenerator(
    rotation_range=20,
    horizontal_flip=True)

model.fit_generator(datagen.flow(x_train, y_train, batch_size=32),
                    steps_per_epoch=len(x_train) / 32, epochs=epochs)
```

Conclusion

Preprocessing of data is an important step before training a deep learning model. A common thread in all of this is that we want it to be as easy as possible for networks to learn the right thing and not be confused by irrelevant features of the input. Getting a balanced training set, creating randomized training batches, and the various ways to normalize the data are all a big part of this.

CHAPTER 2

Getting Unstuck

Deep learning models are often treated as a black box; we pour data in at one end and an answer comes out at the other without us having to care much about how our network learns. While it is true that deep neural nets can be remarkably good at distilling a signal out of complex input data, the flip side of treating these networks as black boxes is that it isn't always clear what to do when things get stuck.

A common theme among the techniques we discuss here is that we want the network to *generalize* rather than to *memorize*. It is worth pondering the question of why neural networks generalize at all. Some of the models described in this book and used in production contain millions of parameters that would allow the network to memorize inputs with very many examples. If everything goes well, though, it doesn't do this, but rather develops generalized rules about its input.

If things don't go well, you can try the techniques described in this chapter. We'll start out by looking at how we know that we're stuck. We'll then look at various ways in which we can preprocess our input data to make it easier for the network to work with.

2.1 Determining That You Are Stuck

Problem

How do you know when your network is stuck?

Solution

Look at various metrics while the network trains.

The most common signs that things are not well with a neural network are that the network is not learning anything or that it is learning the wrong thing. When we set up the network, we specify the *loss function*. This determines what the network is trying to optimize for. During training the loss is continuously printed. If this value doesn't go down after a few iterations, we're in trouble. The network is not learning anything measured by its own notion of progress.

A second metric that comes in handy is *accuracy*. This shows the percentage of the inputs for which the network is predicting the right answer. As the loss goes down, the accuracy should go up. If accuracy does not go up even though the loss is decreasing, then our network is learning something, but not the thing we were hoping for. Accuracy can take a while, though, to pick up. A complex visual network will take a long time before it gets any labels right while still learning, so take this into account before giving up prematurely.

The third thing to look for, and this is probably the most common way to get stuck, is *overfitting*. With overfitting we see our loss decrease and our accuracy increase, but the accuracy we see over our testing set doesn't keep up. Assuming we have a testing set and have added this to the metrics to track, we can see this each time an epoch finishes. Typically the testing accuracy at first increases with the accuracy of the training set, but then a gap appears, and oftentimes the testing accuracy even starts to drop while the training accuracy keeps increasing.

What's happening here is that our network is learning a direct mapping between the inputs and the expected outputs, rather than learning generalizations. As long as it sees an input it has seen before, everything looks cool. But confronted with a sample from the test set, which it hasn't seen during training, it starts to fail.

Discussion

Paying attention to the metrics that are displayed during training is a good way to keep track of the progress of the learning process. The three metrics we discussed here are the most important, but frameworks like Keras offer many more and the option to build them yourselves.

2.2 Solving Runtime Errors

Problem

What should you do when your network complains about incompatible shapes?

Solution

Look at the network structure and experiment with different numbers.

Keras is a great abstraction over hairier frameworks like TensorFlow or Theano, but like any abstraction, this comes at a cost. When all is well our clearly defined model runs happily on top of TensorFlow or Theano. When it doesn't, though, we get an error from the depths of the underlying framework. These errors are hard to make sense of without understanding the intricacies of those frameworks—which is what we wanted to avoid in the first place by using Keras.

There are two things that can help and don't require us to go on a deep dive. The first is to print the structure of our network. Let's say we have a simple model that takes in five variables and classifies into eight categories:

```
data_in = Input(name='input', shape=(5,))
fc = Dense(12, activation='relu')(data_in)
data_out = Dense(8, activation='sigmoid')(fc)
model = Model(inputs=[data_in], outputs=[data_out])
model.compile(loss='binary_crossentropy',
              optimizer='adam',
              metrics=['accuracy'])
```

We can now inspect the model with:

```
model.summary()
```

Layer (type)	Output Shape	Param #
input (InputLayer)	(None, 5)	0
dense_5 (Dense)	(None, 12)	72
dense_6 (Dense)	(None, 8)	104

```
Total params: 176
Trainable params: 176
Non-trainable params: 0
```

Now if we get a runtime error about an incompatible shape, of the feared form:

```
InvalidArgumentError: Incompatible shapes: X vs. Y
```

we know something internal must be wrong that isn't easy to track down using the stack trace. There are some other things to try, though.

First, take a look at whether any of the shapes are either X or Y. If so, that's probably where the problem is. Knowing that is half the work—which of course still leaves the other half. The other thing to pay attention to is the names of the layers. Often they come back in the error message, sometimes in a mangled form. Keras auto-assigns names to anonymous layers, so looking at the summary is useful in this respect too. If needed we can assign our own names, like with the input layer in the example shown here.

If we can't find the shape or the name that the runtime error is mentioning, we can try something else before having to dive in (or post on StackOverflow): use different numbers.

Neural networks contain loads of hyperparameters, like the sizes of the various layers. These are usually picked because they seem reasonable, given other networks that do similar things. But their actual value is somewhat arbitrary. In our example, does the hidden layer really need 12 units? Would 11 do a lot worse, and would 13 lead to overfitting?

Probably not. We tend to pick numbers that feel nice, often powers of two. So if you are stuck on a runtime error, change these numbers and see what it does to the error message. If the error message remains the same, the variable that you changed has nothing to do with it. Once it starts changing, though, you know you've reached something related.

This can be subtle. For example, some networks require that all batches have the same size. If your data isn't divisible by the batch size, your last batch will be too small and you'll get an error like:

```
Incompatible shapes: [X,784] vs. [Y,784]
```

Here X would be the batch size and Y the size of your last incomplete batch. You might recognize X as your batch size, but Y is hard to place. But if you change the batch size, Y also changes, which provides a hint as to where to look.

Discussion

Understanding errors reported by the framework that is abstracted away by Keras is fundamentally tricky. The abstraction breaks, and we suddenly see the internals of the machinery. The techniques from this recipe allow you to postpone looking into those details by spotting shapes and names in the errors and, failing that, experimenting with numbers and seeing what changes.

2.3 Checking Intermediate Results

Problem

Your network quickly gets to a promising level of accuracy but refuses to go beyond that.

Solution

Check whether it hasn't gotten stuck at an obvious local maximum.

One situation in which this can happen is when one label is far more common than any others, and your network quickly learns that always predicting this outcome gives decent results. It is not hard to verify that this is happening; just feed the network a sample of inputs and look at the outputs. If all outputs are the same, you are stuck this way.

Some of the following recipes in this chapter offer suggestions for how to fix this. Alternatively, you could play with the distribution of the data. If 95% of your examples are dogs and only 5% cats, the network might not see enough cats. By artificially changing the distribution to, say, 65%/35%, you make it a little easier for the network.

This is, of course, not without its own risks. The network might now have more of a chance to learn about cats, but it will also learn the wrong base distribution, or prior. This means that in case of doubt the network will now be more likely to pick "cat" as the answer, even though, all things being equal, "dog" is more likely.

Discussion

Looking at the distribution of output labels of a network for a small sample of inputs is an easy way to get an idea of what is actually being done, yet it is often overlooked. Playing with the distribution is a way to try to get the network unstuck if it focuses on just the top answer, but you should probably consider other techniques too.

There are other things to look out for in the output when a network isn't converging quickly; the occurrence of NaNs is an indication of exploding gradients, and if the outputs of your network seem to be clipped and can't seem to reach the right values, you might have an incorrect activation function on your final layer.

2.4 Picking the Right Activation Function (for Your Final Layer)

Problem

How do you pick the right activation function for your final layer when things are off?

Solution

Make sure that the activation function corresponds with the intention of the network.

A good way to get started with deep learning is to find an example online somewhere and modify it step by step until it does what you want it to do. However, if the intention of the example network is different from what your goal, you might have to change the activation function of the final layer. Let's take a look at some common choices.

The softmax activation function makes sure that the sum of the output vector is exactly 1. This is an appropriate activation function for networks that output exactly one label for a given input (for example, an image classifier). The output vector will then represent the probability distribution—if the entry for "cat" in the output vector is .65, then the network thinks that it sees a cat with 65% certainty. Softmax only works when there is one answer. When multiple answers are possible, give the sigmoid activation a try.

A linear activation function is appropriate for regression problems when we need to predict a numeric value given an input. An example would be to predict a movie rating given a series of movie reviews. The linear activation function will take the values of the previous layer and multiply them with a set of weights such that it best fits the expected output. Just as it is a good idea to normalize the input data into a $[-1, 1]$ range or thereabouts, it often helps to do the same for outputs. So, if our movie ratings are between 0 and 5, we'd subtract 2.5 and divide by the same when creating the training data.

If the network outputs an image, make sure that the activation function you use is in line with how you normalize the pixels. The standard normalization of deducting the mean pixel value and dividing by the standard deviation results in values that center around 0, so it won't work with sigmoid, and since 30% of the values will fall outside the range $[-1, 1]$ tanh won't be a good fit either. You can still use these, but you'd have to change the normalization applied to your output.

Depending on what you know about the output distribution, it might be useful to do something even more fancy. Movie ratings, for example, tend to center around 3.7 or so, so using that as the center could well yield better results. When the actual distribution is skewed such that values around the average are much more likely than outliers, using a tanh activation function can be appropriate. This squashes any value into a $[-1, 1]$ range. By mapping the expected outputs to the same range, keeping the expected distribution in mind, we can mimic any shape of our output data.

Discussion

Picking the right output activation function is crucial, but in most cases not difficult. If your output represents a probability distribution with one possible outcome, softmax is for you; otherwise, you need to experiment.

You also need to make sure that the loss function works with the activation function of the final layer. The loss function steers the training of the network by calculating how "wrong" a prediction is, given an expected value. We saw that a softmax activation function is the right choice when a network does multilabel predictions; in that case you probably want to go with a categorical loss function like Keras's `categorical_crossentropy`.

2.5 Regularization and Dropout

Problem

Once you have detected your network is overfitting, what can you do about it?

Solution

Restrict what the network can do by using regularization and dropout.

A neural network with enough parameters can fit any input/output mapping by memorizing. Accuracy seems great while training, but of course the network fails to perform very well on data it hasn't seen before and so does poorly on the test data or indeed in production. The network is overfitting.

One obvious way to stop the network from overfitting is to reduce the number of parameters that we have by decreasing the number of layers or making each layer smaller. But this of course also reduces the expressive power of our network. Regularization and dropout offer us something in between by restricting the expressive power of our network in a way that doesn't hurt the ability to learn (too much).

With regularization we add penalties to *extreme* values for parameters. The intuition here is that in order to fit an arbitrary input/output mapping, a network would need arbitrary parameters, while learned parameters tend to be in a normal range. So, making it harder to get to those arbitrary parameters should keep the network on the path of learning rather than memorizing.

Application in Keras is straightforward:

```
dense = Dense(128,
              activation='relu',
              kernel_regularizer=regularizers.l2(0.01))(flatten)
```

Regularizers can be applied to the weights of the kernel or the bias of the layer, or to the output of the layer. Which one and what penalty to use is mostly a matter of trial and error. 0.01 seems like a popular starting value.

Dropout is a similar technique, but more radical. Rather than keeping the weights of neurons in check, we randomly ignore a percentage of all neurons during training.

Similar to regularization, this makes it harder for a network to memorize input/output pairs, since it can't rely on specific neurons working during training. This nudges the network into learning general, robust features rather than one-off, specific ones to cover one training instance.

In Keras dropout is applied to a layer using the Dropout (pseudo)layer:

```
max_pool_1x = MaxPooling1D(window)(conv_1x)
dropout_1x = Dropout(0.3)(max_pool_1x)
```

This applies a dropout of 30% to the max-pooling layer, ignoring 30% of its neurons during training.

When doing inference, dropout is not applied. All things being equal this would increase the output of the layer by over 40%, so the framework automatically scales these outputs back.

Discussion

As you make your network more expressive, its tendency to overfit or memorize its inputs rather than learn general features will increase. Both regularization and dropout can play a role to reduce this effect. Both work by reducing the freedom of the network to develop arbitrary features, by punishing extreme values (regularization) or by ignoring the contribution of a percentage of the neurons in a layer (dropout).

An interesting alternative way to look at how networks with dropout work is to consider that if we have N neurons and we randomly switch a certain percentage of the neurons off, we really have created a generator that can create a very large variety of different but related networks. During training these different networks all learn the task at hand, but at evaluation time they all run in parallel and their average opinion is taken. So even if some of them start overfitting, chances are that this is drowned out in the aggregate vote.

2.6 Network Structure, Batch Size, and Learning Rate

Problem

How do you find the best network structure, batch size, and learning rate for a given problem?

Solution

Start small and work your way up.

Once we've identified the sort of network we'll need to solve a specific problem, we still have to make a number of implementation decisions. The more important among those are decisions about the network structure, the learning rate, and the batch size.

Let's start with the network structure. How many layers will we have? How big will each of those layers be? A decent strategy is to start with the smallest sizes that could possibly work. Being all enthusiastic about the "deep" in deep learning, there is a certain temptation to start with many layers. But typically if a one- or two-layer network doesn't perform at all, chances are that adding more layers isn't going to really help.

Continuing with the size of each individual layer, larger layers can learn more, but they also take longer and have more space to hide problems. As with the number of layers, start small and expand from there. If you suspect that the expressive power of a smaller network will be insufficient to make any sense of your data, consider simplifying your data; start with a small network that only distinguishes between the two most popular labels and then gradually increase the complexity of both the data and the network.

The batch size is the number of samples we feed into the network before adjusting the weights. The larger the batch size, the longer it takes to finish one, but the more accurate the gradient is. In order to get results quickly, it is advisable to start with a smallish batch size—32 seems to work well.

The learning rate determines how much we'll change the weights in our network in the direction of the derived gradient. The higher the rate, the quicker we move through the landscapes. Too big a rate, though, and we risk skipping over the good bits and we start thrashing. When we take into account that a smaller batch size leads to a less accurate gradient, it stands to reason that we should combine a small batch size with a smaller learning rate. So, the suggestion here is again to start out small and, when things work, experiment with larger batch rates and higher learning rates.

Training on GPUs impacts this assessment. GPUs efficiently run steps in parallel, so there is no real reason to pick a batch size that is so small that it leaves part of the GPU idle. What batch size that is depends of course on the network, but as long as the time per batch doesn't increase by much when you increase the batch size, you're still on the right side of things. A second consideration when running on GPUs is memory. When a batch no longer fits in the memory of the GPU things start to fail and you'll start to see out of memory messages.

Discussion

Network structure, batch size, and learning rate are some of the important hyper parameters that impact the performance of networks but have little to do with the actual strategy. For all of these a reasonable strategy is to start small (but big enough that things still work) and go bigger step by step, observing that the network still performs.

As we increase the number of layers and the size of each layer, we'll start to see symptoms of overfitting at some point (training and testing accuracy start to diverge, for example). That might be a good time to look at regularization and dropout.

CHAPTER 3

Calculating Text Similarity Using Word Embeddings

Before we get started, this is the first chapter with actual code in it.
Chances are you skipped straight to here, and who would blame
you? To follow the recipes it really helps though if you have the
accompanying code up and running. You can easily do this by exe-
cuting the following commands in a shell:

```
git clone \
  https://github.com/DOsinga/deep_learning_cookbook.git
cd deep_learning_cookbook
python3 -m venv venv3
source venv3/bin/activate
pip install -r requirements.txt
jupyter notebook
```

You can find a more detailed explanation in "What Do You Need to
Know?" on page 9.

In this chapter we'll look at word embeddings and how they can help us to calculate
the similarities between pieces of text. Word embeddings are a powerful technique
used in natural language processing to represent words as vectors in an n-
dimensional space. The interesting thing about this space is that words that have similar meanings will appear close to each other.

The main model we'll use here is a version of Google's Word2vec. This is not a deep
neural model. In fact, it is no more than a big lookup table from word to vector and
therefore hardly a model at all. The Word2vec embeddings are produced as a side
effect of training a network to predict a word from context for sentences taken from
Google News. Moreover, it is possibly the best-known example of an embedding, and
embeddings are an important concept in deep learning.

Once you start looking for them, high-dimensional spaces with semantic properties start popping up everywhere in deep learning. We can build a movie recommender by projecting movies into a high-dimensional space (Chapter 4) or create a map of handwritten digits using only two dimensions (Chapter 13). Image recognition networks project images into a space such that similar images are near to each other (Chapter 10).

In the current chapter we'll focus on just word embeddings. We'll start with using a pretrained word embedding model to calculate word similarities, then show some interesting Word2vec math. We'll then explore how to visualize these high-dimensional spaces.

Next, we'll take a look at how we can exploit the semantic properties of word embeddings like Word2vec for domain-specific ranking. We'll treat the words and their embeddings as the entities they represent, with some interesting results. We'll start with finding entity classes in Word2vec embeddings—in this case, countries. We'll then show how to rank terms against these countries and how to visualize these results on a map.

Word embeddings are a powerful way to map words to vectors and have many uses. They are often used as a preprocessing step for text.

There are two Python notebooks associated with this chapter:

```
03.1 Using pretrained word embeddings
03.2 Domain specific ranking using word2vec cosine distance
```

3.1 Using Pretrained Word Embeddings to Find Word Similarity

Problem

You need to find out whether two words are similar but not equal, for example when you're verifying user input and you don't want to require the user to exactly enter the expected word.

Solution

You can use a pretrained word embedding model. We'll use `gensim` in this example, a useful library in general for topic modeling in Python.

The first step is to acquire a pretrained model. There are a number of pretrained models available for download on the internet, but we'll go with the Google News one. It has embeddings for 3 million words and was trained on roughly 100 billion words taken from the Google News archives. Downloading it will take a while, so we'll cache the file locally:

```
MODEL = 'GoogleNews-vectors-negative300.bin'
path = get_file(MODEL + '.gz',
    'https://s3.amazonaws.com/dl4j-distribution/%s.gz' % MODEL)
unzipped = os.path.join('generated', MODEL)
if not os.path.isfile(unzipped):
    with open(unzipped, 'wb') as fout:
        zcat = subprocess.Popen(['zcat'],
                        stdin=open(path),
                        stdout=fout
                        )
        zcat.wait()

Downloading data from GoogleNews-vectors-negative300.bin.gz
1647050752/1647046227 [==============================] - 71s 0us/step
```

Now that we have the model downloaded, we can load it into memory. The model is quite big and this will take around 5 GB of RAM:

```
model = gensim.models.KeyedVectors.load_word2vec_format(MODEL, binary=True)
```

Once the model has finished loading, we can use it to find similar words:

```
model.most_similar(positive=['espresso'])

[(u'cappuccino', 0.6888186931610107),
 (u'mocha', 0.6686209440231323),
 (u'coffee', 0.6616827249526978),
 (u'latte', 0.6536752581596375),
 (u'caramel_macchiato', 0.6491267681121826),
 (u'ristretto', 0.6485546827316284),
 (u'espressos', 0.6438628435134888),
 (u'macchiato', 0.6428250074386597),
 (u'chai_latte', 0.6308028697967529),
 (u'espresso_cappuccino', 0.6280542612075806)]
```

Discussion

Word embeddings associate an *n*-dimensional vector with each word in the vocabulary in such a way that similar words are near each other. Finding similar words is a mere nearest-neighbor search, for which there are efficient algorithms even in high-dimensional spaces.

Simplifying things somewhat, the Word2vec embeddings are obtained by training a neural network to predict a word from its context. So, we ask the network to predict which word it should pick for X in a series of fragments; for example, "the cafe served a X that really woke me up."

This way words that can be inserted into similar patterns will get vectors that are close to each other. We don't care about the actual task, just about the assigned weights, which we will get as a side effect of training this network.

Later in this book we'll see how word embeddings can also be used to feed words into a neural network. It is much more feasible to feed a 300-dimensional embedding vector into a network than a 3-million-dimensional one that is one-hot encoded. Moreover, a network fed with pretrained word embeddings doesn't have to learn the relationships between the words, but can start with the real task at hand immediately.

3.2 Word2vec Math

Problem

How can you automatically answer questions of the form "A is to B as C is to what?"

Solution

Use the semantic properties of the Word2vec model. The gensim library makes this rather straightforward:

```
def A_is_to_B_as_C_is_to(a, b, c, topn=1):
  a, b, c = map(lambda x:x if type(x) == list else [x], (a, b, c))
  res = model.most_similar(positive=b + c, negative=a, topn=topn)
  if len(res):
    if topn == 1:
      return res[0][0]
    return [x[0] for x in res]
  return None
```

We can now apply this to arbitrary words—for example, to find what relates to "king" the way "son" relates to "daughter":

```
A_is_to_B_as_C_is_to('man', 'woman', 'king')

u'queen'
```

We can also use this approach to look up the capitals of selected countries:

```
for country in 'Italy', 'France', 'India', 'China':
    print('%s is the capital of %s' %
          (A_is_to_B_as_C_is_to('Germany', 'Berlin', country), country))

Rome is the capital of Italy
Paris is the capital of France
Delhi is the capital of India
Beijing is the capital of China
```

or to find the main products of companies (note the # placeholder for any number used in these embeddings):

```
for company in 'Google', 'IBM', 'Boeing', 'Microsoft', 'Samsung':
  products = A_is_to_B_as_C_is_to(
    ['Starbucks', 'Apple'], ['Starbucks_coffee', 'iPhone'], company, topn=3)
```

```
print('%s -> %s' %
        (company, ', '.join(products)))
```

```
Google -> personalized_homepage, app, Gmail
IBM -> DB2, WebSphere_Portal, Tamino_XML_Server
Boeing -> Dreamliner, airframe, aircraft
Microsoft -> Windows_Mobile, SyncMate, Windows
Samsung -> MM_A###, handset, Samsung_SCH_B###
```

Discussion

As we saw in the previous step, the vectors associated with the words encode the meaning of the words—words that are similar to each other have vectors that are close to each other. It turns out that the difference between word vectors also encodes the difference between words, so if we take the vector for the word "son" and deduct the vector for the word "daughter" we end up with a difference that can be interpreted as "going from male to female." If we add this difference to the vector for the word "king" we end up near the vector for the word "queen":

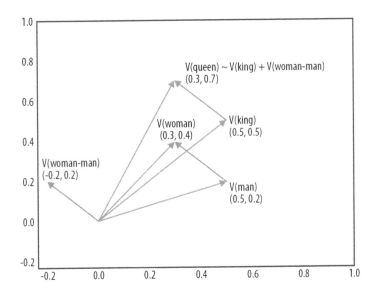

The most_similar method takes one or more positive words and one or more negative words. It looks up the corresponding vectors, then deducts the negative from the positive and returns the words that have vectors nearest to the resulting vector.

So in order to answer the question "A is to B as C is to?" we want to deduct A from B and then add C, or call most_similar with positive = [B, C] and negative = [A]. The example A_is_to_B_as_C_is_to adds two small features to this behavior. If we request only one example, it will return a single item, rather than a list with one item. Similarly, we can return either lists or single items for A, B, and C.

Being able to provide lists turned out to be useful in the product example. We asked for three products per company, which makes it more important to get the vector exactly right than if we only asked for one. By providing "Starbucks" and "Apple," we get a more exact vector for the concept of "is a product of."

3.3 Visualizing Word Embeddings

Problem

You want to get some insight into how word embeddings partition a set of objects.

Solution

A 300-dimensional space is hard to browse, but luckily we can use an algorithm called *t-distributed stochastic neighbor embedding* (t-SNE) to fold a higher-dimensional space into something more comprehensible, like two dimensions.

Let's say we want to look at how three sets of terms are partitioned. We'll pick countries, sports, and drinks:

```
beverages = ['espresso', 'beer', 'vodka', 'wine', 'cola', 'tea']
countries = ['Italy', 'Germany', 'Russia', 'France', 'USA', 'India']
sports = ['soccer', 'handball', 'hockey', 'cycling', 'basketball', 'cricket']

items = beverages + countries + sports
```

Now let's look up their vectors:

```
item_vectors = [(item, model[item])
                for item in items
                if item in model]
```

We can now use t-SNE to find the clusters in the 300-dimensional space:

```
vectors = np.asarray([x[1] for x in item_vectors])
lengths = np.linalg.norm(vectors, axis=1)
norm_vectors = (vectors.T / lengths).T
tsne = TSNE(n_components=2, perplexity=10,
            verbose=2).fit_transform(norm_vectors)
```

Let's use matplotlib to show the results in a nice scatter plot:

```
x=tsne[:,0]
y=tsne[:,1]

fig, ax = plt.subplots()
ax.scatter(x, y)

for item, x1, y1 in zip(item_vectors, x, y):
    ax.annotate(item[0], (x1, y1))

plt.show()
```

The result is:

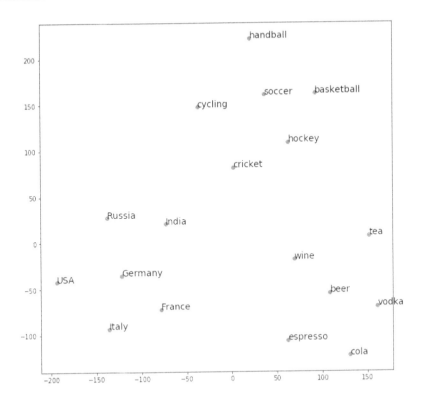

Discussion

t-SNE is a clever algorithm; you give it a set of points in a high-dimensional space, and it iteratively tries to find the best projection onto a lower-dimensional space (usually a plane) that maintains the distances between the points as well as possible. It is therefore very suitable for visualizing higher dimensions like (word) embeddings.

For more complex situations, the `perplexity` parameter is something to play around with. This variable loosely determines the balance between local accuracy and overall accuracy. Setting it to a low value creates small clusters that are locally accurate; setting it higher leads to more local distortions, but with better overall clusters.

3.4 Finding Entity Classes in Embeddings

Problem

In high-dimensional spaces there are often subspaces that contain only entities of one class. How do you find those spaces?

Solution

Apply a support vector machine (SVM) on a set of examples and counterexamples. For example, let's find the countries in the Word2vec space. We'll start by loading up the model again and exploring things similar to a country, Germany:

```
model = gensim.models.KeyedVectors.load_word2vec_format(MODEL, binary=True)
model.most_similar(positive=['Germany'])

[(u'Austria', 0.7461062073707581),
 (u'German', 0.7178748846054077),
 (u'Germans', 0.6628648042678833),
 (u'Switzerland', 0.6506867408752441),
 (u'Hungary', 0.6504981517791748),
 (u'Germnay', 0.649348258972168),
 (u'Netherlands', 0.6437495946884155),
 (u'Cologne', 0.6430779099464417)]
```

As you can see there are a number of countries nearby, but words like "German" and the names of German cities also show up in the list. We could try to construct a vector that best represents the concept of "country" by adding up the vectors of many countries rather than just using Germany, but that only goes so far. The concept of country in the embedding space isn't a point, it is a shape. What we need is a real classifier.

Support vector machines have proven effective for classification tasks like this. Scikit-learn has an easy-to-deploy solution. The first step is to build a training set. For this recipe getting positive examples is not hard since there are only so many countries:

```
positive = ['Chile', 'Mauritius', 'Barbados', 'Ukraine', 'Israel',
    'Rwanda', 'Venezuela', 'Lithuania', 'Costa_Rica', 'Romania',
    'Senegal', 'Canada', 'Malaysia', 'South_Korea', 'Australia',
    'Tunisia', 'Armenia', 'China', 'Czech_Republic', 'Guinea',
    'Gambia', 'Gabon', 'Italy', 'Montenegro', 'Guyana', 'Nicaragua',
    'French_Guiana', 'Serbia', 'Uruguay', 'Ethiopia', 'Samoa',
    'Antarctica', 'Suriname', 'Finland', 'Bermuda', 'Cuba', 'Oman',
    'Azerbaijan', 'Papua', 'France', 'Tanzania', 'Germany' ... ]
```

Having more positive examples is of course better, but for this example using 40–50 will give us a good idea of how the solution works.

We also need some negative examples. We sample these directly from the general vocabulary of the Word2vec model. We could get unlucky and draw a country and put it in the negative examples, but given the fact that we have 3 million words in the model and there are less than 200 countries in the world, we'd have to be very unlucky indeed:

```
negative = random.sample(model.vocab.keys(), 5000)
negative[:4]

[u'Denys_Arcand_Les_Invasions',
 u'2B_refill',
```

```
 u'strained_vocal_chords',
 u'Manifa']
```

Now we'll create a labeled training set based on the positive and negative examples. We'll use 1 as the label for something being a country, and 0 for it not being a country. We'll follow the convention of storing the training data in a variable X and the labels in a variable y:

```
labelled = [(p, 1) for p in positive] + [(n, 0) for n in negative]
random.shuffle(labelled)
X = np.asarray([model[w] for w, l in labelled])
y = np.asarray([l for w, l in labelled])
```

Let's train the model. We'll set aside a fraction of the data to evaluate how we are doing:

```
TRAINING_FRACTION = 0.7
cut_off = int(TRAINING_FRACTION * len(labelled))
clf = svm.SVC(kernel='linear')
clf.fit(X[:cut_off], y[:cut_off])
```

The training should happen almost instantaneously even on a not very powerful computer since our dataset is relatively small. We can have a peek at how we are doing by looking at how many times the model has the right prediction for the bits of the eval set:

```
res = clf.predict(X[cut_off:])

missed = [country for (pred, truth, country) in
             zip(res, y[cut_off:], labelled[cut_off:]) if pred != truth]
100 - 100 * float(len(missed)) / len(res), missed
```

The results you get will depend a bit on the positive countries selected and which negative samples you happened to draw. I mostly get a list of countries that it missed —typically because the country name also means something else, like Jordan, but there are also some genuine misses in there. The precision comes out at 99.9% or so.

We can now run the classifier over all of the words to extract the countries:

```
res = []
for word, pred in zip(model.index2word, all_predictions):
  if pred:
    res.append(word)
    if len(res) == 150:
      break
random.sample(res, 10)

[u'Myanmar',
 u'countries',
 u'Sri_Lanka',
 u'Israelis',
 u'Australia',
 u'Pyongyang',
```

```
u'New_Hampshire',
u'Italy',
u'China',
u'Philippine']
```

The results are pretty good, though not perfect. The word "countries" itself, for example, is classified as a country, as are entities like continents or US states.

Discussion

Support vector machines are effective tools when it comes to finding classes within a higher-dimensional space like word embeddings. They work by trying to find hyperplanes that separate the positive examples from the negative examples.

Countries in Word2vec are all somewhat near to each other since they share a semantic aspect. SVMs help us find the cloud of countries and come up with boundaries. The following diagram visualizes this in two dimensions:

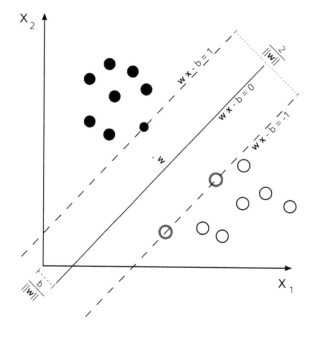

SVMs can be used for all kinds of ad hoc classifiers in machine learning since they are effective even if the number of dimensions is greater than the number of samples, like in this case. The 300 dimensions could allow the model to overfit the data, but because the SVM tries to find a simple model to fit the data, we can still generalize from a dataset as small as a few dozen examples.

The results achieved are pretty good, though it is worth noting that in a situation where we have 3 million negative examples, 99.7% precision would still give us 9,000 false positives, drowning out the actual countries.

3.5 Calculating Semantic Distances Inside a Class

Problem

How do you find the most relevant items from a class for a given criterion?

Solution

Given a class, for example *countries*, we can rank the members of that class against a criterion, by looking at the relative distances:

```
country_to_idx = {country['name']: idx for idx, country in enumerate(countries)}
country_vecs = np.asarray([model[c['name']] for c in countries])
country_vecs.shape
```

```
(184, 300)
```

We can now, as before, extract the vectors for the countries into a numpy array that lines up with the countries:

```
countries = list(country_to_cc.keys())
country_vecs = np.asarray([model[c] for c in countries])
```

A quick sanity check to see which countries are most like Canada:

```
dists = np.dot(country_vecs, country_vecs[country_to_idx['Canada']])
for idx in reversed(np.argsort(dists)[-8:]):
    print(countries[idx], dists[idx])
```

```
Canada 7.5440245
New_Zealand 3.9619699
Finland 3.9392405
Puerto_Rico 3.838145
Jamaica 3.8102934
Sweden 3.8042784
Slovakia 3.7038736
Australia 3.6711009
```

The Caribbean countries are somewhat surprising and a lot of the news about Canada must be related to hockey, given the appearance of Slovakia and Finland in the list, but otherwise it doesn't look unreasonable.

Let's switch gears and do some ranking for an arbitrary term over the set of countries. For each country we'll calculate the distance between the name of the country and the term we want to rank against. Countries that are "closer" to the term are more relevant for the term:

```
def rank_countries(term, topn=10, field='name'):
    if not term in model:
        return []
    vec = model[term]
    dists = np.dot(country_vecs, vec)
    return [(countries[idx][field], float(dists[idx]))
            for idx in reversed(np.argsort(dists)[-topn:])]
```

For example:

```
rank_countries('cricket')

[('Sri_Lanka', 5.92276668548584),
 ('Zimbabwe', 5.336524486541748),
 ('Bangladesh', 5.192488670349121),
 ('Pakistan', 4.948408126831055),
 ('Guyana', 3.9162840843200684),
 ('Barbados', 3.757995128631592),
 ('India', 3.7504401206970215),
 ('South_Africa', 3.6561498641967773),
 ('New_Zealand', 3.642028331756592),
 ('Fiji', 3.608567714691162)]
```

Since the Word2vec model we are using was trained on Google News, the ranker will return countries that are mostly known for the given term in the recent news. India might be more often mentioned for cricket, but as long as it is also covered for other things, Sri Lanka can still win.

Discussion

In spaces where we have members of different classes projected into the same dimensions, we can use the cross-class distances as a measure of affinity. Word2vec doesn't quite represent a conceptual space (the word "Jordan" can refer to the river, the country, or a person), but it is good enough to nicely rank countries on relevance for various concepts.

A similar approach is often taken when building recommender systems. For the Netflix challenge, for example, a popular strategy was to use user ratings for movies as a way to project users and movies into a shared space. Movies that are close to a user are then expected to be rated highly by that user.

In situations where we have two spaces that are not the same, we can still use this trick if we can calculate the projection matrix to go from one space to the other. This is possible if we have enough candidates whose positions we know in both spaces.

3.6 Visualizing Country Data on a Map

Problem

How can you visalize country rankings from an experiment on a map?

Solution

GeoPandas is a perfect tool to visualize numerical data on top of a map.

This nifty library combines the power of Pandas with geographical primitives and comes preloaded with a few maps. Let's load up the world:

```
world = gpd.read_file(gpd.datasets.get_path('naturalearth_lowres'))
world.head()
```

This shows us some basic information about a set of countries. We can add a column to the world object based on our `rank_countries` function:

```
def map_term(term):
    d = {k.upper(): v for k, v in rank_countries(term,
                                                 topn=0,
                                                 field='cc3')}
    world[term] = world['iso_a3'].map(d)
    world[term] /= world[term].max()
    world.dropna().plot(term, cmap='OrRd')

map_term('coffee')
```

This draws, for example, the map for coffee quite nicely, highlighting the coffee consuming countries and the coffee producing countries.

-0.303   1.943

Discussion

Visualizing data is an important technique for machine learning. Being able to look at the data, whether it is the input or the result of some algorithm, allows us to quickly spot anomalies. Do people in Greenland really drink that much coffee? Or are we seeing an artifact because of "Greenlandic coffee" (a variation on Irish coffee)? And those countries in the middle of Africa—do they really neither drink nor produce coffee? Or do we just have no data on them because they don't occur in our embeddings?

GeoPandas is the perfect tool to analyze geographically coded information and builds on the general data capabilities of Pandas, which we'll see more of in Chapter 6.

CHAPTER 4

Building a Recommender System Based on Outgoing Wikipedia Links

Recommender systems are traditionally trained on previously collected ratings from users. We want to predict ratings from users, so starting with historical ratings feels like a natural fit. However, this requires us to have a substantial set of ratings before we can get going and it doesn't allow us to do a good job on new items for which we don't have ratings yet. Moreover, we deliberately ignore the metainformation that we have on items.

In this chapter you'll explore how to build a simple movie recommender system based solely on outgoing Wikipedia links. You'll start by extracting a training set from Wikipedia and then train embeddings based on these links. You'll then implement a simple support vector machine classifier to give recommendations. Finally, you'll explore how you can use your newly trained embeddings to predict review scores for the movies.

The code in this chapter can be found in these notebooks:

```
04.1 Collect movie data from Wikipedia
04.2 Build a recommender system based on outgoing Wikipedia links
```

4.1 Collecting the Data

Problem

You want to obtain a dataset for training for a specific domain, like movies.

Solution

Parse a Wikipedia dump and extract only the pages that are movies.

The code in this recipe shows how to fetch and extract training data from Wikipedia, which is a very useful skill. However, downloading and processing a full dump takes a rather long time. The *data* directory of the notebook folder contains the top 10,000 movies pre-extracted that we'll use in the rest of the chapter, so you don't need to run the steps in this recipe.

Let's start by downloading a recent dump from Wikipedia. You can easily do this using your favorite browser, and if you don't need the very latest version, you should probably pick a nearby mirror. But you can also do it programmatically. Here's how to get the latest dump pages:

```
index = requests.get('https://dumps.wikimedia.org/backup-index.html').text
soup_index = BeautifulSoup(index, 'html.parser')
dumps = [a['href'] for a in soup_index.find_all('a')
            if a.has_attr('href') and a.text[:-1].isdigit()]
```

We'll now go through the dumps and find the newest one that has actually finished processing:

```
for dump_url in sorted(dumps, reverse=True):
    print(dump_url)
    dump_html = index = requests.get(
        'https://dumps.wikimedia.org/enwiki/' + dump_url).text
    soup_dump = BeautifulSoup(dump_html, 'html.parser')
    pages_xml = [a['href'] for a in soup_dump.find_all('a')
                if a.has_attr('href')
                and a['href'].endswith('-pages-articles.xml.bz2')]
    if pages_xml:
        break
    time.sleep(0.8)
```

Note the sleep to stay under the rate limiting of Wikipedia. Now let's fetch the dump:

```
wikipedia_dump = pages_xml[0].rsplit('/')[-1]
url = url = 'https://dumps.wikimedia.org/' + pages_xml[0]
path = get_file(wikipedia_dump, url)
path
```

The dump we retrieved is a bz2-compressed XML file. We'll use `sax` to parse the Wikipedia XML. We're interested in the `<title>` and the `<page>` tags so our `Content Handler` looks like this:

```
class WikiXmlHandler(xml.sax.handler.ContentHandler):
    def __init__(self):
        xml.sax.handler.ContentHandler.__init__(self)
        self._buffer = None
        self._values = {}
        self._movies = []
        self._curent_tag = None
```

```
def characters(self, content):
    if self._curent_tag:
        self._buffer.append(content)

def startElement(self, name, attrs):
    if name in ('title', 'text'):
        self._curent_tag = name
        self._buffer = []

def endElement(self, name):
    if name == self._curent_tag:
        self._values[name] = ' '.join(self._buffer)

    if name == 'page':
        movie = process_article(**self._values)
        if movie:
            self._movies.append(movie)
```

For each <page> tag this collects the contents of the title and of the text into the
self._values dictionary and calls process_article with the collected values.

Although Wikipedia started out as a hyperlinked text-based encyclopedia, over the
years it has developed into a more structured data dump. One way this is done is by
having pages link back to so-called *category pages*. These links function as tags. The
page for the film *One Flew Over the Cuckoo's Nest* links to the category page "1975
films," so we know it is a movie from 1975. Unfortunately, there is no such thing as a
category page for just movies. Fortunately, there is a better way: Wikipedia templates.

Templates started out as a way to make sure that pages that contain similar information have that information rendered in the same way. The "infobox" template is very
useful for data processing. Not only does it contain a list of key/value pairs applicable
to the subject of the page, but it also has a type. One of the types is "film," which
makes the task of extracting all movies a lot easier.

For each movie we want to extract the name, the outgoing links and, just because we
can, the properties stored in the infobox. The aptly named mwparserfromhell does a
decent job of parsing Wikipedia:

```
def process_article(title, text):
    rotten = [(re.findall('\d\d?\d?%', p),
              re.findall('\d\.\d\/\d+|$', p), p.lower().find('rotten tomatoes'))
              for p in text.split('\n\n')]
    rating = next((((perc[0], rating[0]) for perc, rating, idx in rotten
              if len(perc) == 1 and idx > -1), (None, None))
    wikicode = mwparserfromhell.parse(text)
    film = next((template for template in wikicode.filter_templates()
                 if template.name.strip().lower() == 'infobox film'),
                 None)
    if film:
        properties = {param.name.strip_code().strip():
```

```
                      param.value.strip_code().strip()
                      for param in film.params
                      if param.value.strip_code().strip()
                  }
          links = [x.title.strip_code().strip()
                      for x in wikicode.filter_wikilinks()]
          return (title, properties, links) + rating
```

We can now feed the bzipped dump into the parser:

```
parser = xml.sax.make_parser()
handler = WikiXmlHandler()
parser.setContentHandler(handler)
for line in subprocess.Popen(['bzcat'],
                              stdin=open(path),
                              stdout=subprocess.PIPE).stdout:
  try:
    parser.feed(line)
  except StopIteration:
    break
```

Finally, let's save the results so next time we need the data, we don't have to process for hours:

```
with open('wp_movies.ndjson', 'wt') as fout:
  for movie in handler._movies:
    fout.write(json.dumps(movie) + '\n')
```

Discussion

Wikipedia is not only a great resource to answer questions about almost any area of human knowledge; it also is the starting point for many deep learning experiments. Knowing how to parse the dumps and extract the relevant bits is a skill useful for many projects.

At 13 GB the dumps are sizeable downloads. Parsing the Wikipedia markup language comes with its own challenges: the language has grown organically over the years and doesn't seem to have a strong underlying design. But with today's fast connections and some great open source libraries to help with the parsing, it has all become quite doable.

In some situations the Wikipedia API might be more appropriate. This REST interface to Wikipedia allows you to search and query in a number of powerful ways and only fetch the articles that you need. Getting all the movies that way would take a long time given the rate limiting, but for smaller domains it is an option.

If you end up parsing Wikipedia for many projects, it might be worth it to first import the dump into a database like Postgres so you can query the dataset directly.

4.2 Training Movie Embeddings

Problem

How can you use link data between entities to produce suggestions like "If you liked this, you might also be interested in that"?

Solution

Train embeddings using some metainformation as connectors. This recipe builds on the previous one by using the movies and links extracted there. To make the dataset a bit smaller and less noisy, we'll work with only the top 10,000 movies determined by popularity on Wikipedia.

We'll treat the outgoing links as the connectors. The intuition here is that movies that link to the same page are similar. They might have the same director or be of the same genre. As the model trains, it learns not only which movies are similar, but also which links are similar. This way it can generalize and discover that a link to the year 1978 has a similar meaning as a link to 1979, which in turn helps with movie similarity.

We'll start by counting the outgoing links as a quick way to see whether what we have is reasonable:

```
link_counts = Counter()
for movie in movies:
    link_counts.update(movie[2])
link_counts.most_common(3)
```

```
[(u'Rotten Tomatoes', 9393),
 (u'Category:English-language films', 5882),
 (u'Category:American films', 5867)]
```

Our model's task is to determine whether a certain link can be found on the Wikipedia page of a movie, so we need to feed it labeled examples of matches and nonmatches. We'll keep only links that occur at least three times and build a list of all valid (link, movie) pairs, which we'll store for quick lookups later. We keep the same handy as a set for quick lookups later:

```
top_links = [link for link, c in link_counts.items() if c >= 3]
link_to_idx = {link: idx for idx, link in enumerate(top_links)}
movie_to_idx = {movie[0]: idx for idx, movie in enumerate(movies)}
pairs = []
for movie in movies:
    pairs.extend((link_to_idx[link], movie_to_idx[movie[0]])
                 for link in movie[2] if link in link_to_idx)
pairs_set = set(pairs)
```

We are now ready to introduce our model. Schematically, we take both the `link_id` and the `movie_id` as a number and feed those into their respective embedding layers. The embedding layer will allocate a vector of `embedding_size` for each possible input. We then set the dot product of these two vectors to be the output of our model. The model will learn weights such that this dot product will be close to the label. These weights will then project movies and links into a space such that movies that are similar end up in a similar location:

```python
def movie_embedding_model(embedding_size=30):
    link = Input(name='link', shape=(1,))
    movie = Input(name='movie', shape=(1,))
    link_embedding = Embedding(name='link_embedding',
        input_dim=len(top_links), output_dim=embedding_size)(link)
    movie_embedding = Embedding(name='movie_embedding',
        input_dim=len(movie_to_idx), output_dim=embedding_size)(movie)
    dot = Dot(name='dot_product', normalize=True, axes=2)(
        [link_embedding, movie_embedding])
    merged = Reshape((1,))(dot)
    model = Model(inputs=[link, movie], outputs=[merged])
    model.compile(optimizer='nadam', loss='mse')
    return model

model = movie_embedding_model()
```

We'll feed the model using a generator. The generator yields batches of data made up of positive and negative examples.

We sample the positive samples from the pairs array and then fill it up with negative examples. The negative examples are randomly picked and we make sure they are not in the `pairs_set`. We then return the data in a format that our network expects, an input/output tuple:

```python
def batchifier(pairs, positive_samples=50, negative_ratio=5):
    batch_size = positive_samples * (1 + negative_ratio)
    batch = np.zeros((batch_size, 3))
    while True:
        for idx, (link_id, movie_id) in enumerate(
                random.sample(pairs, positive_samples)):
            batch[idx, :] = (link_id, movie_id, 1)
        idx = positive_samples
        while idx < batch_size:
            movie_id = random.randrange(len(movie_to_idx))
            link_id = random.randrange(len(top_links))
            if not (link_id, movie_id) in pairs_set:
                batch[idx, :] = (link_id, movie_id, -1)
                idx += 1
        np.random.shuffle(batch)
        yield {'link': batch[:, 0], 'movie': batch[:, 1]}, batch[:, 2]
```

Time to train the model:

```
positive_samples_per_batch=512

model.fit_generator(
    batchifier(pairs,
                positive_samples=positive_samples_per_batch,
                negative_ratio=10),
    epochs=25,
    steps_per_epoch=len(pairs) // positive_samples_per_batch,
    verbose=2
)
```

Training times will depend on your hardware, but if you start with the 10,000 movie dataset they should be fairly short, even on a laptop without GPU acceleration.

We can now extract the movie embeddings from our model by accessing the weights of the `movie_embedding` layer. We normalize them so we can use the dot product as an approximation of the cosine similarity:

```
movie = model.get_layer('movie_embedding')
movie_weights = movie.get_weights()[0]
lens = np.linalg.norm(movie_weights, axis=1)
normalized = (movie_weights.T / lens).T
```

Now let's see if the embeddings make some sense:

```
def neighbors(movie):
    dists = np.dot(normalized, normalized[movie_to_idx[movie]])
    closest = np.argsort(dists)[-10:]
    for c in reversed(closest):
        print(c, movies[c][0], dists[c])

neighbors('Rogue One')

29 Rogue One 0.9999999
3349 Star Wars: The Force Awakens 0.9722805
101 Prometheus (2012 film) 0.9653338
140 Star Trek Into Darkness 0.9635347
22 Jurassic World 0.962336
25 Star Wars sequel trilogy 0.95218825
659 Rise of the Planet of the Apes 0.9516557
62 Fantastic Beasts and Where to Find Them (film) 0.94662267
42 The Avengers (2012 film) 0.94634
37 Avatar (2009 film) 0.9460137
```

Discussion

Embeddings are a useful technique, and not just for words. In this recipe we've trained a simple network and produced embeddings for movies with reasonable results. This technique can be applied any time we have a way to connect items. In this case we used the outgoing Wikipedia links, but we could also use incoming links or the words that appear on the page.

The model we trained here is extremely simple. All we do is ask it to come up with an embedding space such that the combination of the vector for the movie and the vector for the link can be used to predict whether or not they will co-occur. This forces the network to project movies into a space such that similar movies end up in a similar location. We can use this space to find similar movies.

In the Word2vec model we use the context of a word to predict the word. In the example of this recipe we don't use the context of the link. For outgoing links it doesn't seem like a particularly useful signal, but if we were using incoming links, it might have made sense. Pages linking to movies do this in a certain order, and we could use the context of the links to improve our embedding.

Alternatively, we could use the actual Word2vec code and run it over any of the pages that link to movies, but keep the links to movies as special tokens. This would then create a mixed movie and word embedding space.

4.3 Building a Movie Recommender

Problem

How can you build a recommender system based on embeddings?

Solution

Use a support vector machine to separate the positively ranked items from the negatively ranked items.

The previous recipe let us cluster movies and make suggestions like "If you liked *Rogue One*, you should also check out *Interstellar*." In a typical recommender system we want to show suggestions based on a series of movies that the user has rated. As we did in Chapter 3, we can use an SVM to do just this. Let's take the best and worst movies according to *Rolling Stone* from 2015 and pretend they are user ratings:

```
best = ['Star Wars: The Force Awakens', 'The Martian (film)',
        'Tangerine (film)', 'Straight Outta Compton (film)',
        'Brooklyn (film)', 'Carol (film)', 'Spotlight (film)']
worst = ['American Ultra', 'The Cobbler (2014 film)',
         'Entourage (film)', 'Fantastic Four (2015 film)',
         'Get Hard', 'Hot Pursuit (2015 film)', 'Mortdecai (film)',
         'Serena (2014 film)', 'Vacation (2015 film)']
y = np.asarray([1 for _ in best] + [0 for _ in worst])
X = np.asarray([normalized_movies[movie_to_idx[movie]]
                for movie in best + worst])
```

Constructing and training a simple SVM classifier based on this is easy:

```
clf = svm.SVC(kernel='linear')
clf.fit(X, y)
```

We can now run the new classifier over all the movies in our dataset and print the best five and the worst five:

```
estimated_movie_ratings = clf.decision_function(normalized_movies)
best = np.argsort(estimated_movie_ratings)
print('best:')
for c in reversed(best[-5:]):
    print(c, movies[c][0], estimated_movie_ratings[c])

print('worst:')
for c in best[:5]:
    print(c, movies[c][0], estimated_movie_ratings[c])

best:
(6870, u'Goodbye to Language', 1.24075226186855)
(6048, u'The Apu Trilogy', 1.2011876298842317)
(481, u'The Devil Wears Prada (film)', 1.1759994747169913)
(307, u'Les Mis\xe9rables (2012 film)', 1.1646775074857494)
(2106, u'A Separation', 1.1483743944891462)
worst:
(7889, u'The Comebacks', -1.5175929012505527)
(8837, u'The Santa Clause (film series)', -1.4651252650867073)
(2518, u'The Hot Chick', -1.464982008376793)
(6285, u'Employee of the Month (2006 film)', -1.4620595013243951)
(7339, u'Club Dread', -1.4593221506016203)
```

Discussion

As we saw in the previous chapter, we can use support vector machines to efficiently construct a classifier that distinguishes between two classes. In this case, we have it distinguish between good movies and bad movies based on the embeddings that we have previously learned.

Since an SVM finds one or more hyperplanes that separate the "good" examples from the "bad" examples, we can use this as the personalization function—the movies that are the furthest from the separating hyperplane and on the right side are the movies that should be liked best.

4.4 Predicting Simple Movie Properties

Problem

You want to predict simple movie properties, like Rotten Tomatoes ratings.

Solution

Use a linear regression model on the learned vectors of the embedding model to predict movie properties.

Let's try this for Rotten Tomatoes ratings. Luckily they are already present in our data in movie[-2] as a string of the form N%:

```
rotten_y = np.asarray([float(movie[-2][:-1]) / 100
                       for movie in movies if movie[-2]])
rotten_X = np.asarray([normalized_movies[movie_to_idx[movie[0]]]
                       for movie in movies if movie[-2]])
```

This should get us data for about half our movies. Let's train on the first 80%:

```
TRAINING_CUT_OFF = int(len(rotten_X) * 0.8)
regr = LinearRegression()
regr.fit(rotten_X[:TRAINING_CUT_OFF], rotten_y[:TRAINING_CUT_OFF])
```

Now let's see how we're doing on the last 20%:

```
error = (regr.predict(rotten_X[TRAINING_CUT_OFF:]) -
         rotten_y[TRAINING_CUT_OFF:])
'mean square error %2.2f' % np.mean(error ** 2)

mean square error 0.06
```

That looks really impressive! But while it is a testament to how effective linear regression can be, there is an issue with our data that makes predicting the Rotten Tomatoes score easier: we've been training on the top 10,000 movies, and while popular movies aren't always better, on average they do get better ratings.

We can get an idea of how well we're doing by comparing our predictions with just always predicting the average score:

```
error = (np.mean(rotten_y[:TRAINING_CUT_OFF]) - rotten_y[TRAINING_CUT_OFF:])
'mean square error %2.2f' % np.mean(error ** 2)

'mean square error 0.09'
```

Our model does perform quite a bit better, but the underlying data makes it easy to produce a reasonable result.

Discussion

Complex problems often need complex solutions, and deep learning can definitely give us those. However, starting with the simplest thing that could possibly work is often a good approach. It gets us started quickly and gives us an idea of whether we're looking in the right direction: if the simple model doesn't produce any useful results at all it's not that likely that a complex model will help, whereas if the simple model does work there's a good chance that a more complex model can help us achieve better results.

Linear regression models are as simple as they come. The model tries to find a set of factors such that the linear combination of these factors and our vectors approach the target value as closely as possible. One nice aspect of these models compared to most machine learning models is that we can actually see what the contribution of each of the factors is.

CHAPTER 5

Generating Text in the Style of an Example Text

In this chapter we'll look at how we can use recurrent neural networks (RNNs) to generate text in the style of a body of text. This makes for fun demos. People have used this type of network to generate anything from names of babies to descriptions of colors. These demos are a good way to get comfortable with recurrent networks. RNNs have their practical uses too—later in the book we'll use them to train a chatbot and build a recommender system for music based on harvested playlists, and RNNs have been used in production to track objects in video.

The recurrent neural network is a type of neural network that is helpful when working with time or sequences. We'll first look at Project Gutenberg as a source of free books and download the collected works of William Shakespeare using some simple code. Next, we'll use an RNN to produce texts that seem Shakespearean (if you don't pay too much attention) by training the network on downloaded text. We'll then repeat the trick on Python code, and see how to vary the output. Finally, since Python code has a predictable structure, we can look at which neurons fire on which bits of code and visualize the workings of our RNN.

The code for this chapter can be found in the following Python notebook:

```
05.1 Generating Text in the Style of an Example Text
```

5.1 Acquiring the Text of Public Domain Books

Problem

You want to download the full text of some public domain books to use to train your model.

Solution

Use the Python API for Project Gutenberg.

Project Gutenberg contains the complete texts of over 50,000 books. There is a handy Python API available to browse and download these books. We can download any book if we know the ID:

```
shakespeare = load_etext(100)
shakespeare = strip_headers(shakespeare)
```

We can get a book's ID either by browsing the website and extracting it from the book's URL or by querying *http://www.gutenberg.org/* by author or title. Before we can query, though, we need to populate the metainformation cache. This will create a local database of all books available. It takes a bit of time, but only needs to be done once:

```
cache = get_metadata_cache()
cache.populate()
```

We can now discover all works by Shakespeare:

```
for text_id in get_etexts('author', 'Shakespeare, William'):
    print(text_id, list(get_metadata('title', text_id))[0])
```

Discussion

Project Gutenberg is a volunteer project to digitize books. It focuses on making available the most important books in English that are out of copyright in the United States, though it also has books in other languages. It was started in 1971, long before the invention of the World Wide Web by Michael Hart.

Any work published in the US before 1923 is in the public domain, so most books found in the Gutenberg collection are older than that. This means that the language can be somewhat dated, but for natural language processing the collection remains an unrivalled source of training data. Going through the Python API not only makes access easy but also respects the restrictions that the site puts up for automatic downloading of texts.

5.2 Generating Shakespeare-Like Texts

Problem

How do you generate text in a specific style?

Solution

Use a character-level RNN.

Let's start by acquiring Shakespeare's collected works. We'll drop the poems, so we're left with a more consistent set of just the plays. The poems happen to be collected in the first entry:

```
shakespeare = strip_headers(load_etext(100))
plays = shakespeare.split('\nTHE END\n', 1)[-1]
```

We're going to feed the text in character by character and we'll one-hot encode each character—that is, every character will be encoded as a vector containing all 0s and one 1. For this, we need to know which characters we're going to encounter:

```
chars = list(sorted(set(plays)))
char_to_idx = {ch: idx for idx, ch in enumerate(chars)}
```

Let's create our model that will take a sequence of characters and predict a sequence of characters. We'll feed the sequence into a number of LSTM layers that do the work. The TimeDistributed layer lets our model output a sequence again:

```
def char_rnn_model(num_chars, num_layers, num_nodes=512, dropout=0.1):
    input = Input(shape=(None, num_chars), name='input')
    prev = input
    for i in range(num_layers):
        prev = LSTM(num_nodes, return_sequences=True)(prev)
    dense = TimeDistributed(Dense(num_chars, name='dense',
                                  activation='softmax'))(prev)
    model = Model(inputs=[input], outputs=[dense])
    optimizer = RMSprop(lr=0.01)
    model.compile(loss='categorical_crossentropy',
                  optimizer=optimizer, metrics=['accuracy'])
    return model
```

We are going to feed in random fragments from the plays to the network, so a generator seems appropriate. The generator will yield blocks of pairs of sequences, where the sequences of the pairs are just one character apart:

```
def data_generator(all_text, num_chars, batch_size):
    X = np.zeros((batch_size, CHUNK_SIZE, num_chars))
    y = np.zeros((batch_size, CHUNK_SIZE, num_chars))
    while True:
        for row in range(batch_size):
            idx = random.randrange(len(all_text) - CHUNK_SIZE - 1)
            chunk = np.zeros((CHUNK_SIZE + 1, num_chars))
            for i in range(CHUNK_SIZE + 1):
                chunk[i, char_to_idx[all_text[idx + i]]] = 1
            X[row, :, :] = chunk[:CHUNK_SIZE]
            y[row, :, :] = chunk[1:]
        yield X, y
```

Now we'll train the model. We'll set steps_per_epoch such that each character should have a decent chance to be seen by the network:

```
model.fit_generator(
    data_generator(plays, len(chars), batch_size=256),
```

```
        epochs=10,
        steps_per_epoch=2 * len(plays) / (256 * CHUNK_SIZE),
        verbose=2
    )
```

After training we can generate some output. We pick a random fragment from the plays and let the model guess what the next character is. We then add the next character to the fragment and repeat until we've reached the required number of characters:

```
def generate_output(model, start_index=None, diversity=1.0, amount=400):
    if start_index is None:
        start_index = random.randint(0, len(plays) - CHUNK_SIZE - 1)
    fragment = plays[start_index: start_index + CHUNK_SIZE]
    generated = fragment
    for i in range(amount):
        x = np.zeros((1, CHUNK_SIZE, len(chars)))
        for t, char in enumerate(fragment):
            x[0, t, char_to_idx[char]] = 1.
        preds = model.predict(x, verbose=0)[0]
        preds = np.asarray(preds[len(generated) - 1])
        next_index = np.argmax(preds)
        next_char = chars[next_index]

        generated += next_char
        fragment = fragment[1:] + next_char
    return generated

for line in generate_output(model).split('\n'):
    print(line)
```

After 10 epochs we should see some text that reminds us of Shakespeare, but we need around 30 for it to start to look like it could fool a casual reader that is not paying too close attention:

```
FOURTH CITIZEN. They were all the summer hearts.
    The King is a virtuous mistress.
CLEOPATRA. I do not know what I have seen him damn'd in no man
    That we have spoken with the season of the world,
    And therefore I will not speak with you.
    I have a son of Greece, and my son
    That we have seen the sea, the seasons of the world
    I will not stay the like offence.

OLIVIA. If it be aught and servants, and something
    have not been a great deal of state)) of the world, I will not stay
    the forest was the fair and not by the way.
SECOND LORD. I will not serve your hour.
FIRST SOLDIER. Here is a princely son, and the world
    in a place where the world is all along.
SECOND LORD. I will not see thee this:
    He hath a heart of men to men may strike and starve.
    I have a son of Greece, whom they say,
    The whiteneth made him like a deadly hand
```

```
And make the seasons of the world,
And then the seasons and a fine hands are parted
To the present winter's parts of this deed.
The manner of the world shall not be a man.
The King hath sent for thee.
The world is slain.
```

It's somewhat suspicious that both Cleopatra and the Second Lord have a son of Greece, but the present winter and the world being slain are appropriately *Game of Thrones*.

Discussion

In this recipe we saw how we can use RNNs to generate text in a certain style. The results are quite convincing, especially given the fact that the model predicts on a character-by-character level. Thanks to the LSTM architecture, the network is capable of learning relationships that span quite large sequences—not just words, but sentences, and even the basic structure of the layout of Shakespeare's plays.

Even though the example shown here isn't very practical, RNNs can be. Any time we want a network to learn a sequence of items, an RNN is probably a good choice.

Other toy apps people have built using this technique have generated baby names, names for paint colors, and even recipes.

More practical RNNs can be used to predict the next character a user is going to type for a smartphone keyboard app, or predict the next move in a chess game when trained on a set of openings. This type of network has also been used to predict sequences like weather patterns or even stock market prices.

Recurrent networks are quite fickle, though. Seemingly small changes to the network architecture can lead to a situation where they no longer converge because of the so-called *exploding gradient problem*. Sometimes during training, after making progress for a number of epochs, the network seems to collapse and starts forgetting what it learns. As always, it is best to start with something simple that works and add complexity step by step, while keeping track of what was changed.

For a slightly more in-depth discussion of RNNs, see Chapter 1.

5.3 Writing Code Using RNNs

Problem

How can you generate Python code using a neural network?

Solution

Train a recurrent neural network over the Python code that comes with the Python distribution that runs your scripts.

We can in fact use pretty much the same model as in the previous recipe for this task. As is often the case with deep learning, the key thing is to get the data. Python ships with the source code of many modules. Since they are stored in the directory where the *random.py* module sits, we can collect them using:

```python
def find_python(rootdir):
    matches = []
    for root, dirnames, filenames in os.walk(rootdir):
        for fn in filenames:
            if fn.endswith('.py'):
                matches.append(os.path.join(root, fn))

    return matches
srcs = find_python(random.__file__.rsplit('/', 1)[0])
```

We could then read in all these source files and concatenate them into one document and start generating new snippets, just as we did with the Shakespearean text in the previous recipe. This works reasonably well, but when generating snippets, it becomes clear that a good chunk of Python source code is actually English. English appears both in the form of comments and the contents of strings. We want our model to learn Python, not English!

Stripping out the comments is easy enough:

```python
COMMENT_RE = re.compile('#.*')
src = COMMENT_RE.sub('', src)
```

Removing the contents of strings is slightly more involved. Some strings contain useful patterns, rather than English. As a rough rule, we're going to replace any bit of text that has more than six letters and at least one space with "MSG":

```python
def replacer(value):
    if ' ' in value and sum(1 for ch in value if ch.isalpha()) > 6:
        return 'MSG'
    return value
```

Finding the occurrences of string literals can be done concisely with a regular expression. Regular expressions are rather slow though, and we're running them over a sizeable amount of code. In this case it's better to just scan the strings:

```python
def replace_literals(st):
    res = []
    start_text = start_quote = i = 0
    quote = ''
    while i < len(st):
        if quote:
```

```
        if st[i: i + len(quote)] == quote:
            quote = ''
            start_text = i
            res.append(replacer(st[start_quote: i]))
    elif st[i] in '"\'':
        quote = st[i]
        if i < len(st) - 2 and st[i + 1] == st[i + 2] == quote:
            quote = 3 * quote
        start_quote = i + len(quote)
        res.append(st[start_text: start_quote])
    if st[i] == '\n' and len(quote) == 1:
        start_text = i
        res.append(quote)
        quote = ''
    if st[i] == '\\':
        i += 1
    i += 1
return ''.join(res) + st[start_text:]
```

Even cleaned up this way, we end up with megabytes of pure Python code. We can now train the model as before, but on Python code rather than on plays. After 30 epochs or so, we should have something workable and can generate code.

Discussion

Generating Python code is no different from writing a Shakespearean-style play—at least for a neural network. We've seen that cleaning up the input data is an important aspect of data processing for neural networks. In this case we made sure to remove most traces of English from the source code. This way the network can focus on learning Python and not be distracted by also having to allocate neurons to learning English.

We could further regularize the input. For example, we could pipe all the source code first through a "pretty printer" so that it would all have the same layout and our network could focus on learning that, rather than the diversity found in the current code. One step further would be to tokenize the Python code using the built-in tokenizer, and then let the network learn this parsed version and use untokenize to generate the code.

5.4 Controlling the Temperature of the Output

Problem

You want to control the variability of the generated code.

Solution

Use the predictions as a probability distribution, rather than picking the highest value.

In the Shakespeare example, we picked the character in the predictions that had the highest score. This approach results in the output that is the best liked by the model. The drawback is that we get the same output for every start. Since we picked a random start sequence from the actual Shakespearean texts that didn't matter much. But if we want to generate Python functions, it would be nice to always start in the same way—let's say with /ndef—and look at various solutions.

The predictions of our network are the result of a softmax activation function and can therefore be seen as a probability distribution. So, rather than picking the maximum value, we can let `numpy.random.multinomial` give us an answer. `multinomial` runs n experiments and takes the probability of how likely the outcomes are. By running it with $n = 1$, we get what we want.

At this point we can introduce the notion of temperature in how we draw the outcomes. The idea is that the higher the temperature is, the more random the outcomes are, while lower temperatures are closer to the pure deterministic outcomes we saw earlier. We do this by scaling the logs of the predictions accordingly and then applying the softmax function again to get back to probabilities. Putting this all together we get:

```python
def generate_code(model, start_with='\ndef ',
                  end_with='\n\n', diversity=1.0):
    generated = start_with
    yield generated
    for i in range(2000):
        x = np.zeros((1, len(generated), len(chars)))
        for t, char in enumerate(generated):
            x[0, t, char_to_idx[char]] = 1.
        preds = model.predict(x, verbose=0)[0]

        preds = np.asarray(preds[len(generated) - 1]).astype('float64')
        preds = np.log(preds) / diversity
        exp_preds = np.exp(preds)
        preds = exp_preds / np.sum(exp_preds)
        probas = np.random.multinomial(1, preds, 1)
        next_index = np.argmax(probas)
        next_char = chars[next_index]
        yield next_char

        generated += next_char
        if generated.endswith(end_with):
            break
```

We're finally ready to have some fun. At `diversity=1.0` the following code is produced. Note how the model generated our `"MSG"` placeholder and, apart from confusing `val` and `value`, almost got us running code:

```
def _calculate_ratio(val):
    """MSG"""
    if value and value[0] != '0':
        raise errors.HeaderParseError(
            "MSG".format(Storable))
    return value
```

Discussion

Using the output of the softmax activation function as a probability distribution allows us to get a variety of results that correspond to what the model "intends." An added bonus is that it allows us to introduce the notion of temperature, so we can control how "random" the output is. In Chapter 13 we'll look at how *variational autoencoders* use a similar technique to control the randomness of what is generated.

The generated Python code can certainly pass for the real thing if we don't pay attention to the details. One way to improve the results further would be to call the com pile function on the generated code and only keep code that compiles. That way we can make sure that it is at least syntactically correct. A slight variation of that approach would be to not start over on a syntax error, but just drop the line where the error occurs and everything that follows and try again.

5.5 Visualizing Recurrent Network Activations

Problem

How can you gain insight into what a recurrent network is doing?

Solution

Extract the activations from the neurons while they process text. Since we're going to visualize the neurons, it makes sense to reduce their number. This will degrade the performance of the model a bit, but makes things simpler:

```
flat_model = char_rnn_model(len(py_chars), num_layers=1, num_nodes=512)
```

This model is a bit simpler and gets us slightly less accurate results, but it is good enough for visualizations. Keras has a handy method called `function` that allows us to specify an input and an output layer and will then run whatever part of the network is needed to convert from one to the other. The following method provides the network with a bit of text (a sequence of characters) and gets the activations for a specific layer back:

```
def activations(model, code):
    x = np.zeros((1, len(code), len(py_char_to_idx)))
    for t, char in enumerate(code):
        x[0, t, py_char_to_idx[char]] = 1.
    output = model.get_layer('lstm_3').output
    f = K.function([model.input], [output])
    return f([x])[0][0]
```

Now the question is which neurons to look at. Even our simplified model has 512 neurons. Activations in an LSTM are between –1 and 1, so a simple way to find interesting neurons is to just pick the highest value corresponding to each character. `np.argmax(act, axis=1)` will get us that. We can visualize those neurons using:

```
img = np.full(((len(neurons) + 1, len(code), 3), 128)
scores = (act[:, neurons].T + 1) / 2
img[1:, :, 0] = 255 * (1 - scores)
img[1:, :, 1] = 255 * scores
```

This will produce a small bitmap. After we enlarge the bitmap and plot the code on top, we get:

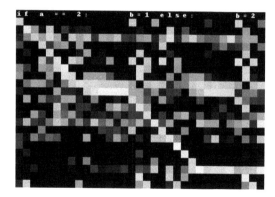

This looks interesting. The top neuron seems to keep track of where new statements start. The one with the green bars keeps track of spaces, but only in as far as they are used for indentation. The last-but-one neuron seems to fire when there is an = sign, but not when there is a ==, suggesting the network learned the difference between assignment and equality.

Discussion

Deep learning models can be very effective, but their results are notoriously hard to explain. We more or less understand the mechanics of the training and inference, but it is often difficult to explain a concrete result, other than pointing to the actual calculations. Visualizing activations is one way of making what the network learned a little clearer.

Looking at the neurons with the highest activation for each character quickly gets us a set of neurons that might be of interest. Alternatively, we could explicitly try to look for neurons that fire in specific circumstances, for example inside brackets.

Once we have a specific neuron that looks interesting, we can use the same coloring technique to highlight larger chunks of code.

CHAPTER 6

Question Matching

We've now seen a few examples of how we can construct and use word embeddings to compare terms with one another. It's natural to ask how we can extend this idea to larger blocks of text. Can we create semantic embeddings of entire sentences or paragraphs? In this chapter, we'll try to do just that: we're going to use data from Stack Exchange to build embeddings for entire questions; we can then use those embeddings to find similar documents or questions.

We'll start out by downloading and parsing our training data from the Internet Archive. Then we'll briefly explore how Pandas can be helpful for analyzing data. We let Keras do the heavy lifting when it comes to featurizing our data and building a model for the task at hand. We then look into how to feed this model from a Pandas `DataFrame` and how we can run it to draw conclusions.

The code for this chapter can be found in the following notebook:

```
06.1 Question matching
```

6.1 Acquiring Data from Stack Exchange

Problem

You need to access a large set of questions to kick-start your training.

Solution

Use the Internet Archive to retrieve a dump of questions.

A Stack Exchange data dump is freely available on the Internet Archive (*https://archive.org/details/stackexchange*), which hosts a number of interesting datasets (as well as striving to provide an archive of the entire web). The data is laid out with one

ZIP file for each area on Stack Exchange (e.g., travel, sci-fi, etc.). Let's download the file for the travel section:

```
xml_7z = utils.get_file(
    fname='travel.stackexchange.com.7z',
    origin=('https://ia800107.us.archive.org/27/'
            'items/stackexchange/travel.stackexchange.com.7z'),
)
```

While the input is technically an XML file, the structure is simple enough that we can get away with just reading individual lines and splitting out the fields. This is a bit brittle, of course. We will limit ourselves to processing 1 million records from the dataset; this keeps our memory usage from blowing up and should be enough data for us to work with. We'll save the processed data as a JSON file so we won't have to do the processing again the next time around:

```
def extract_stackexchange(filename, limit=1000000):
    json_file = filename + 'limit=%s.json' % limit

    rows = []
    for i, line in enumerate(os.popen('7z x -so "%s" Posts.xml'
                            % filename)):
        line = str(line)
        if not line.startswith('  <row'):
            continue

        if i % 1000 == 0:
            print('\r%05d/%05d' % (i, limit), end='', flush=True)

        parts = line[6:-5].split('"')
        record = {}
        for i in range(0, len(parts), 2):
            k = parts[i].replace('=', '').strip()
            v = parts[i+1].strip()
            record[k] = v
        rows.append(record)

        if len(rows) > limit:
            break

    with open(json_file, 'w') as fout:
        json.dump(rows, fout)

    return rows


rows = download_stackexchange()
```

Discussion

The Stack Exchange datasets is a great source for question/answer pairs that comes with a nice reuse license. As long as you give attribution you can use it in pretty much any way you want. Converting the zipped XML into the more easily consumable JSON format is a good preprocessing step.

6.2 Exploring Data Using Pandas

Problem

How do you quickly explore a large dataset so you can make sure it contains what you expect?

Solution

Use Python's Pandas.

Pandas is a powerful framework for data processing in Python. In some ways it is comparable to a spreadsheet; the data is stored in rows and columns and we can quickly filter, convert, and aggregate on the records. Let's start by converting our rows of Python dictionaries into a `DataFrame`. Pandas tries to "guess" the types of some columns. We'll coerce the columns we care about into the right format:

```
df = pd.DataFrame.from_records(rows)
df = df.set_index('Id', drop=False)
df['Title'] = df['Title'].fillna('').astype('str')
df['Tags'] = df['Tags'].fillna('').astype('str')
df['Body'] = df['Body'].fillna('').astype('str')
df['Id'] = df['Id'].astype('int')
df['PostTypeId'] = df['PostTypeId'].astype('int')
```

With `df.head` we can now see what's going on in our database.

We can also use Pandas to take a quick look at popular questions in our data:

```
list(df[df['ViewCount'] > 2500000]['Title'])

['How to horizontally center a &lt;div&gt; in another &lt;div&gt;?',
 'What is the best comment in source code you have ever encountered?',
 'How do I generate random integers within a specific range in Java?',
 'How to redirect to another webpage in JavaScript/jQuery?',
 'How can I get query string values in JavaScript?',
 'How to check whether a checkbox is checked in jQuery?',
 'How do I undo the last commit(s) in Git?',
 'Iterate through a HashMap',
 'Get selected value in dropdown list using JavaScript?',
 'How do I declare and initialize an array in Java?']
```

As you might expect, the most popular questions are general questions about frequently used languages.

Discussion

Pandas is a great tool for many types of data analysis, whether you just want to have a casual look at the data or you want to do in-depth analysis. It can be tempting to try to leverage Pandas for many tasks, but unfortunately the Pandas interface is not at all regular and for complex operations the performance can be significantly worse than using a real database. Lookups in Pandas are significantly more expensive than using a Python dictionary, so be careful!

6.3 Using Keras to Featurize Text

Problem

How do you quickly create feature vectors from text?

Solution

Use the `Tokenizer` class from Keras.

Before we can feed text into a model, we need to convert it into feature vectors. A common way to do this is to assign an integer to each of the top *N* words in a text and then replace each word by its integer. Keras makes this really straightforward:

```
from keras.preprocessing.text import Tokenizer
VOCAB_SIZE = 50000

tokenizer = Tokenizer(num_words=VOCAB_SIZE)
tokenizer.fit_on_texts(df['Body'] + ' ' + df['Title'])
```

Now let's tokenize the titles and bodies of our whole dataset:

```
df['title_tokens'] = tokenizer.texts_to_sequences(df['Title'])
df['body_tokens'] = tokenizer.texts_to_sequences(df['Body'])
```

Discussion

Converting text to a series of numbers by using a tokenizer is one of the classic ways of making text consumable by a neural network. In the previous chapter we converted text on a per-character basis. Character-based models take as input individual characters (removing the need for a tokenizer). The trade-off is in how long it takes to train the model: because you're forcing the model to learn how to tokenize and stem words, you need more training data and more time.

One of the drawbacks of processing texts on a per-word basis is the fact that there is no practical upper limit to the number of different words that can appear in the texts, especially if we have to handle typos and errors. In this recipe we only pay attention to words that appear in the top 50,000 by count, which is one way around this problem.

6.4 Building a Question/Answer Model

Problem

How do you calculate embeddings for questions?

Solution

Train a model to predict whether a question and an answer from the Stack Exchange dataset match.

Whenever we construct a model, the first question we should ask is: "What is our objective?" That is, what is the model going to try to classify?

Ideally we'd have a list of "similar questions to this one," which we could use to train our model. Unfortunately, it would be very expensive to acquire such a dataset! Instead, we'll rely on a surrogate objective: let's see if we can train our model to, given a question, distinguish between the matching answer and an answer from a random question. This will force the model to learn a good representation of titles and bodies.

We start off our model by defining our inputs. In this case we have two inputs, the title (question) and body (answer):

```
title = layers.Input(shape=(None,), dtype='int32', name='title')
body = layers.Input(shape=(None,), dtype='int32', name='body')
```

Both are of varying length, so we have to pad them. The data for each field will be a list of integers, one for each word in the title or the body.

Now we want to define a shared set of layers that both inputs will be passed through. We're first going to construct an embedding for the inputs, then mask out the invalid values, and add all of the words' values together:

```
embedding = layers.Embedding(
        mask_zero=True,
        input_dim=vocab_size,
        output_dim=embedding_size
    )

mask = layers.Masking(mask_value=0)
def _combine_sum(v):
    return K.sum(v, axis=2)
```

```
sum_layer = layers.Lambda(_combine_sum)
```

Here, we've specified a `vocab_size` (how many words are in our vocabulary) and an `embedding_size` (how wide our embedding of each word should be; the GoogleNews vectors are 300 dimensions, for example).

Now let's apply these layers to our word inputs:

```
title_sum = sum_layer(mask(embedding(title)))
body_sum = sum_layer(mask(embedding(body)))
```

Now that we have a single vector for our title and body, we can compare them to each other with a cosine distance, just like we did in Recipe 4.2. In Keras, that is expressed via the dot layer:

```
sim = layers.dot([title_sum, word_sum], normalize=True, axes=1)
```

Finally, we can define our model. It takes the title and the body in and outputs the similarity between the two:

```
sim_model = models.Model(inputs=[title,body], outputs=[sim])
sim_model.compile(loss='mse', optimizer='rmsprop')
```

Discussion

The model we've built here learns to match questions and answers but really the only freedom we give it is to change the embeddings of the words such that the sums of the embeddings of the title and the body match. This should get us embeddings for questions such that questions that are similar will have similar embeddings, because similar questions will have similar answers.

Our training model is compiled with two parameters telling Keras how to improve the model:

The loss function
> This tells the system how "wrong" a given answer is. For example, if we told the network that `title_a` and `body_a` should output 1.0, but the network predicts 0.8, how bad of an error is that? This becomes a more complex problem when we have multiple outputs, but we'll cover that later. For this model, we're going to use *mean squared error*. For the previous example, this means we would penalize the model by (1.0–0.8) ** 2, or 0.04. This loss will be propagated back through the model and improve the embeddings each time the model sees an example.

The optimizer
> There are many ways that loss can be used to improve our model. These are called *optimization strategies*, or *optimizers*. Fortunately, Keras comes with a number of reliable optimizers built in, so we won't have to worry much about

this: we can just pick a suitable one. In this case, we're using the `rmsprop` optimizer, which tends to perform very well across a wide range of problems.

6.5 Training a Model with Pandas

Problem

How do you train a model on data contained in Pandas?

Solution

Build a data generator that leverages the filter and sample features of Pandas.

As in the previous recipe, we are going to train our model to distinguish between a question title and the correct answer (body) versus the answer to another random question. We can write that out as a generator that iterates over our dataset. It will output a 1 for the correct question title and body and a 0 for a random title and body:

```
def data_generator(batch_size, negative_samples=1):
    questions = df[df['PostTypeId'] == 1]
    all_q_ids = list(questions.index)

    batch_x_a = []
    batch_x_b = []
    batch_y = []

    def _add(x_a, x_b, y):
        batch_x_a.append(x_a[:MAX_DOC_LEN])
        batch_x_b.append(x_b[:MAX_DOC_LEN])
        batch_y.append(y)

    while True:
        questions = questions.sample(frac=1.0)

        for i, q in questions.iterrows():
            _add(q['title_tokens'], q['body_tokens'], 1)

            negative_q = random.sample(all_q_ids, negative_samples)
            for nq_id in negative_q:
                _add(q['title_tokens'],
                     df.at[nq_id, 'body_tokens'], 0)

            if len(batch_y) >= batch_size:
                yield ({
                    'title': pad_sequences(batch_x_a, maxlen=None),
                    'body': pad_sequences(batch_x_b, maxlen=None),
                }, np.asarray(batch_y))

                batch_x_a = []
```

```
batch_x_b = []
batch_y = []
```

The only complication here is the batching of the data. This is not strictly necessary, but extremely important for performance. All deep learning models are optimized to work on chunks of data at a time. The best batch size to use depends on the problem you're working on. Using larger batches means your model sees more data for each update and therefore can more accurately update its weights, but on the flip side it can't update as often. Bigger batch sizes also take more memory. It's best to start small and keep doubling the batch size until the results no longer improve.

Now let's train the model:

```
sim_model.fit_generator(
    data_generator(batch_size=128),
    epochs=10,
    steps_per_epoch=1000
)
```

We'll train it for 10,000 steps, divided into 10 epochs of 1,000 steps each. Each step will process 128 documents, so our network will end up seeing 1.28M training examples. If you have a GPU, you'll be surprised how quickly this runs!

6.6 Checking Similarities

Problem

You'd like to use Keras to predict values by using the weights of another network.

Solution

Construct a second model that uses different input and output layers from the original network, but shares some of the other layers.

Our `sim_model` has been trained and as part of that learned how to go from a title to a `title_sum`, which is really what we are after. The model that just does that is:

```
embedding_model = models.Model(inputs=[title], outputs=[title_sum])
```

We can now use the "embedding" model to compute a representation for each question in our dataset. Let's wrap this up in a class for easy reuse:

```
questions = df[df['PostTypeId'] == 1]['Title'].reset_index(drop=True)
question_tokens = pad_sequences(tokenizer.texts_to_sequences(questions))

class EmbeddingWrapper(object):
    def __init__(self, model):
        self._questions = questions
        self._idx_to_question = {i:s for (i, s) in enumerate(questions)}
        self._weights = model.predict({'title': question_tokens},
```

```
                                        verbose=1, batch_size=1024)
        self._model = model
        self._norm = np.sqrt(np.sum(self._weights * self._weights
                                 + 1e-5, axis=1))

    def nearest(self, question, n=10):
        tokens = tokenizer.texts_to_sequences([sentence])
        q_embedding = self._model.predict(np.asarray(tokens))[0]
        q_norm= np.sqrt(np.dot(q_embedding, q_embedding))
        dist = np.dot(self._weights, q_embedding) / (q_norm * self._norm)

        top_idx = np.argsort(dist)[-n:]
        return pd.DataFrame.from_records([
            {'question': self._r[i], 'similarity': float(dist[i])}
            for i in top_idx
        ])
```

And now we can use it:

```
lookup = EmbeddingWrapper(model=sum_embedding_trained)
lookup.nearest('Python Postgres object relational model')
```

This produces the following results:

Similarity	Question
0.892392	working with django and sqlalchemy but backend...
0.893417	Python ORM that auto-generates/updates tables ...
0.893883	Dynamic Table Creation and ORM mapping in SqlA...
0.896096	SQLAlchemy with count, group_by and order_by u...
0.897706	SQLAlchemy: Scan huge tables using ORM?
0.902693	Efficiently updating database using SQLAlchemy...
0.911446	What are some good Python ORM solutions?
0.922449	python orm
0.924316	Python libraries to construct classes from a r...
0.930865	python ORM allowing for table creation and bul...

In a very short training time, our network managed to figure out that "SQL," "query,"
and "INSERT" are all related to Postgres!

Discussion

In this recipe we saw how we can use part of a network to predict the values we're
after, even if the overall network was trained to predict something else. The func‐
tional API of Keras provides a nice separation between the layers, how they are con‐
nected, and which combination of input and output layers forms a model.

As we'll see later in this book, this gives us a lot of flexibility. We can take a pre-trained network and use one of the middle layers as an output layer, or we can take one of those middle layers and add some new layers (see Chapter 9). We can even run the network backwards (see Chapter 12).

CHAPTER 7

Suggesting Emojis

In this chapter we'll build a model to suggest emojis given a small piece of text. We'll start by developing a simple sentiment classifier based on a public set of tweets labeled with various sentiments, like happiness, love, surprise, etc. We'll first try a Bayesian classifier to get an idea of the baseline performance and take a look at what this classifier can learn. We'll then switch to a convolutional network and look at various ways to tune this classifier.

Next we'll look at how we can harvest tweets using the Twitter API ourselves, and then we'll apply the convolutional model from Recipe 7.3 before moving on to a word-level model. We'll then construct and apply a recurrent word-level network, and compare the three different models.

Finally, we'll combine all three models into an ensemble model that outperforms any of the three.

The final model does a very decent job and just needs to be rolled into a mobile app!

The code for this chapter can be found in these notebooks:

```
07.1 Text Classification
07.2 Emoji Suggestions
07.3 Tweet Embeddings
```

7.1 Building a Simple Sentiment Classifier

Problem

How can you determine the sentiment expressed in a piece of text?

Solution

Find a dataset consisting of sentences where the sentiment is labeled and run a simple classifier over them.

Before trying something complicated, it is a good idea to first try the simplest thing we can think of on a dataset that is readily available. In this case we'll try to build a simple sentiment classifier based on a published dataset. In the following recipes we'll try to do something more involved.

A quick Google search leads us to a decent dataset from CrowdFlower containing tweets and sentiment labels. Since sentiment labels are similar to emojis on some level, this is a good start. Let's download the file and take a peek:

```
import pandas as pd
from keras.utils.data_utils import get_file
import nb_utils

emotion_csv = get_file('text_emotion.csv',
                       'https://www.crowdflower.com/wp-content/'
                       'uploads/2016/07/text_emotion.csv')
emotion_df = pd.read_csv(emotion_csv)

emotion_df.head()
```

This results in:

tweet_id	sentiment	author	content
0	1956967341	empty	xoshayzers @tiffanylue i know i was listenin to bad habi...
1	1956967666	sadness	wannamama Layin n bed with a headache ughhhh...waitin o...
2	1956967696	sadness	coolfunky Funeral ceremony...gloomy friday...
3	1956967789	enthusiasm	czareaquino wants to hang out with friends SOON!
4	1956968416	neutral	xkilljoyx @dannycastillo We want to trade with someone w...

We can also check how frequently the various emotions occur:

```
emotion_df['sentiment'].value_counts()
neutral       8638
worry         8459
happiness     5209
sadness       5165
love          3842
surprise      2187
```

Some of the simplest models that often give surprisingly good results are from the naive Bayes family. We'll start by encoding the data using the methods that sklearn provides. TfidfVectorizer assigns weights to words according to their inverse document frequency; words that occur often get a lower weight since they tend to be less informative. LabelEncoder assigns unique integers to the different labels it sees:

```
tfidf_vec = TfidfVectorizer(max_features=VOCAB_SIZE)
label_encoder = LabelEncoder()
linear_x = tfidf_vec.fit_transform(emotion_df['content'])
linear_y = label_encoder.fit_transform(emotion_df['sentiment'])
```

With this data in hand, we can now construct the Bayesian model and evaluate it:

```
bayes = MultinomialNB()
bayes.fit(linear_x, linear_y)
pred = bayes.predict(linear_x)
precision_score(pred, linear_y, average='micro')

0.28022727272727271
```

We get 28% right. If we always predicted the most likely category we would get a bit over 20%, so we're off to a good start. There are some other simple classifiers to try that might do a little better, but tend to be slower:

```
classifiers = {'sgd': SGDClassifier(loss='hinge'),
               'svm': SVC(),
               'random_forrest': RandomForestClassifier()}

for lbl, clf in classifiers.items():
    clf.fit(X_train, y_train)
    predictions = clf.predict(X_test)
    print(lbl, precision_score(predictions, y_test, average='micro'))

random_forrest 0.283939393939
svm 0.218636363636
sgd 0.325454545455
```

Discussion

Trying out "the simplest thing that could possibly work" helps us get started quickly and gives us an idea of whether the data has enough signal in it to do the job that we want to do.

Bayesian classifiers proved very effective in the early days of email spam fighting. However, they assume the contributions of each factor are independent from each other—so in this case, each word in a tweet has a certain effect on the predicted label, independent from the other words—which is clearly not always the case. A simple example is that inserting the word *not* into a sentence can negate the sentiment expressed. Still the model is easy to construct, and gets us results very quickly, and the results are understandable. As a rule, if a Bayesian model does not produce any good results on your data, using something more complex will probably not help much.

Bayesian models often seem to work even better than we'd naively expect. There has been some interesting research on why this is. Before machine learning they helped break the Enigma code, and they helped power the first email spam detectors.

7.2 Inspecting a Simple Classifier

Problem

How can you see what a simple classifier has learned?

Solution

Look at the contributing factors that make the classifier output a result.

One of the advantages of using a Bayesian approach is that we get a model that we can understand. As we discussed in the previous recipe, Bayesian models assume that the contribution of each word is independent of the other words, so to get an idea of what our model has learned, we can just ask the model's opinion on the individual words.

Now remember, the model expects a series of documents, each encoded as a vector whose length is equal to the size of the vocabulary, with each element encoding the relative frequency of the corresponding word in this document versus all the documents. So, a collection of documents that each contained just one word would be a square matrix with ones on the diagonal; the nth document would have zeros for all words in the vocabulary, except for word n. Now we can for each word predict the likelihoods for the labels:

```
d = eye(len(tfidf_vec.vocabulary_))
word_pred = bayes.predict_proba(d)
```

Then we can go through all the predictions and find the word scores for each class. We store this in a Counter object so we can easily access the top contributing words:

```
by_cls = defaultdict(Counter)
for word_idx, pred in enumerate(word_pred):
    for class_idx, score in enumerate(pred):
        cls = label_encoder.classes_[class_idx]
        by_cls[cls][inverse_vocab[word_idx]] = score
```

Let's print the results:

```
for k in by_cls:
    words = [x[0] for x in by_cls[k].most_common(5)]
    print(k, ':', ' '.join(words))

happiness : excited woohoo excellent yay wars
hate : hate hates suck fucking zomberellamcfox
```

```
boredom : squeaking ouuut cleanin soooooo candyland3
enthusiasm : lena_distractia foolproofdiva attending krisswouldhowse tatt
fun : xbox bamboozle sanctuary oldies toodaayy
love : love mothers mommies moms loved
surprise : surprise wow surprised wtf surprisingly
empty : makinitrite conversating less_than_3 shakeyourjunk kimbermuffin
anger : confuzzled fridaaaayyyyy aaaaaaaaaaa transtelecom filthy
worry : worried poor throat hurts sick
relief : finally relax mastered relief inspiration
sadness : sad sadly cry cried miss
neutral : www painting souljaboytellem link frenchieb
```

Discussion

Inspecting what a simple model learns before diving into something more complex is a useful exercise. As powerful as deep learning models are, the fact is that it is hard to really tell what they are doing. We can get a general idea of how they work, but truly understanding the millions of weights that result from training is almost impossible.

The results from our Bayesian model here are in line with what we would expect. The word "sad" is an indication for the class "sadness" and "wow" is an indication for surprise. Touchingly, the word "mothers" is a strong indication for love.

We do see a bunch of odd words, like "kimbermuffin" and "makinitrite." On inspection it turns out that these are Twitter handles. "foolproofdiva" is just a very enthusiastic person. Depending on the goal, we might consider filtering these out.

7.3 Using a Convolutional Network for Sentiment Analysis

Problem

You'd like to try using a deep network to determine the sentiment expressed in a piece of text using a deep network.

Solution

Use a convolutional network.

CNNs are more commonly associated with image recognition (see Chapter 9), but they do also work well with certain text classification tasks. The idea is to slide a window over the text and that way convert a sequence of items into a (shorter) sequence of features. The items in this case would be characters. The same weights are used for each step, so we don't have to learn the same thing multiple times—the word "cat" means "cat" wherever it occurs in a tweet:

```
char_input = Input(shape=(max_sequence_len, num_chars), name='input')

conv_1x = Conv1D(128, 6, activation='relu', padding='valid')(char_input)
```

```
max_pool_1x = MaxPooling1D(6)(conv_1x)
conv_2x = Conv1D(256, 6, activation='relu', padding='valid')(max_pool_1x)
max_pool_2x = MaxPooling1D(6)(conv_2x)

flatten = Flatten()(max_pool_2x)
dense = Dense(128, activation='relu')(flatten)
preds = Dense(num_labels, activation='softmax')(dense)

model = Model(char_input, preds)
model.compile(loss='sparse_categorical_crossentropy',
              optimizer='rmsprop',
              metrics=['acc'])
```

For the model to run, we first have to vectorize our data. We'll use the same one-hot encoding we saw in the previous recipe, encoding each character as a vector filled with all zeros, except for the nth entry, where n corresponds to the character we're encoding:

```
chars = list(sorted(set(chain(*emotion_df['content']))))
char_to_idx = {ch: idx for idx, ch in enumerate(chars)}
max_sequence_len = max(len(x) for x in emotion_df['content'])

char_vectors = []
for txt in emotion_df['content']:
    vec = np.zeros((max_sequence_len, len(char_to_idx)))
    vec[np.arange(len(txt)), [char_to_idx[ch] for ch in txt]] = 1
    char_vectors.append(vec)
char_vectors = np.asarray(char_vectors)
char_vectors = pad_sequences(char_vectors)
labels = label_encoder.transform(emotion_df['sentiment'])
```

Let's split our data into a training and a test set:

```
def split(lst):
    training_count = int(0.9 * len(char_vectors))
    return lst[:training_count], lst[training_count:]

training_char_vectors, test_char_vectors = split(char_vectors)
training_labels, test_labels = split(labels)
```

We can now train the model and evaluate it:

```
char_cnn_model.fit(training_char_vectors, training_labels,
                   epochs=20, batch_size=1024)
char_cnn_model.evaluate(test_char_vectors, test_labels)
```

After 20 epochs, the training accuracy reaches 0.39, but the test accuracy is only 0.31. The difference is explained by overfitting; the model doesn't just learn general aspects of the data that are also applicable to the test set, but starts to memorize part of the training data. This is similar to a student learning which answers match which questions, without understanding why.

Discussion

Convolutional networks work well in situations where we want our network to learn things independently of where they occur. For image recognition, we don't want the network to learn separately for each pixel; we want it to learn to recognize features independently of where they occur in the image.

Similarly, for text, we want the model to learn that if the word "love" appears anywhere in the tweet, "love" would be a good label. We don't want the model to learn this for each position separately. A CNN accomplishes this by running a sliding window over the text. In this case we use a window of size 6, so we take 6 characters at a time; for a tweet containing 125 characters, we would apply this 120 times.

The crucial thing is that each of those 120 neurons uses the same weights, so they all learn the same thing. After the convolution, we apply a `max_pooling` layer. This layer will take groups of six neurons and output the maximum value of their activations. We can think of this as forwarding the strongest theory that any of the neurons have to the next layer. It also reduces the size by a factor of six.

In our model we have two convolutional/max-pooling layers, which changes the size from an input of 167×100 to 3×256. We can think of these as steps that increase the level of abstraction. At the input level, we only know for each of the 167 positions which of any of the 100 different characters occurs. After the last convolution, we have 3 vectors of 256 each, which encode what is happening at the beginning, the middle, and the end of the tweet.

7.4 Collecting Twitter Data

Problem

How can you collect a large amount of Twitter data for training purposes automatically?

Solution

Use the Twitter API.

The first thing to do is to head over to *https://apps.twitter.com* to register a new app. Click the Create New App button and fill in the form. We're not going to do anything on behalf of users, so you can leave the Callback URL field empty.

After completion, you should have two keys and two secrets that allow access to the API. Let's store them in their corresponding variables:

```
CONSUMER_KEY = '<your value>'
CONSUMER_SECRET = '<your value>'
ACCESS_TOKEN = '<your value>'
ACCESS_SECRET = '<your value>'
```

We can now construct an authentication object:

```
auth=twitter.OAuth(
    consumer_key=CONSUMER_KEY,
    consumer_secret=CONSUMER_SECRET,
    token=ACCESS_TOKEN,
    token_secret=ACCESS_SECRET,
)
```

The Twitter API has two parts. The REST API makes it possible to call various functions to search for tweets, get the status for a user, and even post to Twitter. In this recipe we'll use the streaming API, though.

If you pay Twitter, you'll get a stream that contains all tweets as they are happening. If you don't pay, you get a sample of all tweets. That's good enough for our purpose:

```
status_stream = twitter.TwitterStream(auth=auth).statuses
```

The `stream` object has an iterator, `sample`, which will yield tweets. Let's take a look at some of these using `itertools.islice`:

```
[x['text'] for x in itertools.islice(stream.sample(), 0, 5) if x.get('text')]
```

In this case we only want tweets that are in English and contain at least one emoji:

```
def english_has_emoji(tweet):
    if tweet.get('lang') != 'en':
        return False
    return any(ch for ch in tweet.get('text', '') if ch in emoji.UNICODE_EMOJI)
```

We can now get a hundred tweets containing at least one emoji with:

```
tweets = list(itertools.islice(
    filter(english_has_emoji, status_stream.sample()), 0, 100))
```

We get two to three tweets a second, which is not bad, but it will take a while until we have a sizeable training set. We only care about the tweets that have only one type of emoji, and we only want to keep that emoji and the text:

```
stripped = []
for tweet in tweets:
    text = tweet['text']
    emojis = {ch for ch in text if ch in emoji.UNICODE_EMOJI}
    if len(emojis) == 1:
        emoiji = emojis.pop()
        text = ''.join(ch for ch in text if ch != emoiji)
        stripped.append((text, emoiji))
```

Discussion

Twitter can be a very useful source of training data. Each tweet has a wealth of metadata associated with it, from the account that posted the tweet to the images and hash tags. In this chapter we only use the language metainformation, but it is a rich area for exploring.

7.5 A Simple Emoji Predictor

Problem

How can you predict the emoji that best matches a piece of text?

Solution

Repurpose the sentiment classifier from Recipe 7.3.

If you collected a sizeable amount of tweets in the previous step, you can use those. If not, you can find a good sample in *data/emojis.txt*. Let's read those into a Pandas Data Frame. We're going to filter out any emoji that occurs less than 1,000 times:

```
all_tweets = pd.read_csv('data/emojis.txt',
        sep='\t', header=None, names=['text', 'emoji'])
tweets = all_tweets.groupby('emoji').filter(lambda c:len(c) > 1000)
tweets['emoji'].value_counts()
```

This dataset is too large to keep in memory in vectorized form, so we'll train using a generator. Pandas comes conveniently with a sample method, which allows us to have the following data_generator:

```
def data_generator(tweets, batch_size):
    while True:
        batch = tweets.sample(batch_size)
        X = np.zeros((batch_size, max_sequence_len, len(chars)))
        y = np.zeros((batch_size,))
        for row_idx, (_, row) in enumerate(batch.iterrows()):
            y[row_idx] = emoji_to_idx[row['emoji']]
            for ch_idx, ch in enumerate(row['text']):
                X[row_idx, ch_idx, char_to_idx[ch]] = 1
        yield X, y
```

We can now train the model from Recipe 7.3 without modifications using:

```
train_tweets, test_tweets = train_test_split(tweets, test_size=0.1)
BATCH_SIZE = 512
char_cnn_model.fit_generator(
    data_generator(train_tweets, batch_size=BATCH_SIZE),
    epochs=20,
    steps_per_epoch=len(train_tweets) / BATCH_SIZE,
```

```
        verbose=2
    )
```

The model trains to about 40% precision. This sounds pretty good, even if we take into account that the top emojis occur a lot more often than the bottom ones. If we run the model over the evaluation set the precision score drops from 40% to a little over 35%:

```
char_cnn_model.evaluate_generator(
    data_generator(test_tweets, batch_size=BATCH_SIZE),
    steps=len(test_tweets) / BATCH_SIZE
)

[3.0898117224375405, 0.35545459692028986]
```

Discussion

With no changes to the model itself, we are able to suggest emojis for a tweet instead of running sentiment classification. This is not too surprising; in a way emojis are sentiment labels applied by the author. That the performance is about the same for both tasks is maybe less expected, since we have so many more labels and since we would expect the labels to be more noisy.

7.6 Dropout and Multiple Windows

Problem

How can you increase the performance of your network?

Solution

Increase the number of trainable variables while introducing dropout, a technique that makes it harder for a bigger network to overfit.

The easy way to increase the expressive power of a neural network is to make it bigger, either by making the individual layers bigger or by adding more layers to the network. A network with more variables has a higher capacity for learning and can generalize better. This doesn't come for free, though; at some point the network starts to *overfit*. (Recipe 1.3 describes this problem in more detail.)

Let's start by expanding our current network. In the previous recipe we used a step size of 6 for our convolutions. Six characters seems like a reasonable amount to capture local information, but it is also slightly arbitrary. Why not four or five? We can in fact do all three and then join the results:

```
layers = []
for window in (4, 5, 6):
    conv_1x = Conv1D(128, window, activation='relu',
```

```
                       padding='valid')(char_input)
        max_pool_1x = MaxPooling1D(4)(conv_1x)
        conv_2x = Conv1D(256, window, activation='relu',
                       padding='valid')(max_pool_1x)
        max_pool_2x = MaxPooling1D(4)(conv_2x)
        layers.append(max_pool_2x)

    merged = Concatenate(axis=1)(layers)
```

Precision goes up to 47% during training using this network with its extra layers. But unfortunately the precision on the test set reaches only 37%. That is still slightly better than what we had before, but the overfitting gap has increased by quite a bit.

There are a number of techniques to stop overfitting, and they all have in common that they restrict what the model can learn. One of the most popular is adding a Drop out layer. During training, Dropout randomly sets the weights of a fraction of all neurons to zero. This forces the network to learn more robustly since it can't rely on a specific neuron to be present. During prediction, all neurons work, which averages the results and makes outliers less likely. This slows the overfitting down.

In Keras we add Dropout just like any other layer. Our model then becomes:

```
    for window in (4, 5, 6):
        conv_1x = Conv1D(128, window,
                         activation='relu', padding='valid')(char_input)
        max_pool_1x = MaxPooling1D(4)(conv_1x)
        dropout_1x = Dropout(drop_out)(max_pool_1x)
        conv_2x = Conv1D(256, window,
                         activation='relu', padding='valid')(dropout_1x)
        max_pool_2x = MaxPooling1D(4)(conv_2x)
        dropout_2x = Dropout(drop_out)(max_pool_2x)
        layers.append(dropout_2x)

    merged = Concatenate(axis=1)(layers)

    dropout = Dropout(drop_out)(merged)
```

Picking the dropout value is a bit of an art. A higher value means a more robust model, but one that also trains more slowly. Running with 0.2 brings the training precision to 0.43 and the test precision to 0.39, suggesting that we could still go higher.

Discussion

This recipe gives an idea of some of the techniques we can use to improve the performance of our networks. By adding more layers, trying different windows, and introducing Dropout layers at various places, we have a lot of knobs to turn to optimize our network. The process of finding the best values is called *hyperparameter tuning*.

There are frameworks that can automatically find the best parameters by trying various combinations. Since they do need to train the model many times, you need to either be patient or have access to multiple instances to train your models in parallel.

7.7 Building a Word-Level Model

Problem

Tweets are words, not just random characters. How can you take advantage of this fact?

Solution

Train a model that takes as input sequences of word embeddings, rather than sequences of characters.

The first thing to do is to tokenize our tweets. We'll construct a tokenizer that keeps the top 50,000 words, apply it to our training and test sets, and then pad both so they have a uniform length:

```
VOCAB_SIZE = 50000
tokenizer = Tokenizer(num_words=VOCAB_SIZE)
tokenizer.fit_on_texts(tweets['text'])
training_tokens = tokenizer.texts_to_sequences(train_tweets['text'])
test_tokens = tokenizer.texts_to_sequences(test_tweets['text'])
max_num_tokens = max(len(x) for x in chain(training_tokens, test_tokens))
training_tokens = pad_sequences(training_tokens, maxlen=max_num_tokens)
test_tokens = pad_sequences(test_tokens, maxlen=max_num_tokens)
```

We can have our model get started quickly by using pretrained embeddings (see Chapter 3). We'll load the weights with a utility function, load_wv2, which will load the Word2vec embeddings and match them to the words in our corpus. This will construct a matrix with a row for each of our tokens containing the weights from the Word2vec model:

```
def load_w2v(tokenizer=None):
    w2v_model = gensim.models.KeyedVectors.load_word2vec_format(
        word2vec_vectors, binary=True)

    total_count = sum(tokenizer.word_counts.values())
    idf_dict = {k: np.log(total_count/v)
                for (k,v) in tokenizer.word_counts.items()}

    w2v = np.zeros((tokenizer.num_words, w2v_model.syn0.shape[1]))
    idf = np.zeros((tokenizer.num_words, 1))

    for k, v in tokenizer.word_index.items():
        if < tokenizer.num_words and k in w2v_model:
            w2v[v] = w2v_model[k]
```

```
        idf[v] = idf_dict[k]

    return w2v, idf
```

We can now create a model very similar to our character model, mostly just changing how we process the input. Our input takes a sequence of tokens and the embedding layer looks each of those tokens up in the matrix we just created:

```
message = Input(shape=(max_num_tokens,), dtype='int32', name='title')
embedding = Embedding(mask_zero=False, input_dim=vocab_size,
                      output_dim=embedding_weights.shape[1],
                      weights=[embedding_weights],
                      trainable=False,
                      name='cnn_embedding')(message)
```

This model works, but not as well as the character model. We can fiddle with the various hyperparameters, but the gap is quite big (38% precision for the character-level model versus 30% for the word-level model). There is one thing we can change that does make a difference—setting the embedding layer's `trainable` property to `True`. This helps to get the precision for the word-level model up to 36%, but it also means that we're using the wrong embeddings. We'll take a look at fixing that in the next recipe.

Discussion

A word-level model has a bigger view of the input data than a character-level model because it looks at clusters of words rather than clusters of characters. Rather than using the one-hot encoding we used for characters, we use word embeddings to get started quickly. Here, we represent each word by a vector representing the semantic value of that word as an input to the model. (See Chapter 3 for more information on word embeddings.)

The model presented in this recipe doesn't outperform our character-level model and doesn't do much better than the Bayesian model we saw in Recipe 7.1. This indicates that the weights from our pretrained word embeddings are a bad match for our problem. Things work a lot better if we set the embedding layer to trainable; the model improves if we allow it to change those embeddings. We'll look at this in more detail in the next recipe.

That the weights aren't a good match is not all that surprising. The Word2vec model was trained on Google News, which has a rather different use of language than what we find on average on social media. Popular hashtags, for example, won't occur in the Google News corpus, while they seem rather important for classifying tweets.

7.8 Constructing Your Own Embeddings

Problem

How can you acquire word embeddings that match your corpus?

Solution

Train your own word embeddings.

The gensim package not only lets us use a pretrained embedding model, it also makes it possible to train new embeddings. The only thing it needs to do so is a generator that produces sequences of tokens. It will use this to build up a vocabulary and then go on to train a model by going through the generator multiple times. The following object will go through a stream of tweets, clean them up, and tokenize them:

```python
class TokensYielder(object):
    def __init__(self, tweet_count, stream):
        self.tweet_count = tweet_count
        self.stream = stream

    def __iter__(self):
        print('!')
        count = self.tweet_count
        for tweet in self.stream:
            if tweet.get('lang') != 'en':
                continue
            text = tweet['text']
            text = html.unescape(text)
            text = RE_WHITESPACE.sub(' ', text)
            text = RE_URL.sub(' ', text)
            text = strip_accents(text)
            text = ''.join(ch for ch in text if ord(ch) < 128)
            if text.startswith('RT '):
                text = text[3:]
            text = text.strip()
            if text:
                yield text_to_word_sequence(text)
                count -= 1
                if count <= 0:
                    break
```

We can now train the model. The sensible way to do it is to collect a week or so of tweets, save them in a set of files (one JSON document per line is a popular format), and then pass a generator that goes through the files into the TokensYielder.

Before we set off to do this and wait a week for our tweets to dribble in, we can test if this works at all by just getting 100,000 filtered tweets:

```
tweets = list(TokensYielder(100000,
              twitter.TwitterStream(auth=auth).statuses.sample()))
```

And then construct the model with:

```
model = gensim.models.Word2Vec(tweets, min_count=2)
```

Looking at the closest neighbors of the word "love" shows us that we have indeed our own domain-specific embeddings—only on Twitter is "453" related to "love," since online it is short for "cool story, bro":

```
model.wv.most_similar(positive=['love'], topn=5)

[('hate', 0.7243724465370178),
 ('loved', 0.7227891087532043),
 ('453', 0.707709789276123),
 ('melanin', 0.7069753408432007),
 ('appreciate', 0.696381688117981)]
```

"Melanin" is slightly less expected.

Discussion

Using existing word embeddings is a great way to get started quickly but is only suitable to the extent that the text we're processing is similar to the text that the embeddings were trained on. In situations where this is not the case and where we have access to a large body of text similar to what we are training on, we can easily train our own word embeddings.

As we saw in the previous recipe, an alternative to training fresh embeddings is to take existing embeddings but set the `trainable` property of the layer to `True`. This will make the network adjust the weights of the words in the embedding layer and find new ones where they are missing.

7.9 Using a Recurrent Neural Network for Classification

Problem

Surely there's a way to take advantage of the fact that a tweet is a sequence of words. How can you do this?

Solution

Use a word-level recurrent network to do the classification.

Convolutional networks are good for spotting local patterns in an input stream. For sentiment analysis this often works quite well; certain phrases influence the sentiment of a sentence independently of where they appear. The task of suggesting emojis has a time element in it, though, that we don't take advantage of using a CNN. The emoji associated with a tweet is often the conclusion of the tweet. In this sort of situation, an RNN can be a better fit.

We saw how we can teach RNNs to generate texts in Chapter 5. We can use a similar approach for suggesting emojis. Just like with the word-level CNN, we'll feed in words converted to their embeddings. A one-layer LSTM does quite well:

```
def create_lstm_model(vocab_size, embedding_size=None, embedding_weights=None):
    message = layers.Input(shape=(None,), dtype='int32', name='title')
    embedding = Embedding(mask_zero=False, input_dim=vocab_size,
                          output_dim=embedding_weights.shape[1],
                          weights=[embedding_weights],
                          trainable=True,
                          name='lstm_embedding')(message)

    lstm_1 = layers.LSTM(units=128, return_sequences=False)(embedding)
    category = layers.Dense(units=len(emojis), activation='softmax')(lstm_1)

    model = Model(
        inputs=[message],
        outputs=[category],
    )
    model.compile(loss='sparse_categorical_crossentropy',
                  optimizer='rmsprop', metrics=['accuracy'])
    return model
```

After 10 epochs we reach a precision of 50% on training and 40% on the test set, out-performing the CNN model by quite a bit.

Discussion

The LSTM model we used here strongly outperforms our word-level CNN. We can attribute this superior performance to the fact that tweets are sequences, where what happens at the end of a tweet has a different impact from what happens at the beginning.

Since our character-level CNN tended to do better than our word-level CNN and our word-level LSTM does better than our character-level CNN, we might wonder if a character-level LSTM wouldn't be even better. It turns out it isn't.

The reason for this is that if we feed an LSTM one character at a time, it will mostly have forgotten what happened at the beginning of the tweet by the time it gets to the end. If we feed the LSTM one word at a time, it's able to overcome this. Note also that our character-level CNN doesn't actually handle the input one character at a time. We use sequences of four, five, or six characters at a time and have multiple convolutions stacked on top of each other, such that the average tweet has at the highest level only three feature vectors left.

We could try to combine the two, though, by creating a CNN that compresses the tweet into fragments with a higher level of abstraction and then feeding those vectors into an LSTM to draw the final conclusion. This is of course close to how our word-level LSTM works. Instead of using a CNN to classify fragments of text, we use the pretrained word embeddings to do the same on a per-word level.

7.10 Visualizing (Dis)Agreement

Problem

You'd like to visualize how the different models you've built compare in practice.

Solution

Use Pandas to show where they agree and disagree.

Precision gives us an idea of how well our models are doing. Suggesting emojis is a rather noisy task though, so it can be very useful to take a look at how our various models are doing side-by-side. Pandas is a great tool for this.

Let's start by getting the test data for our character model in as a vector, rather than a generator:

```
test_char_vectors, _ = next(data_generator(test_tweets, None))
```

Now let's run predictions on the first 100 items:

```
predictions = {
    label: [emojis[np.argmax(x)] for x in pred]
    for label, pred in (
        ('lstm', lstm_model.predict(test_tokens[:100])),
        ('char_cnn', char_cnn_model.predict(test_char_vectors[:100])),
        ('cnn', cnn_model.predict(test_tokens[:100])),
    )
}
```

Now we can construct and display a Pandas `DataFrame` with the first 25 predictions for each model next to the tweet text and the original emoji:

```
pd.options.display.max_colwidth = 128
test_df = test_tweets[:100].reset_index()
eval_df = pd.DataFrame({
    'content': test_df['text'],
    'true': test_df['emoji'],
    **predictions
})
eval_df[['content', 'true', 'char_cnn', 'cnn', 'lstm']].head(25)
```

This results in:

#	content	true	char_cnn	cnn	lstm
0	@Gurmeetramrahim @RedFMIndia @rjraunac #8DaysToLionHeart Great	😻	😹	😻	😂
1	@suchsmallgods I can't wait to show him these tweets	😈	😹	💜	😹
2	@Captain_RedWolf I have like 20 set lol WAYYYYYY ahead of you	😹	😹	😹	😹
3	@OtherkinOK were just at @EPfestival, what a set! Next stop is @whelanslive on Friday 11th November 2016.	😊	😌	💜	😊
4	@jochendria: KathNiel with GForce Jorge. #PushAwardsKathNiels	💜	💜	💜	💜
5	Okay good	😹	😹	😹	😹
6	"Distraught means to be upset" "So that means confused right?" -@ReevesDakota	😹	😹	💜	😹
7	@JennLiri babe wtf call bck I'm tryna listen to this ring tone	😄	😄	©	😩
8	does Jen want to be friends? we can so be friends. love you, girl. #BachelorInParadise	💜	😹	💜	💜
9	@amwalker38: Go Follow these hot accounts @the1stMe420 @DanaDeelish @So_deelish @aka_teemoney38 @CamPromoXXX @SexyLThings @l...	😌	🙏	🙏	
10	@gspisak: I always made fun of the parents that show up 30+ mins early to pick up their kids today thats me At least I got a...	😭	😌		😹
11	@ShawnMendes: Toronto Billboard. So cool! @spotify #ShawnXSpotify go find them in your city	😄	😄	😄	😄
12	@kayleeburt77 can I have your number? I seem to have lost mine.	😹	😹	😹	😄
13	@KentMurphy: Tim Tebow hits a dinger on his first pitch seen in professional ball	😄	😄	😄	😄
14	@HailKingSoup...	😹	😹	😹	😹
15	@RoxeteraRibbons Same and I have to figure to prove it	😹	😹	😹	😄
16	@theseoulstory: September comebacks: 2PM, SHINee, INFINITE, BTS, Red Velvet, Gain, Song Jieun, Kanto...	🔥	🔥	🔥	🔥
17	@VixenMusicLabel - Peace & Love	😌	💜	😌	💜
18	@iDrinkGallons sorry	😕	😹	😹	😹
19	@StarYouFollow: 19- Frisson	😶	😏	😊	
20	@RapsDaily: Don't sleep on Ugly God	🙏	🙏	🙏	🙏
21	How tf do all my shifts get picked up so quickly?! Wtf	😩	😩	😹	😩
22	@ShadowhuntersTV: #Shadowhunters fans, how many s would YOU give this father-daughter #FlashbackFriday bonding moment betwee...	💜	💜	💜	💜
23	@mbaylisxo: thank god I have a uniform and don't have to worry about what to wear everyday	😹	😹	💜	😊
24	Mood swings like...	😹	😹	😹	😕

Browsing these results, we can see that often when the models get it wrong, they land on an emoji that is very similar to the one in the original tweet. Sometimes the predictions seem to make more sense than what was actually used, and sometimes none of the models do very well.

Discussion

Looking at the actual data can help us see where our models go wrong. In this case a simple thing to improve performance would be to treat all the emojis that are similar as the same. The different hearts and different smiley faces express more or less the same things.

One alternative would be to learn embeddings for the emojis. This would give us a notion of how related emojis are. We could then have a loss function that takes this similarity into account, rather than a hard correct/incorrect measure.

7.11 Combining Models

Problem

You'd like to harness the combined prediction power of your models to get a better answer.

Solution

Combine the models into an ensemble model.

The idea of the wisdom of crowds—that the average of the opinions of a group is often more accurate than any specific opinion—also goes for machine learning models. We can combine all three models into one by using three inputs and combining the outputs of our models using the Average layer from Keras:

```
def prediction_layer(model):
    layers = [layer for layer in model.layers
                if layer.name.endswith('_predictions')]
    return layers[0].output

def create_ensemble(*models):
    inputs = [model.input for model in models]
    predictions = [prediction_layer(model) for model in models]
    merged = Average()(predictions)
    model = Model(
        inputs=inputs,
        outputs=[merged],
    )
    model.compile(loss='sparse_categorical_crossentropy',
                optimizer='rmsprop',
                metrics=['accuracy'])
    return model
```

We need a different data generator to train this model; rather than specifying one input, we now have three. Since they have different names, we can have our data generator yield a dictionary to feed the three inputs. We also need to do some wrangling to get the character-level data to line up with the word-level data:

```
def combined_data_generator(tweets, tokens, batch_size):
    tweets = tweets.reset_index()
    while True:
        batch_idx = random.sample(range(len(tweets)), batch_size)
        tweet_batch = tweets.iloc[batch_idx]
        token_batch = tokens[batch_idx]
        char_vec = np.zeros((batch_size, max_sequence_len, len(chars)))
        token_vec = np.zeros((batch_size, max_num_tokens))
        y = np.zeros((batch_size,))
        it = enumerate(zip(token_batch, tweet_batch.iterrows()))
        for row_idx, (token_row, (_, tweet_row)) in it:
            y[row_idx] = emoji_to_idx[tweet_row['emoji']]
            for ch_idx, ch in enumerate(tweet_row['text']):
                char_vec[row_idx, ch_idx, char_to_idx[ch]] = 1
            token_vec[row_idx, :] = token_row
        yield {'char_cnn_input': char_vec,
               'cnn_input': token_vec,
               'lstm_input': token_vec}, y
```

We can then train the model using:

```
BATCH_SIZE = 512
ensemble.fit_generator(
    combined_data_generator(train_tweets, training_tokens, BATCH_SIZE),
    epochs=20,
    steps_per_epoch=len(train_tweets) / BATCH_SIZE,
    verbose=2,
    callbacks=[early]
)
```

Discussion

Combined models or ensemble models are a great way to combine various approaches to a problem in one model. It is not a coincidence that in popular machine learning competitions like Kaggle the winners almost always are based on this technique.

Instead of keeping the models almost completely separate and then joining them up at the very end using the Average layer, we could also join them earlier, for example by concatenating the first dense layer of each of the models. Indeed, this is to some extent what we did with the more complex CNN, where we used various window sizes for small subnets that then were concatenated for a final conclusion.

CHAPTER 8

Sequence-to-Sequence Mapping

In this chapter we'll look at using sequence-to-sequence networks to learn transformations between pieces of text. This is a relatively new technique with tantalizing possibilities. Google claims to have made huge improvements to its Google Translate product using this technique; moreover, it has open sourced a version that can learn language translations purely based on parallel texts.

We won't go that far to start with. Instead, we'll start out with a simple model that learns the rules for pluralization in English. After that we'll extract dialogue from 19th-century novels from Project Gutenberg and train a chatbot on them. For this last project we'll have to abandon the safety of Keras running in a notebook and will use Google's open source seq2seq toolkit.

The following notebooks contain the code relevant for this chapter:

```
08.1 Sequence to sequence mapping
08.2 Import Gutenberg
08.3 Subword tokenizing
```

8.1 Training a Simple Sequence-to-Sequence Model

Problem

How do you train a model to reverse engineer a transformation?

Solution

Use a sequence-to-sequence mapper.

In Chapter 5 we saw how we can use recurrent networks to "learn" the rules of a sequence. The model learns how to best represent a sequence such that it can predict what the next element will be. Sequence-to-sequence mapping builds on this, but now the model learns to predict a different sequence based on the first one.

We can use this to learn all kinds of transformations. Let's consider converting singular nouns into plural nouns in English. At first sight it might seem that this is just a matter of appending an *s* to a word, but when you look more closely it turns out that the rules are really quite a bit more complicated.

The model is very similar to what we were using in Chapter 5, but now it is not just the input that is a sequence, but also the output. This is achieved using the RepeatVector layer, which allows us to map from the input to the output vector:

```
def create_seq2seq(num_nodes, num_layers):
    question = Input(shape=(max_question_len, len(chars),
                    name='question'))
    repeat = RepeatVector(max_expected_len)(question)
    prev = input
    for _ in range(num_layers)::
        lstm = LSTM(num_nodes, return_sequences=True,
                name='lstm_layer_%d' % (i + 1))(prev)
        prev = lstm
    dense = TimeDistributed(Dense(num_chars, name='dense',
                        activation='softmax'))(prev)
    model = Model(inputs=[input], outputs=[dense])
    optimizer = RMSprop(lr=0.01)
    model.compile(loss='categorical_crossentropy',
                optimizer=optimizer,
                metrics=['accuracy'])
    return model
```

Preprocessing of the data happens much as before. We read in the data from the file *data/plurals.txt* and vectorize it. One trick to consider is whether to reverse the strings in the input. If the input is reversed, then generating the output is like unrolling the processing, which might be easier.

It takes the model quite a bit of time to reach a precision in the neighborhood of 99%. Most of this time, though, is spent on learning to reproduce the prefixes that the singular and plural forms of the words share. In fact, when we check the model's performance when it has reached over 99% precision, we see that most of the errors are still in that area.

Discussion

Sequence-to-sequence models are powerful tools that, given enough resources, can learn almost any transformation. Learning the rules for going from singular to plural in English is just a simple example. These models are essential elements of the state-of-the-art machine translation solutions offered by the leading tech companies.

Simpler models like the one from this recipe can learn how to add numbers in Roman notation or learn to translate between written English and phonetic English, which is a useful first step when building a text-to-speech system.

In the next few recipes we'll see how we can use this technique to train a chatbot based on dialogues extracted from 19th-century novels.

8.2 Extracting Dialogue from Texts

Problem

How can you acquire a large corpus of dialogues?

Solution

Parse some texts available from Project Gutenberg and extract all the dialogue.

Let's start with downloading a set of books from Project Gutenberg. We could download all of them, but here we'll focus on works whose authors were born after 1835. This keeps the dialogue somewhat modern. The *data/books.json* document contains the relevant references:

```
with open('data/gutenberg_index.json') as fin:
    authors = json.load(fin)
recent = [x for x in authors
            if 'birthdate' in x and x['birthdate'] > 1830]
[(x['name'], x['birthdate'], x['english_books']) for x in recent[:5]]
```

```
[('Twain, Mark', 1835, 210),
 ('Ebers, Georg', 1837, 164),
 ('Parker, Gilbert', 1862, 135),
 ('Fenn, George Manville', 1831, 128),
 ('Jacobs, W. W. (William Wymark)', 1863, 112)]
```

The books are mostly laid out consistently in ASCII. Paragraphs are separated by double newlines, and dialogue almost always uses double quotes. A small fraction of books also use single quotes, but we'll just ignore those, since single quotes also occur elsewhere in the texts. We'll assume a conversation continues as long as the text outside of the quotes is less than 100 characters long (as in "Hi," he said, "How are you doing?"):

```
def extract_conversations(text, quote='"'):
    paragraphs = PARAGRAPH_SPLIT_RE.split(text.strip())
    conversations = [['']]
    for paragraph in paragraphs:
        chunks = paragraph.replace('\n', ' ').split(quote)
        for i in range((len(chunks) + 1) // 2):
            if (len(chunks[i * 2]) > 100
                or len(chunks) == 1) and conversations[-1] != ['']:
```

```
                if conversations[-1][-1] == '':
                    del conversations[-1][-1]
                conversations.append([''])
            if i * 2 + 1 < len(chunks):
                chunk = chunks[i * 2 + 1]
                if chunk:
                    if conversations[-1][-1]:
                        if chunk[0] >= 'A' and chunk[0] <= 'Z':
                            if conversations[-1][-1].endswith(','):
                                conversations[-1][-1] = \
                                    conversations[-1][-1][:-1]
                                conversations[-1][-1] += '.'
                            conversations[-1][-1] += ' '
                        conversations[-1][-1] += chunk
        if conversations[-1][-1]:
            conversations[-1].append('')

    return [x for x in conversations if len(x) > 1]
```

Processing this over the top 1,000 authors gets us a good set of dialogue data:

```
for author in recent[:1000]:
    for book in author['books']:
        txt = strip_headers(load_etext(int(book[0]))).strip()
        conversations += extract_conversations(txt)
```

This takes some time, so we'd better save the results to a file:

```
with open('gutenberg.txt', 'w') as fout:
    for conv in conversations:
        fout.write('\n'.join(conv) + '\n\n')
```

Discussion

As we saw in Chapter 5, Project Gutenberg is a good source for freely usable texts, as long as we don't mind that they are a little bit older since they have to be out of copyright.

The project was started at a time before concerns around layout and illustrations played a role, and therefore all documents are produced in pure ASCII. While this isn't the best format for actual books, it makes parsing relatively easy. Paragraphs are separated by double newlines and there's no mucking around with smart quotes or any markup.

8.3 Handling an Open Vocabulary

Problem

How do you tokenize a text completely with only a fixed number of tokens?

Solution

Use subword units for tokenizing.

In the previous chapter we just skipped words that weren't found in our vocabulary of the top 50,000 words. With subword-unit tokenizing, we break up words that don't appear very often into subunits that do. We continue doing so until all words and subunits fit our fixed-size vocabulary.

For example, if we have the words *working* and *worked*, we could break them up into *work-*, *-ed* and *-ing*. These three tokens will most likely overlap with others in our vocabulary, so this could reduce the size of our overall vocabulary. The algorithm used is straightforward. We split all tokens up into their individual letters. At this point each letter is a subword token, and presumably we have less than our maximum number of tokens. We then find which pair of subword tokens occurs most in our tokens. In English that would typically be (t, h). We then join those subword tokens. This will usually increase the number of subword tokens by one, unless one of the items in our pair is now exhausted. We keep doing this until we have the desired number of subword and word tokens.

Even though the code is not complicated, it makes sense to use the open source version of this algorithm (*https://github.com/rsennrich/subword-nmt*). The tokenizing is a three-step process.

The first step is to tokenize our corpus. The default tokenizer just splits the text, which means that it keeps all punctuation, usually attached to the previous word. We want something more advanced. We want all punctuation stripped except for the question mark. We'll also convert everything to lowercase and replace underscores with spaces:

```
RE_TOKEN = re.compile('(\w+|\?)', re.UNICODE)
token_counter = Counter()
with open('gutenberg.txt') as fin:
    for line in fin:
        line = line.lower().replace('_', ' ')
        token_counter.update(RE_TOKEN.findall(line))
with open('gutenberg.tok', 'w') as fout:
    for token, count in token_counter.items():
        fout.write('%s\t%d\n' % (token, count))
```

Now we can learn the subword tokens:

```
./learn_bpe.py -s 25000 < gutenberg.tok > gutenberg.bpe
```

And then we can apply them to any text:

```
./apply_bpe.py -c gutenberg.bpe < some_text.txt > some_text.bpe.txt
```

The resulting *some_text.bpe.txt* looks like our original corpus, except that rare tokens are broken up and end with @@ indicating the continuation.

Discussion

Tokenizing a text into words is an effective way of reducing the size of a document. As we saw in Chapter 7, it also allows us to kick-start our learning by loading up pretrained word embeddings. There is a drawback, though: larger texts contain so many different words that we can't hope to cover them all. One solution is to just skip the words that are not in our vocabulary, or replace them with a fixed UNKNOWN token. This doesn't work too badly for sentiment analysis, but for tasks where we want to generate an output text it is rather unsatisfactory. Subword-unit tokenizing is a good solution in this situation.

Another option that has in recent times gotten some traction is to train a character-level model to produce embeddings for words that are not in the vocabulary.

8.4 Training a seq2seq Chatbot

Problem

You want to train a deep learning model to reproduce the characteristics of a dialogue corpus.

Solution

Use Google's seq2seq framework.

The model from Recipe 8.1 is capable of learning relations between sequences—even fairly complex ones. However, sequence-to-sequence models are hard to tune for performance. In early 2017, Google published seq2seq, a library specifically developed for this type of application that runs directly on TensorFlow. It lets us focus on the model hyperparameters, rather than the nitty-gritty of the code.

The seq2seq framework wants its input split up into training, evaluation, and development sets. Each set should contain a source and a target file, with matching lines defining the input and the output of the model. In our case the source should contain the prompt of the dialogue, and the target the answer. The model will then try to learn how to convert from prompt to answer, effectively learning how to conduct a dialogue.

The first step is to split our dialogues into (source, target) pairs. For each consecutive pair of lines in the dialogues, we extract the first and last sentence as a source and target:

```
RE_TOKEN = re.compile('(\w+|\?)', re.UNICODE)
def tokenize(st):
    st = st.lower().replace('_', ' ')
    return ' '.join(RE_TOKEN.findall(st))
```

```
pairs = []
prev = None
with open('data/gutenberg.txt') as fin:
    for line in fin:
        line = line.strip()
        if line:
            sentences = nltk.sent_tokenize(line)
            if prev:
                pairs.append((prev, tokenize(sentences[0])))
            prev = tokenize(sentences[-1])
        else:
            prev = None
```

Now let's shuffle our pairs and split them into our three groups, with the dev and test sets each representing 5% of our data:

```
random.shuffle(pairs)
ss = len(pairs) // 20

data = {'dev': pairs[:ss],
        'test': pairs[ss:ss * 2],
        'train': pairs[ss * 2:]}
```

Next we need to unpack the pairs and put them into the right directory structure:

```
for tag, pairs2 in data.items():
    path = 'seq2seq/%s' % tag
    if not os.path.isdir(path):
        os.makedirs(path)
    with open(path + '/sources.txt', 'wt') as sources:
        with open(path + '/targets.txt', 'wt') as targets:
            for source, target in pairs2:
                sources.write(source + '\n')
                targets.write(target + '\n')
```

Time to train the network. Clone the seq2seq repository and install the dependencies. You might want to do this in a separate `virtualenv`:

```
git clone https://github.com/google/seq2seq.git
cd seq2seq
pip install -e .
```

Now let's set an environment variable pointing to the data we've put together:

```
Export SEQ2SEQROOT=/path/to/data/seq2seq
```

The seq2seq library contains a number of configuration files that we can mix and match in the *example_configs* directory. In this case, we want to train a large model with:

```
python -m bin.train \
    ./example_configs/train_seq2seq.yml" \
  --model_params "
```

```
      vocab_source: $SEQ2SEQROOT/gutenberg.tok
      vocab_target: $SEQ2SEQROOT/gutenberg.tok" \
  --input_pipeline_train "
    class: ParallelTextInputPipeline
    params:
      source_files:
        - $SEQ2SEQROOT/train/sources.txt
      target_files:
        - $SEQ2SEQROOT/train/targets.txt" \
  --input_pipeline_dev "
    class: ParallelTextInputPipeline
    params:
      source_files:
        - $SEQ2SEQROOT/dev/sources.txt
      target_files:
        - $SEQ2SEQROOT/dev/targets.txt" \
  --batch_size 1024  --eval_every_n_steps 5000 \
  --train_steps 5000000 \
  --output_dir $SEQ2SEQROOT/model_large
```

Unfortunately, even on a system with a capable GPU it will take days and days before we get some decent results. The *zoo* folder in the notebook contains a pretrained model though, if you can't wait.

The library doesn't provide a way to run the model interactively. In Chapter 16 we'll look into how we can do this, but for now we can quickly get some results by adding our test questions to a file (for example, */tmp/test_questions.txt*) and running:

```
python -m bin.infer \
  --tasks "
    - class: DecodeText" \
  --model_dir $SEQ2SEQROOT/model_large \
  --input_pipeline "
    class: ParallelTextInputPipeline
    params:
      source_files:
        - '/tmp/test_questions.txt'"
```

A simple conversation works:

```
> hi
hi
> what is your name ?
sam barker
> how do you feel ?
Fine
> good night
good night
```

With more complex sentences it is a bit hit or miss.

Discussion

The seq2seq model's primary use case seems to be automatic translation, although it has also been effective for captioning images and summarizing texts. The documentation contains a tutorial (*https://google.github.io/seq2seq/nmt/*) on how to train a model that learns decent English–German translations in weeks or months, depending on your hardware. Google claims that making a sequence-to-sequence model central to its machine translation efforts has improved the quality dramatically.

One interesting way to think about sequence-to-sequence mapping is to see it as an embedding process. For translations, both the source and the target sentence are projected into a multidimensional space and the model learns a projection such that sentences that mean the same thing end up around the same point in that space. This leads to the intriguing possibility of "zero-shot" translations; if a model learns to translate between Finnish and English and then later between English and Greek and it uses the same semantic space, it can also be used to directly translate between Finnish and Greek. This then opens up the possibility of "thought vectors," embeddings for relatively complex ideas that have similar properties to the "word vectors" we saw in Chapter 3.

CHAPTER 9

Reusing a Pretrained Image Recognition Network

Image recognition and computer vision is one of the areas where deep learning has made some significant impacts. Networks with dozens of layers, sometimes more than a hundred, have proven to be very effective in image classification tasks, to the point where they outperform humans.

Training such networks, though, is very involved, both in terms of processing power and the amount of training images needed. Fortunately, we often don't have to start from scratch, but can reuse an existing network.

In this chapter we'll walk through how to load one of the five pretrained networks that are supported by Keras, go into the preprocessing that is needed before we can feed an image into a network, and finally show how we can run the network in inference mode, where we ask it what it thinks the image contains.

We'll then look into what is known as *transfer learning*—taking a pretrained network and partly retraining it on new data for a new task. We'll first acquire a set of images from Flickr containing cats and dogs. We'll then teach our network to tell them apart. This will be followed by an application where we use this network to improve upon Flickr's search results. Finally, we'll download a set of images that contain pictures of 37 different types of pets and train a network that beats the average human at labeling them.

The following notebooks contain the code referred to in this chapter:

```
09.1 Reusing a pretrained image recognition network
09.2 Images as embeddings
09.3 Retraining
```

9.1 Loading a Pretrained Network

Problem

You'd like to know how to instantiate a pretrained image recognition network.

Solution

Use Keras to load up a pretrained network, downloading the weights if necessary.

Keras doesn't only make it easier to compose networks, it also ships with references to a variety of pretrained networks that we can easily load:

```
model = VGG16(weights='imagenet', include_top=True)
model.summary()
```

This will also print a summary of the network, showing its various layers. This is useful when we want to use the network, since it not only shows the names of the layers but also their sizes and how they are connected.

Discussion

Keras ships with access to a number of popular image recognition networks that can be readily downloaded. The downloads are cached in ~/.keras/models/, so you'll usually only have to wait for the download the first time.

In total we can use five different networks (VGG16, VGG19, ResNet50, Inception V3, and Xception). They differ in complexity and architecture, though for most simpler applications it probably doesn't matter which model you pick. VGG16 has "only" a depth of 16 layers, which makes it easier to inspect. Inception is a much deeper network but has 85% fewer variables, which makes it quicker to load and less memory-intensive.

9.2 Preprocessing Images

Problem

You've loaded a pretrained network, but now you need to know how to preprocess an image before feeding it into the network.

Solution

Crop and resize the image to the right size and normalize the colors.

All of the pretrained networks included in Keras expect their inputs to be square and of a certain size. They also expect the color channels to be normalized. Normalizing the images while training makes it easier for the networks to focus on the things that matter and not get "distracted."

We can use PIL/Pillow to load and center-crop an image:

```
img = Image.open('data/cat.jpg')
w, h = img.size
s = min(w, h)
y = (h - s) // 2
x = (w - s) // 2
img = img.crop((x, y, s, s))
```

We can get the desired size from the first layer of the network by querying the input_shape property. This property also contains the color depth, but depending on the architecture this might be the first or the last dimension. By calling max on it we'll get the right number:

```
target_size = max(model.layers[0].input_shape)
img = img.resize((target_size, target_size), Image.ANTIALIAS)
imshow(np.asarray(img))
```

Finally, we need to convert the image to a format suitable for the network to process. This involves converting the image to an array, expanding the dimensions so it's a batch, and normalizing the colors:

```
np_img = image.img_to_array(img)
img_batch = np.expand_dims(np_img, axis=0)
pre_processed = preprocess_input(img_batch)
pre_processed.shape
```

```
(1, 224, 224, 3)
```

We are now ready to classify the image!

Discussion

Center cropping is not the only option. In fact, Keras has a function in the image module called load_img that will load and resize an image, but doesn't do the cropping. It is a good general-purpose strategy for converting an image to the size that the network expects, though.

Center cropping is often the best strategy, since what we want to classify typically sits in the middle of our image and straightforward resizing distorts the picture. But in some cases, special strategies might work better. For example, if we have very tall images on a white background, then center cropping might cut off too much of the actual image, while resizing leads to large distortions. In this case a better solution might be to pad the image with white pixels on either side to make it square.

9.3 Running Inference on Images

Problem

If you have an image, how do you find out what it shows?

Solution

Run inference on the image using the pretrained network.

Once we have the image in the right format, we can call `predict` on the model:

```
features = model.predict(pre_processed)
features.shape
```

```
(1, 1000)
```

The predictions are returned as a `numpy` array shaped (1, 1,000)—a vector of 1,000 for each image in the batch. Each entry in the vector corresponds to a label, while the value of the entry indicates how likely it is that the image represents the label.

Keras has the convenient `decode_predictions` function to find the best-scoring entries and return the labels and corresponding scores:

```
decode_predictions(features, top=5)
```

Here are the results for the image in the previous recipe:

```
[[(u'n02124075', u'Egyptian_cat', 0.14703247),
  (u'n04040759', u'radiator', 0.12125628),
  (u'n02123045', u'tabby', 0.097638465),
  (u'n03207941', u'dishwasher', 0.047418527),
  (u'n02971356', u'carton', 0.047036409)]]
```

The network thinks we're looking at a cat. The second guess of it being a radiator is a bit of surprise, although the background does look a bit like a radiator.

Discussion

The last layer of this network has a softmax activation function. The softmax function makes sure that the sum for the activations of all the classes is equal to 1. Because of how the network learns when it is training, these activations can be thought of as the likelihood that the image matches the class.

The pretrained networks all come with a thousand classes of images they can recognize. The reason for this is that they are all trained for the ImageNet competition (*http://www.image-net.org/challenges/LSVRC/*). This makes it easy to compare their relative performance, but unless we happen to want to detect the images that are part of this competition, it is not immediately useful for practical purposes. In the next chapter we'll see how we can use these pretrained networks to classify images of our own choosing.

Another restriction is that these types of networks only return one answer, while often there are multiple objects in an image. We'll look into resolving this in Chapter 11.

9.4 Using the Flickr API to Collect a Set of Labeled Images

Problem

How do you quickly put together a set of labeled images for experimentation?

Solution

Use the `search` method of the Flickr API.

To use the Flickr API you need to have an application key, so head over to *https://www.flickr.com/services/apps/create* to register your app. Once you have a key and a secret, you can search for images using the `flickrapi` library:

```
flickr = flickrapi.FlickrAPI(FLICKR_KEY, FLICKR_SECRET, format='parsed-json')
res = flickr.photos.search(text='"cat"', per_page='10', sort='relevance')
photos = res['photos']['photo']
```

The photos returned by Flickr don't by default contain a URL. We can compose the URL from the record though:

```
def flickr_url(photo, size=''):
    url = 'http://farm{farm}.staticflickr.com/{server}/{id}_{secret}{size}.jpg'
    if size:
        size = '_' + size
    return url.format(size=size, **photo)
```

The HTML method is the easiest way to display images inside a notebook:

```
tags = ['<img src="{}" width="150" style="display:inline"/>'
        .format(flickr_url(photo)) for photo in photos]
HTML(''.join(tags))
```

This should show us a bunch of cat pictures. After we've confirmed that we have decent images, let's download a slightly bigger test set:

```
def fetch_photo(dir_name, photo):
    urlretrieve(flickr_url(photo), os.path.join(dir_name, photo['id'] + '.jpg'))

def fetch_image_set(query, dir_name=None, count=250, sort='relevance'):
    res = flickr.photos.search(text='"{}"'.format(query),
                               per_page=count, sort=sort)['photos']['photo']
    dir_name = dir_name or query
    if not os.path.exists(dir_name):
        os.makedirs(dir_name)
    with multiprocessing.Pool() as p:
        p.map(partial(fetch_photo, dir_name), res)

fetch_image_set('cat')
```

Discussion

Getting good training data is always a key concern when running experiments in deep learning. When it comes to images, it is hard to beat the Flickr API, giving us access to billions of images. Not only can we find images based on keywords and tags, but also on where they were taken. We can also filter on how we can use the images. For random experiments that isn't really a factor, but if we want to republish the images in some way this certainly comes in handy.

The Flickr API gives us access to general, user-generated images. There are other APIs available that, depending on your purpose, might work better. In Chapter 10 we look at how we can acquire images directly from Wikipedia. Getty Images (*http://developers.gettyimages.com/*) provides a good API for stock images, while 500px (*https://github.com/500px/api-documentation*) provides access to high-quality images through its API. The last two have strict requirements for republishing, but are great for experimentation.

9.5 Building a Classifier That Can Tell Cats from Dogs

Problem

You'd like to be able to classify images into one of two categories.

Solution

Train a support vector machine on top of the features coming out of a pretrained network.

Let's start by fetching a training set for dogs:

```
fetch_image_set('dog')
```

Load the images as one vector with the cats first, followed by the dogs:

```
images = [image.load_img(p, target_size=(224, 224))
          for p in glob('cat/*jpg') + glob('dog/*jpg')]
vector = np.asarray([image.img_to_array(img) for img in images])
```

Now load the pretrained model and construct a new model out of it with fc2 as its output. fc2 is the last fully connected layer before the network assigns labels. The values of this layer for an image describe the image in an abstract way. Another way to put this is to say that this projects the image into a high-dimensional semantic space:

```
base_model = VGG16(weights='imagenet')
model = Model(inputs=base_model.input,
              outputs=base_model.get_layer('fc2').output)
```

Now we'll run the model over all our images:

```
vectors = model.predict(vector)
vectors.shape
```

For every one of our 500 images, we now have a 4,096-dimensional vector characterizing that image. As in Chapter 4 we can construct a support vector machine to find the distinction between cats and dogs in this space.

Let's run the SVM and print our performance:

```
X_train, X_test, y_train, y_test = train_test_split(
    p, [1] * 250 + [0] * 250, test_size=0.20, random_state=42)

clf = svm.SVC(kernel='rbf')
clf.fit(X_train, y_train)
sum(1 for p, t in zip(clf.predict(X_test), y_test) if p != t)
```

Depending on which of the images we fetched, we should see precision around 90%. We can take a look at the images for which we predicted the wrong class with the following code:

```
mm = {tuple(a): b for a, b in zip(p, glob('cat/*jpg') + glob('dog/*jpg'))}
wrong = [mm[tuple(a)] for a, p, t in zip(X_test,
                                         clf.predict(X_test),
                                         y_test) if p != t]

for x in wrong:
    display(Image(x, width=150))
```

All in all, our network is not doing too badly. We would be confused too about some of these images labeled as cats or dogs!

Discussion

As we saw in Recipe 4.3, support vector machines are a good choice when we need a classifier on top of high-dimensional spaces. Here we extract the output of an image recognition network and treat those vectors as image embeddings. We let the SVM find hyperplanes that separate the cats from the dogs. This works well for binary cases. We can use SVMs for situations where we have more than two classes, but things get more complicated and it might make more sense to add a layer to our network to do the heavy lifting. Recipe 9.7 shows how to do this.

A lot of the times the classifier doesn't get the right answer, you can really blame the quality of the search results. In the next recipe, we'll take a look at how we can improve search results using the image features we've extracted.

9.6 Improving Search Results

Problem

How do you filter out the outliers from a set of images?

Solution

Treat the features from the highest-but-one layer of the image classifier as image embeddings and find the outliers in that space.

As we saw in the previous recipe, one of the reasons why our network sometimes failed to distinguish between cats and dogs was that the images it saw weren't very good. Sometimes the images weren't pictures of cats or dogs at all and the network just had to guess.

The Flickr search API doesn't return images that match the supplied text query, but images whose tags, descriptions, or titles match the text. Even major search engines have only recently started to take into account what can actually be seen in the images they return. (So, a search for "cat" might return a picture of a lion captioned "look at this big cat.")

As long as the majority of the returned images do match the intent of the user, we can improve upon the search by filtering out the outliers. For a production system it might be worth exploring something more sophisticated; in our case, where we have at most a few hundred images and thousands of dimensions, we can get away with something simpler.

Let's start by getting some recent cat pictures. Since we sort by recent and not relevance here, we expect the search results to be slightly less accurate:

```
fetch_image_set('cat', dir_name='maybe_cat', count=100, sort='recent')
```

As before, we load the images as one vector:

```
maybe_cat_fns = glob('maybe_cat/*jpg')
maybe_cats = [image.load_img(p, target_size=(224, 224))
              for p in maybe_cat_fns]
maybe_cat_vectors = np.asarray([image.img_to_array(img)
                                for img in maybe_cats])
```

We'll look for outliers by first finding the average point in the "maybe cat" space:

```
centroid = maybe_cat_vectors.sum(axis=0) / len(maybe_cats)
```

Then we calculate the distances of the cat vectors to the centroid:

```
diffs = maybe_cat_vectors - centroid
distances = numpy.linalg.norm(diffs, axis=1)
```

And now we can take a look at the things that are least like the average cat:

```
sorted_idxs = np.argsort(distances)
for worst_cat_idx in sorted_idxs[-10:]:
    display(Image(maybe_cat_fns[worst_cat_idx], width=150))
```

Filtering out the noncats this way works reasonably well, but since the outliers disproportionately influence the average vector, the top of our list looks a bit noisy. One way to improve upon this is to repeatedly recalculate the centroid only on top of the results so far, like a poor man's outlier filter:

```
to_drop = 90
sorted_idxs_i = sorted_idxs
for i in range(5):
    centroid_i = maybe_cat_vectors[sorted_idxs_i[:-to_drop]].sum(axis=0) /
        (len(maybe_cat_fns) - to_drop)
    distances_i = numpy.linalg.norm(maybe_cat_vectors - centroid_i, axis=1)
    sorted_idxs_i = np.argsort(distances_i)
```

This results in very decent top results.

Discussion

In this recipe we used the same technique from Recipe 9.5 to improve upon the search results from Flickr. We can imagine the high-dimensional space with our images as a large "point cloud."

Rather than finding a hyperplane that separates the dogs from the cats, we try to find the most central cat. We then assume that the distance to this archetypical cat is a good measure for "catness."

We've taken a simplistic approach to finding the most central cat; just average the coordinates, throw out the outliers, take the average again, and repeat. Ranking outliers in high-dimensional spaces is an active area of research and there are many interesting algorithms being developed.

9.7 Retraining Image Recognition Networks

Problem

How do you train a network to recognize images in a specialized category?

Solution

Train a classifier on top of the features extracted from a pretrained network.

Running an SVM on top of a pretrained network is a good solution if we have two categories of images, but less suitable if we have a large number of classes to choose from. The Oxford-IIIT Pet Dataset, for example, contains 37 different pet categories, each of which has around 200 pictures.

Training a network from scratch would take a lot of time and might not be super effective—7,000 images isn't a lot when it comes to deep learning. What we'll do instead is take a pretrained network minus the top layers and build on top of that. The intuition here is that the bottom layers of the pretrained layer recognize features in the images that the layers that we provide can use to learn how to distinguish these pets from each other.

Let's load the Inception model, minus the top layers, and freeze the weights. Freezing the weights means that they are no longer changed during training:

```
base_model = InceptionV3(weights='imagenet', include_top=False)
for layer in base_model.layers:
    layer.trainable = False
```

Now let's add some trainable layers on top. With one fully connected layer in between, we ask the model to predict our animal pet classes:

```
pool_2d = GlobalAveragePooling2D(name='pool_2d')(base_model.output)
dense = Dense(1024, name='dense', activation='relu')(pool_2d)
predictions = Dense(len(idx_to_labels), activation='softmax')(dense)
model = Model(inputs=base_model.input, outputs=predictions)
model.compile(optimizer='rmsprop',
              loss='categorical_crossentropy',
              metrics=['accuracy'])
```

Let's load up the data from the unpacked *tar.gz* provided by the Oxford-IIIT Pet Dataset. The filenames are of the format *<class_name>_<idx>.jpg*, so we can split off the *<class_name>* while updating the label_to_idx and idx_to_label tables:

```
pet_images_fn = [fn for fn in os.listdir('pet_images') if fn.endswith('.jpg')]
labels = []
idx_to_labels = []
label_to_idx = {}
for fn in pet_images_fn:
    label, _ = fn.rsplit('_', 1)
    if not label in label_to_idx:
        label_to_idx[label] = len(idx_to_labels)
        idx_to_labels.append(label)
    labels.append(label_to_idx[label])
```

Next, we convert the images into training data:

```
def fetch_pet(pet):
    img = image.load_img('pet_images/' + pet, target_size=(299, 299))
    return image.img_to_array(img)
img_vector = np.asarray([fetch_pet(pet) for pet in pet_images_fn])
```

And set up the labels as one-hot encoded vectors:

```
y = np.zeros((len(labels), len(idx_to_labels)))
for idx, label in enumerate(labels):
    y[idx][label] = 1
```

Training the model for 15 epochs produces decent results with over 90% precision:

```
model.fit(
    img_vector, y,
    batch_size=128,
    epochs=30,
    verbose=2
)
```

What we've done so far is called *transfer learning*. We can do a bit better by unfreezing the top layers of the pretrained network to give it some more leeway to train. mixed9 is a layer in the network about two-thirds of the way up:

```
unfreeze = False
for layer in base_model.layers:
    if unfreeze:
        layer.trainable = True
    if layer.name == 'mixed9':
        unfreeze = True
model.compile(optimizer=SGD(lr=0.0001, momentum=0.9),
              loss='categorical_crossentropy', metrics=['accuracy'])
```

We can continue training:

```
model.fit(
    img_vector, y,
    batch_size=128,
    epochs=15,
    verbose=2
)
```

And we should see that performance improves even more, up to 98%!

Discussion

Transfer learning is a key concept in deep learning. The world's leaders in machine learning often publish the architectures of their top-performing networks, which makes for a good start if we want to reproduce their results, but we don't always have easy access to the training data they used to get those results. And even if we do have access, training these world-class networks takes a lot of computing resources.

Having access to the actual trained networks is extremely useful if we want to do the same things the networks were trained for, but using transfer learning also can help us a lot when we want to perform similar tasks. Keras ships with a variety of models, but if they don't suffice, we can adapt models built for different frameworks.

CHAPTER 10

Building an Inverse Image Search Service

In the previous chapter we saw how to use a pretrained network on our own images, first by running a classifier on top of the network and then in a more complex example in which we trained only part of a network to recognize new classes of images. In this chapter we will use a similar approach to build a reverse image search engine, or a search by example.

We'll start by looking at how we can acquire a good base set of images from Wikipedia by querying Wikidata. We'll then use a pretrained network to extract values for each of those images to get embeddings. Once we have those embeddings, finding similar images is a mere matter of nearest neighbor search. Finally, we'll look at principal components analysis (PCA) as a way to visualize relationships between images.

The code for this chapter can be found in the following notebook:

```
10.1 Building an inverse image search service
```

10.1 Acquiring Images from Wikipedia

Problem

How do you get a clean set of images from Wikipedia covering the major categories of things?

Solution

Use Wikidata's metainformation to find Wikipedia pages that represent a class of things.

Wikipedia contains a great number of pictures that can be used for most purposes. The vast majority of those pictures, though, represent concrete instances, which is not really what we need for a reverse search engine. We want to return a picture representative of a cat as a species, not a specific cat like Garfield.

Wikidata, the structured cousin of Wikipedia, is based around triplets of the form (subject, relation, object) and has a great number of predicates encoded, partly on top of Wikipedia. One of those "instance of" is represented by P31. What we are after is a list of images of the objects in the instance-of relationships. We can use the Wikidata query language to ask for this:

```
query = """SELECT DISTINCT ?pic
WHERE
{
    ?item wdt:P31 ?class .
    ?class wdt:P18 ?pic
}
"""
```

We can call the query backend of Wikidata using requests and unroll the resulting JSON into a list of image references:

```
url = 'https://query.wikidata.org/bigdata/namespace/wdq/sparql'
data = requests.get(url, params={'query': query, 'format': 'json'}).json()
images = [x['pic']['value'] for x in data['results']['bindings']]
```

The references returned are URLs to the image pages, not the images themselves. Images in the various wiki projects are supposed to be stored in *http://upload.wikimedia.org/wikipedia/commons/*, but unfortunately this isn't always the case yet—some are still stored in the folder for a specific language. So, we'll also have to check at least the English folder (*en*). The actual URL for the image is determined by the filename and the first two characters of the hexdigest of the MD5 hash of the file name. Caching the image locally helps if we have to do this multiple times:

```
def center_crop_resize(img, new_size):
    w, h = img.size
    s = min(w, h)
    y = (h - s) // 2
    x = (w - s) // 2
    img = img.crop((x, y, s, s))
    return img.resize((new_size, new_size))

def fetch_image(image_cache, image_url):
    image_name = image_url.rsplit('/', 1)[-1]
    local_name = image_name.rsplit('.', 1)[0] + '.jpg'
    local_path = os.path.join(image_cache, local_name)
    if os.path.isfile(local_path):
        img = Image.open(local_path)
        img.load()
        return center_crop_resize(img, 299)
    image_name = unquote(image_name).replace(' ', '_')
    m = md5()
    m.update(image_name.encode('utf8'))
```

```
    c = m.hexdigest()
    for prefix in ('http://upload.wikimedia.org/wikipedia/en',
                   'http://upload.wikimedia.org/wikipedia/commons'):
        url = '/'.join((prefix, c[0], c[0:2], image_name))
        r = requests.get(url)
        if r.status_code != 404:
            try:
                img = Image.open(BytesIO(r.content))
                if img.mode != 'RGB':
                    img = img.convert('RGB')
                img.save(local_path)
                return center_crop_resize(img, 299)
            except IOError:
                pass
    return None
```

Even this doesn't always seem to work. The notebook for this chapter contains some more corner case–handling code to increase the yield of images.

Now all we need to do is fetch the images. This can take a long time, so we use tqdm to show our progress:

```
valid_images = []
for image_name in tqdm(images):
    img = fetch_image(IMAGE_DIR, image_name)
    if img:
        valid_images.append(img)
```

Discussion

Wikidata's query language is not widely known, but it's an effective way to access structured data. The example here is quite straightforward, but online you can find more complex queries, for example, to return the largest cities in the world with a female mayor or the most popular surnames for fictional characters. A lot of this data can also be extracted from Wikipedia, but running a Wikidata query is usually faster, more precise, and more fun.

The Wikimedia universe is also a good source for images. There are tens of millions of images available, all with a friendly reuse license. Moreover, using Wikidata we can get access to all kinds of properties for these images. It would be easy to expand this recipe to return not just the image URLs, but also the names of the objects in the images in a language of our choice.

 The fetch_image function described here works most of the time, but not always. We can improve upon this by fetching the contents of the URL returned from the Wikidata query and extracting the <img> tag from the HTML code.

10.2 Projecting Images into an N-Dimensional Space

Problem

Given a set of images, how do you organize them such that images that look similar are near each other?

Solution

Treat the weights of the last-but-one layer of an image recognition net as image embeddings. This layer is connected directly to the softmax layer that draws the conclusions. Anything that the network thinks is a cat should therefore have similar values.

Let's load and instantiate the pretrained network. We'll use Inception again—let's peek at its structure using .summary():

```
base_model = InceptionV3(weights='imagenet', include_top=True)
base_model.summary()
```

As you can see, we need the avg_pool layer, which has a size of 2,048:

```
model = Model(inputs=base_model.input,
              outputs=base_model.get_layer('avg_pool').output)
```

Now we can run the model on an image or a set of images:

```
def get_vector(img):
    if not type(img) == list:
        images = [img]
    else:
        images = img
    target_size = int(max(model.input.shape[1:]))
    images = [img.resize((target_size, target_size), Image.ANTIALIAS)
              for img in images]
    np_imgs = [image.img_to_array(img) for img in images]
    pre_processed = preprocess_input(np.asarray(np_imgs))
    return model.predict(pre_processed)
```

and index the images we acquired in the previous recipe in chunks (of course, if you have enough memory, you can try to do the entire shot in one go):

```
chunks = [get_vector(valid_images[i:i+256])
          for i in range(0, len(valid_images), 256)]
vectors = np.concatenate(chunks)
```

Discussion

In this recipe we used the last-but-one layer of the network to extract the embeddings. Since this layer is directly connected to the softmax layer that determines the

---

actual output layers, we expect the weights to form a semantic space that puts all the cat images in roughly the same space. But what happens if we pick a different layer?

One way to think about convolutional networks that do image recognition is to treat the successive layers as feature detectors of increasing levels of abstraction. The lowest level works directly on the pixel values and will detect very local patterns. The last layer detects concepts like "catness."

Picking a lower layer should result in similarity on a lower level of abstractness, so instead of returning things that are cat-like, we would expect to see images that have similar textures.

10.3 Finding Nearest Neighbors in High-Dimensional Spaces

Problem

How do you find the points that are closest to each other in a high-dimensional space?

Solution

Use scikit-learn's *k*-nearest neighbors implementation.

The *k*-nearest neighbors algorithm builds a model that can quickly return nearest neighbors. It does so with some loss of accuracy, but is much faster than doing the precise calculations. Effectively, it builds a distance index on our vectors:

```
nbrs = NearestNeighbors(n_neighbors=10,
                        balgorithm='ball_tree').fit(vectors)
```

With this distance index we can now quickly return near matches from our set of images given an input image. We have arrived at our reverse image search implementation! Let's put it all together to find more cats:

```
cat = get_vector(Image.open('data/cat.jpg'))
distances, indices = nbrs.kneighbors(cat)
```

And display the top results using inline HTML images:

```
html = []
for idx, dist in zip(indices[0], distances[0]):
    b = BytesIO()
    valid_images[idx].save(b, format='jpeg')
    b64_img = base64.b64encode(b.getvalue()).decode('utf-8'))
    html.append("<img src='data:image/jpg;base64,{0}'/>".format(b64_img)
HTML(''.join(html))
```

You should see a nice list of images dominated by cats!

Discussion

Fast computation of nearest neighbors is an active area of research in machine learning. The most naive neighbor search implementation involves the brute-force computation of distances between all pairs of points in the dataset, which quickly gets out of hand if we have a large number of points in a high-dimensional space.

Scikit-learn provides us with a number of algorithms that precalculate a tree that can help us find nearest neighbors fast, at the cost of some memory. The different approaches are discussed in the documentation (*http://scikit-learn.org/stable/modules/neighbors.html*), but the general approach is to use an algorithm to recursively split the space into subspaces, this way building a tree. This allows us to quickly identify which subspaces to check when looking for neighbors.

10.4 Exploring Local Neighborhoods in Embeddings

Problem

You'd like to explore what local clusters of images look like.

Solution

Use principal component analysis to find the dimensions among a local set of images that discriminate the most between images.

For example, let's say we have the 64 images that are the closest match to our cat image:

```
nbrs64 = NearestNeighbors(n_neighbors=64, algorithm='ball_tree').fit(vectors)
distances64, indices64 = nbrs64.kneighbors(cat)
```

PCA allows us to reduce the dimensionality of a space in such a way that the original space can be constructed with as little loss as possible. If we reduce the dimensionality to two, PCA will find the plane that the examples provided can be projected upon with as little loss as possible. If we then look at where the examples landed on that plane, we get a good idea of the structure of the local neighborhood. TruncatedSVD is the implementation we'll use in this case:

```
vectors64 = np.asarray([vectors[idx] for idx in indices64[0]])
svd = TruncatedSVD(n_components=2)
vectors64_transformed = svd.fit_transform(vectors64)
```

vectors64_transformed now has a shape of 64×2. We are going to draw the 64 images on an 8×8 grid with a cell size of 75×75. Let's start by normalizing the coordinates onto a 0 to 1 scale:

```
mins = np.min(vectors64_transformed, axis=0)
maxs = np.max(vectors64_transformed, axis=0)
xys = (vectors64_transformed - mins) / (maxs - mins)
```

Now we can draw and display the local area:

```
img64 = Image.new('RGB', (8 * 75, 8 * 75), (180, 180, 180))

for idx, (x, y) in zip(indices64[0], xys):
    x = int(x * 7) * 75
    y = int(y * 7) * 75
    img64.paste(valid_images[idx].resize((75, 75)), (x, y))

img64
```

We see a cat image roughly in the middle, with one corner dominated by animals and the rest of the images matched because of other reasons. Note that we plot over existing images, so the grid won't actually be filled completely.

Discussion

In Recipe 3.3 we used t-SNE to fold a higher-dimensional space into a two-dimensional plane. In this recipe we used principal component analysis instead. The two algorithms accomplish the same thing, reducing the dimensions of a space, but do so in different ways.

t-SNE tries to keep the distances between points in the space the same, despite the reduction of dimensionality. Some information is of course lost in this transformation, so we can make a choice as to whether we want to try to keep clusters locally intact (distances between points that were close to each other in the higher dimensions are kept similar) or keep distances between clusters intact (distances between points that were far from each other in the higher dimensions are kept similar).

PCA tries to find an N-dimensional hyperplane that is the closest possible to all the items in the space. If N is 2, we're talking about a normal plane, and so it tries to find the plane in our high-dimensional space that is closest to all images. In other words, it captures the two most important dimensions (the principal components), which we then use to visualize the cat space.

CHAPTER 11

Detecting Multiple Images

In the previous chapters we saw how we can work with pretrained classifiers to detect images and learn new categories. In all those experiments, though, we always assumed there was only one thing to see in our images. In the real world this is not always the case—we might have an image with both a cat and a dog, for example.

This chapter explores some techniques to overcome this limitation. We start out with building on a pretrained classifier and modifying the setup in such a way that we get multiple answers. We then look at a state-of-the art solution to solving this problem.

This is an area of active research, and the most advanced algorithms are tricky to reproduce inside a Python notebook on top of Keras. Instead, we use an open source library in the second and third recipes of this chapter to demonstrate what is possible.

The code for this chapter can be found in the following notebook:

```
11.1 Detecting Multiple Images
```

11.1 Detecting Multiple Images Using a Pretrained Classifier

Problem

How do you find multiple image classes in a single image?

Solution

Use the outputs of the middle layers as a feature map and run a sliding window over them.

Using a pretrained neural network to do image classifying is not very difficult once we have everything set up. If there are multiple objects to detect in the image, we don't do so well though: the pretrained network will return the likelihood that the image represents any of the classes. If it sees two different objects, it might split the score returned. It will also split the score if it sees one object but isn't sure whether it is one of two classes.

One idea is to run a sliding window over the image. Rather than downsampling the image to 224×224, we downsample it to 448×448, double the original. We then feed all the different crops that we can get out of the larger image:

Let's create the crops from the larger image:

```
cat_dog2 = preprocess_image('data/cat_dog.jpg', target_size=(448, 448))
crops = []
for x in range(7):
    for y in range(7):
        crops.append(cat_dog2[0,
                              x * 32: x * 32 + 224,
                              y * 32: y * 32 + 224,
                              :])
crops = np.asarray(crops)
```

Classifiers run over batches, so we can feed the crops object into the classifier that we've loaded before in the same fashion:

```
preds = base_model.predict(vgg16.preprocess_input(crops))
l = defaultdict(list)
for idx, pred in enumerate(vgg16.decode_predictions(preds, top=1)):
    _, label, weight = pred[0]
    l[label].append((idx, weight))
l.keys()

dict_keys(['Norwegian_elkhound', 'Egyptian_cat', 'standard_schnauzer',
           'kuvasz', 'flat-coated_retriever', 'tabby', 'tiger_cat',
           'Labrador_retriever'])
```

The classifier mostly seems to think that the various tiles are either cats or dogs, but isn't really sure what type. Let's take a look at the crops that have the highest value for a given tag:

```
def best_image_for_label(l, label):
    idx = max(l[label], key=lambda t:t[1])[0]
    return deprocess_image(crops[idx], 224, 224)

showarray(best_image_for_label(crop_scores, 'Egyptian_cat'))
```

```
showarray(best_image_for_label(crop_scores, 'Labrador_retriever'))
```

This approach works, but is rather expensive. And we duplicate a lot of work. Remember that the way a CNN works is by way of running a convolution over the image, which is very similar to doing all those crops. Moreover, if we load a pre-trained network without its top layers, it can run on an image of any size:

```
bottom_model = vgg16.VGG16(weights='imagenet', include_top=False)

(1, 14, 14, 512)
```

The top layer of the network expects an input of 7×7×512. We can recreate the top layer of the network based on the network we already loaded and copy the weights:

```
def top_model(base_model):
    inputs = Input(shape=(7, 7, 512), name='input')
    flatten = Flatten(name='flatten')(inputs)
    fc1 = Dense(4096, activation='relu', name='fc1')(flatten)
    fc2 = Dense(4096, activation='relu', name='fc2')(fc1)
    predictions = Dense(1000, activation='softmax',
                        name='predictions')(fc2)
    model = Model(inputs,predictions, name='top_model')
    for layer in model.layers:
        if layer.name != 'input':
            print(layer.name)
            layer.set_weights(
                base_model.get_layer(layer.name).get_weights())
    return model

model = top_model(base_model)
```

Now we can do the cropping based on the output of the bottom model and feed that into the top model, which means we only run the bottom model on 4 times the pixels of the original image, rather than 64 times as we did before. First, let's run the image through the bottom model:

```
bottom_out = bottom_model.predict(cat_dog2)
```

Now, we'll create the crops of the output:

```
vec_crops = []
for x in range(7):
    for y in range(7):
        vec_crops.append(bottom_out[0, x: x + 7, y: y + 7, :])
vec_crops = np.asarray(vec_crops)
```

And run the top classifier:

```
crop_pred = top_model.predict(vec_crops)
l = defaultdict(list)
for idx, pred in enumerate(vgg16.decode_predictions(crop_pred, top=1)):
    _, label, weight = pred[0]
    l[label].append((idx, weight))
l.keys()
```

This should give us the same results as before, but much faster!

Discussion

In this recipe we've taken advantage of the fact that the lower layers of a neural network have spatial information about what the network sees, even though this information is discarded at prediction time. This trick is based on some of the work done around Faster RCNN (see the next recipe), but doesn't require the expensive training step.

The fact that our pretrained classifier works on images with a fixed size (224×224 pixels, in this case) somewhat limits the approach here. The output regions always have the same size, and we have to decide into how many cells we split the original image. However, it does work well to find interesting subimages and is easy to deploy.

Faster RNN itself doesn't have the same drawbacks, but is much more costly to train. We'll take a look at this in the next recipe.

11.2 Using Faster RCNN for Object Detection

Problem

How do you find multiple objects in an image with tight bounding boxes?

Solution

Use a (pretrained) Faster RCNN network.

Faster RCNN is a neural network solution for finding bounding boxes of objects in an image. Unfortunately, the algorithm is too complex to easily reproduce in a Python notebook; instead, we'll rely on an open source implementation and treat that code more or less as a black box. Let's clone it from GitHub:

```
git clone https://github.com/yhenon/keras-frcnn.git
```

After we've installed the dependencies from *requirements.txt*, we can train the network. We can either train it using our own data or on the standard dataset from the Visual Object Challenge (*http://host.robots.ox.ac.uk/pascal/VOC/*). The latter contains many images with bounding boxes and 20 classes.

After we've downloaded the VOC 2007/2012 dataset and unpacked it, we can start training with:

```
python train_frcnn.py -p <downloaded-data-set>
```

 This takes quite a long time—about a day on a serious GPU, and much longer on just CPUs. If you'd prefer to skip this step, there's a pretrained network available at *https://storage.googleapis.com/deep-learning-cookbook/model_frcnn.hdf5*.

The training script saves the weights of the model every time it sees an improvement. Instantiation of the model for testing purposes is somewhat complex:

```
img_input = Input(shape=input_shape_img)
roi_input = Input(shape=(c.num_rois, 4))
feature_map_input = Input(shape=input_shape_features)

shared_layers = nn.nn_base(img_input, trainable=True)

num_anchors = len(c.anchor_box_scales) * len(c.anchor_box_ratios)
rpn_layers = nn.rpn(shared_layers, num_anchors)

classifier = nn.classifier(feature_map_input,
                           roi_input,
                           c.num_rois,
                           nb_classes=len(c.class_mapping),
                           trainable=True)

model_rpn = Model(img_input, rpn_layers)
model_classifier_only = Model([feature_map_input, roi_input], classifier)

model_classifier = Model([feature_map_input, roi_input], classifier)
```

We now have two models, one that is able to suggest regions that might have something interesting going on and the other able to tell us what it is. Let's load the weights of the models and compile:

```
model_rpn.load_weights('data/model_frcnn.hdf5', by_name=True)
model_classifier.load_weights('data/model_frcnn.hdf5', by_name=True)

model_rpn.compile(optimizer='sgd', loss='mse')
model_classifier.compile(optimizer='sgd', loss='mse')
```

Now let's feed our image into the region suggester model. We'll reshape the output in a way that will make it easier to run the next step. After this, r2 is a three-dimensional structure with the last dimension holding the predictions:

```
img_vec, ratio = format_img(cv2.imread('data/cat_dog.jpg'), c)
y1, y2, f = model_rpn.predict(img_vec)
r = keras_frcnn.roi_helpers.rpn_to_roi(y1, y2, c, K.image_dim_ordering(),
                                       overlap_thresh=0.7)
roi_count = R.shape[0] // c.num_rois
r2 = np.zeros((roi_count * c.num_rois, r.shape[1]))
r2 = r[:r2.shape[0],:r2.shape[1]]
r2 = np.reshape(r2, (roi_count, c.num_rois, r.shape[1]))
```

The image classifier runs over one-dimensional batches, so we have to feed in the two dimensions of r2 one by one. p_cls will contain the detected classes and p_regr fine-tuning information for the boxes:

```
p_cls = []
p_regr = []
for i in range(r2.shape[0]):
    pred = model_classifier_only.predict([F, r2[i: i + 1]])
    p_cls.append(pred[0][0])
    p_regr.append(pred[1][0])
```

Putting the three arrays together to get the actual boxes, labels, and certainty is a matter of looping through the two dimensions:

```
boxes = []
w, h, _ = r2.shape
for x in range(w):
    for y in range(h):
        cls_idx = np.argmax(p_cls[x][y])
        if cls_idx == len(idx_to_class) - 1:
            continue
        reg = p_regr[x, y, 4 * cls_idx:4 * (cls_idx + 1)]
        params = list(r2[x][y])
        params += list(reg / c.classifier_regr_std)
        box = keras_frcnn.roi_helpers.apply_regr(*params)
        box = list(map(lambda i: i * c.rpn_stride, box))
        boxes.append((idx_to_class[cls_idx], p_cls[x][y][cls_idx], box))
```

The list boxes now contains the detected cats and dogs. There are a lot of overlapping rectangles that can be resolved into each other.

Discussion

The Faster RCNN algorithm is an evolution of the Fast RCNN algorithm, which in turn was an improvement on the original RCNN. All these algorithms work similarly; a region proposer comes up with possible rectangles that might contain interesting images and the image classifier then detects what—if anything—can be seen there. The approach is not so different from what we did in the previous recipe, where our region proposer just produced 64 subcrops of an image.

Jian Sun, who came up with Faster RCNN, quite cleverly observed that the CNN that produces the feature map we used in the previous recipe could also be a good source for region proposals. So instead of treating the problem of region proposing separately, Faster RCNN trains the region proposal in parallel on the same feature map on which the image classification is done.

You can read more about the evolution of RCNN to Faster RCNN and how these algorithms work in the Athelas blog post "A Brief History of CNNs in Image Segmentation: From R-CNN to Mask-CNN." (*https://bit.ly/2oUCh88*)

11.3 Running Faster RCNN over Our Own Images

Problem

You'd like to train a Faster RCNN model, but don't want to have to start from scratch.

Solution

Start training from a pretrained model.

Training from scratch requires a lot of labeled data. The VOC dataset contains more than 20,000 labeled images for 20 classes. So what do we do if we don't have that much labeled data? We can use the transfer learning trick we came across first in Chapter 9.

The training script already loads weights if it is restarted; what we need to do is convert the weights from the network trained on the VOC dataset to our own. In the previous recipe we constructed a dual network and loaded weights. As long as our new task is similar to the VOC classification task, all we need to do is change the number of classes, write back the weights, and start training.

The easiest way to do this is to let the training script run just long enough for it to write its configuration file and then use that configuration file and the previously loaded model to get to these weights. For training our own data, it is best to use the comma-separated format described on GitHub with the format:

```
filepath,x1,y1,x2,y2,class_name
```

Here, `filepath` should be the full path to the image and x1, y1, x2, and y2 form the bounding box in pixels on that image. We can now train the model with:

```
python train_frcnn.py -o simple -p my_data.txt \
    --config_filename=newconfig.pickle
```

Now, after we've loaded the pretrained model as before, we can load the new configuration file with:

```
new_config = pickle.load(open('data/config.pickle', 'rb'))
Now construct the model for training and load the weights:

img_input = Input(shape=input_shape_img)
roi_input = Input(shape=(None, 4))
shared_layers = nn.nn_base(img_input, trainable=True)

num_anchors = len(c.anchor_box_scales) * len(c.anchor_box_ratios)
rpn = nn.rpn(shared_layers, num_anchors)

classifier = nn.classifier(shared_layers, roi_input, c.num_rois,
                           len(c.class_mapping), trainable=True)

model_rpn = Model(img_input, rpn[:2])
model_classifier = Model([img_input, roi_input], classifier)
model_all = Model([img_input, roi_input], rpn[:2] + classifier)

model_rpn.load_weights('data/model_frcnn.hdf5', by_name=True)
model_classifier.load_weights('data/model_frcnn.hdf5', by_name=True)
```

We can see that the training model only depends on the number of classes for the classifier object. So, we want to reconstruct the classifier object and any object that depend on it, then save the weights. That way we've constructed our new model based on the old weights. If we peek into the code that constructs the classifier, we see that it all depends on the third-to-last layer. So let's copy that code, but run it using the `new_config`:

```
new_nb_classes = len(new_config.class_mapping)
out = model_classifier_only.layers[-3].output
new_out_class = TimeDistributed(Dense(new_nb_classes,
                 activation='softmax', kernel_initializer='zero'),
                 name='dense_class_{}'.format(new_nb_classes))(out)
new_out_regr = TimeDistributed(Dense(4 * (new_nb_classes-1),
                 activation='linear', kernel_initializer='zero'),
                 name='dense_regress_{}'.format(new_nb_classes))(out)
new_classifer =  [new_out_class, new_out_regr]
```

With the new classifier in hand, we can construct the model as before and save the weights. These weights will retain what the model learned before, but have zeros for the classifier bit that is specific to the new training task:

```
new_model_classifier = Model([img_input, roi_input], classifier)
new_model_rpn = Model(img_input, rpn[:2])
new_model_all = Model([img_input, roi_input], rpn[:2] + classifier)
new_model_all.save_weights('data/model_frcnn_new.hdf5')
```

We can now continue training with:

```
python train_frcnn.py -o simple -p my_data.txt \
       --config_filename=newconfig.pickle \
       --input_weight_path=data/model_frcnn_new.hdf5
```

Discussion

Most examples of transfer learning are based on image recognition networks. This is partly because of the easy availability of pretrained networks and the fact that getting a training set of labeled images is straightforward. In this recipe we saw that we can apply this technique in other situations too. All we need is a pretrained network and an insight into how the network is constructed. By loading up the network weights, modifying the network for the new dataset, and saving the weights again, we can increase the speed of learning dramatically.

Even in situations where we don't have a pretrained network available, but where there is a large set of public training data available and our own dataset is small, it might make sense to first train on the public dataset and then transfer that learning to our own set. For the bounding box case discussed in this recipe, this could easily be the case.

 If your own dataset is small, it might make sense to experiment with setting part of the network to untrainable as we did in Recipe 9.7.

CHAPTER 12

Image Style

In this chapter we'll explore some techniques to visualize what convolutional networks see when they classify images. We'll do this by running the networks in reverse —rather than giving the network an image and asking it what it is, we tell the network what to see and ask it to modify the image in a way that makes it see the detected item more exaggeratedly.

We'll start by doing this for a single neuron. This will show us what sorts of patterns that neuron reacts to. We'll then expand on this by introducing the concept of octaves, where we zoom in while we optimize the image to get more detail. Finally, we will look at applying this technique to existing images and visualize what the network "almost" sees in an image, a technique known as deep dreaming.

We'll then switch gears and look at how combinations of "lower" layers of a network determine the artistic style of an image and how we can visualize just the style of an image. This uses the concept of gram matrices and how they represent the style of a painting.

Next, we look at how we can combine this notion with a way to stabilize an image, which allows us to generate an image that only copies the style of an image. We then move on to apply this technique to existing images, which makes it possible to render a recent photograph in the style of Vincent van Gogh's *Starry Skies*. Finally, we'll use two style images and render versions of the same picture somewhere between the two styles.

The following notebooks contain the code for this chapter:

```
12.1 Activation Optimization
12.2 Neural Style
```

12.1 Visualizing CNN Activations

Problem

You'd like to see what is actually happening inside the image recognition network.

Solution

Maximize the activation of a neuron to see which pixels it reacts to most strongly.

In the previous chapter we saw that convolutional neural networks are the networks of choice when it comes to image recognition. The lowest layers work directly on the pixels of the image, and as we go up in the stack of layers we speculate that the abstraction level of the features recognized goes up. The final layers are capable of actually recognizing things in the image.

This makes intuitive sense. These networks are designed this way analogously to how we think the human visual cortex works. Let's take a look at what the individual neurons are doing to see if this is actually the case. We'll start by loading the network up as before. We use the VGG16 here because of its simpler architecture:

```
model = vgg16.VGG16(weights='imagenet', include_top=False)
layer_dict = dict([(layer.name, layer) for layer in model.layers[1:]])
```

We'll now run the network backwards. That is, we'll define a loss function that optimizes the activation for one specific neuron and then ask the network to calculate in what direction to change an image to optimize the value for that neuron. In this case we randomly pick the layer block3_conv and the neuron at index 1:

```
input_img = model.input
neuron_index  = 1
layer_output = layer_dict['block3_conv1'].output
loss = K.mean(layer_output[:, neuron_index, :, :])
```

To run the network backwards, we need to define a Keras function called iterate. It will take an image and return the loss and the gradient (the changes we need to make to the network). We also need to normalize the gradient:

```
grads = K.gradients(loss, input_img)[0]
grads = normalize(grads)
iterate = K.function([input_img], [loss, grads])
```

We'll start with a random noise image and feed it repeatedly into the iterate function we just defined, and then add the returned gradient to our image. This changes the image step by step in the direction where the neuron and layer we picked will have a maximum activation—20 steps should do the trick:

```
for i in range(20):
    loss_value, grads_value = iterate([input_img_data])
    input_img_data += grads_value * step
```

Before we can display the resulting image, it needs normalization and clipping of the values to the usual RGB range:

```
def visstd(a, s=0.1):
    a = (a - a.mean()) / max(a.std(), 1e-4) * s + 0.5
    return np.uint8(np.clip(a, 0, 1) * 255)
```

Once we have done that, we can display the image:

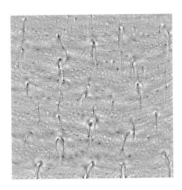

This is cool. It gives us a glimpse of what the network is doing at this particular level. The overall network, though, has millions of neurons; inspecting them one by one is not a very scalable strategy to get an insight into what is going on.

A good way to get an impression is to pick some layers of increasing abstraction:

```
layers = ['block%d_conv%d' % (i, (i + 1) // 2) for i in range(1, 6)]
```

For each of those layers we'll find eight representative neurons and add them to a grid:

```
grid = []
layers = [layer_dict['block%d_conv%d' % (i, (i + 1) // 2)]
          for i in range(1, 6)]
for layer in layers:
    row = []
    neurons = random.sample(range(max(x or 0
                            for x in layers[0].output_shape)
    for neuron in tqdm(neurons), sample_size), desc=layer.name):
        loss = K.mean(layer.output[:, neuron, :, :])
        grads = normalize(K.gradients(loss, input_img)[0])
        iterate = K.function([input_img], [loss, grads])
        img_data = np.random.uniform(size=(1, 3, 128, 128, 3)) + 128.
        for i in range(20):
            loss_value, grads_value = iterate([img_data])
            img_data += grads_value
```

```
            row.append((loss_value, img_data[0]))
        grid.append([cell[1] for cell in
                    islice(sorted(row, key=lambda t: -t[0]), 10)])
```

Converting the grid and displaying it in the notebook is similar to what we did in Recipe 3.3:

```
img_grid = PIL.Image.new('RGB',
                         (8 * 100 + 4, len(layers) * 100 + 4), (180, 180, 180))
for y in range(len(layers)):
    for x in range(8):
        sub = PIL.Image.fromarray(
                visstd(grid[y][x])).crop((16, 16, 112, 112))
        img_grid.paste(sub,
                       (x * 100 + 4, (y * 100) + 4))
display(img_grid)
```

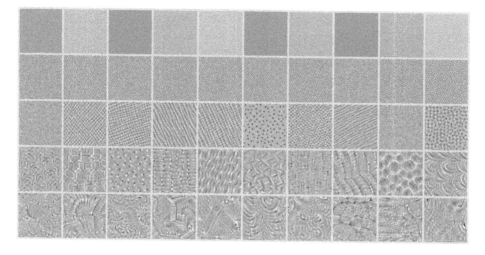

Discussion

Maximizing the activation of a neuron in a neural network is a good way to visualize the function of that neuron in the overall task of the network. By sampling neurons from different layers we can even visualize the increasing complexity of the features that the neurons detect as we go up in the stack.

The results we see contain mostly small patterns. The way that we update the pixels makes it hard for larger objects to emerge, since a group of pixels has to move in unison and they all are optimized against their local contents. This means that it is harder for the more abstract layers to "get what they want" since the patterns that they recognize are of a larger size. We can see this in the grid image we generated. In the next recipe we'll explore a technique to help with this.

You might wonder why we only try to activate neurons in low and middle layers. Why not try to activate the final predictions layer? We could find the prediction for "cat" and tell the network to activate that, and we'd expect to end up with a picture of a cat.

Sadly, this doesn't work. It turns out that the universe of all images that a network will classify as a "cat" is staggeringly large, but only very few of those images would be recognizable to us as cats. So, the resulting image almost always looks like noise to us, but the network thinks it is a cat.

In Chapter 13 we'll look at some techniques to generate more realistic images.

12.2 Octaves and Scaling

Problem

How do you visualize larger structures that activate a neuron?

Solution

Zoom in while optimizing the image for maximum neuron activation.

In the previous step we saw that we can create images that maximize the activation of a neuron, but the patterns remain rather local. An interesting way to get around this is to start with a small image and then do a series of steps where we optimize it using the algorithm from the previous recipe followed by an enlargement of the image. This allows the activation step to first set out the overall structure of the image before filling in the details. Starting with a 64×64 image:

```
img_data = np.random.uniform(size=(1, 3, size, size)) + 128.
```

we can now do the zoom/optimize thing 20 times:

```
for octave in range(20):
    if octave>0:
        size = int(size * 1.1)
        img_data = resize_img(img_data, (size, size))
    for i in range(10):
        loss_value, grads_value = iterate([img_data])
        img_data += grads_value
    clear_output()
    showarray(visstd(img_data[0]))
```

Using the `block5_conv1` layer and neuron 4 gives a nice organic-looking result:

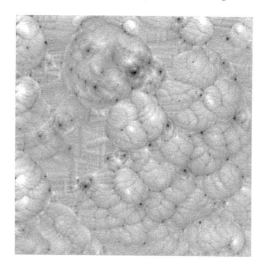

Discussion

Octaves and scaling are a great way to let a network produce images that somehow represent what it can see.

There's a lot to explore here. In the code in the Solution we only optimize the activation for one neuron, but we can optimize multiple neurons at the same time for a more mixed picture. We can assign different weights to them or even negative weights to some of them, forcing the network to stay away from certain activations.

The current algorithm sometimes produces too many high frequencies, especially in the first octaves. We can counteract this by applying a Gaussian blur to the first octaves to produce a less sharp result.

And why stop resizing when the image has reached our target size? Instead we could continue resizing, but also crop the image to keep it the same size. This would create a video sequence where we keep zooming while new patterns unfold.

Once we're making movies, we could also change the set of neurons that we activate and explore the network that way. The *movie_dream.py* script combines some of these ideas and produces mesmerizing movies, an example of which you can find on YouTube (*https://youtu.be/rubLdCdfDSk*).

12.3 Visualizing What a Neural Network Almost Sees

Problem

Can you exaggerate what a network detects, to get a better idea of what it's seeing?

Solution

Expand the code from the previous recipe to operate on existing images.

There are two things we need to change to make the existing algorithm work. First, upscaling an existing image would make it rather blocky. Second, we want to keep some similarity with the original image, as otherwise we might as well start out with a random image. Fixing these two issues reproduces Google's famous DeepDream experiment, where eerie pictures appear out of skies and mountain landscapes.

We can achieve those two goals by keeping track of the loss of detail because of the upscaling and injecting that lost detail back into the generated image; this way we undo the scaling artifacts, plus we "steer" the image back to the original at every octave. In the following code, we get all the shapes we want to go through and then upscale the image step by step, optimize the image for our loss function, and then add the lost detail by comparing what gets lost between upscaling and downscaling:

```
successive_shapes = [tuple(int(dim / (octave_scale ** i))
                     for dim in original_shape)
                     for i in range(num_octave - 1, -1, -1)]

original_img = np.copy(img)
shrunk_original_img = resize_img(img, successive_shapes[0])

for shape in successive_shapes:
    print('Processing image shape', shape)
    img = resize_img(img, shape)
    for i in range(20):
        loss_value, grads_value = iterate([img])
        img += grads_value
    upscaled_shrunk_original_img = resize_img(shrunk_original_img, shape)
    same_size_original = resize_img(original_img, shape)
    lost_detail = same_size_original - upscaled_shrunk_original_img

    img += lost_detail
    shrunk_original_img = resize_img(original_img, shape)
```

This gives a pretty nice result:

The original Google algorithm for deep dreaming was slightly different, though. What we just did was tell the network to optimize the image to maximize the activation for a particular neuron. What Google did instead was to have the network exaggerate what it already was seeing.

It turns out we can optimize the image to increase the current activations by adjusting the loss function that we previously defined. Instead of taking into account one neuron, we are going to use entire layers. For this to work, we have to modify our loss function such that it maximizes activations that are already high. We do this by taking the sum of the squares of the activations.

Let's start by specifying the three layers we want to optimize and their respective weights:

```
settings = {
        'block3_pool': 0.1,
        'block4_pool': 1.2,
        'block5_pool': 1.5,
}
```

Now we define the loss as a sum of those, avoiding border artifacts by only involving nonborder pixels in the loss:

```
loss = K.variable(0.)
for layer_name, coeff in settings.items():
```

```
x = layer_dict[layer_name].output
scaling = K.prod(K.cast(K.shape(x), 'float32'))
if K.image_data_format() == 'channels_first':
    loss += coeff * K.sum(K.square(x[:, :, 2: -2, 2: -2])) / scaling
else:
    loss += coeff * K.sum(K.square(x[:, 2: -2, 2: -2, :])) / scaling
```

The `iterate` function remains the same, as does the function to generate the image. The only change we make is that where we add the gradient to the image, we slow down the speed by multiplying the `grad_value` by 0.1:

```
for i in range(20):
    loss_value, grads_value = iterate([img])
    img += grads_value * 0.10
```

Running this code, we see eyes and something animal face–like appear in the landscape:

You can play around with the layers, their weights, and the speed factor to get different images.

Discussion

Deep dreaming seems like a playful way to generate hallucinogenic images, and it certainly allows for endless exploring and experimentation. But it is also a way to understand what neural networks see in an image. Ultimately this is a reflection on the images that the networks were trained on: a network trained on cats and dogs will "see" cats and dogs in an image of a cloud.

We can exploit this by using the techniques from Chapter 9. If we have a large set of images that we use for retraining an existing network, but we set only one layer of that network to trainable, the network has to put all its "prejudices" into that layer. When we then run the deep dreaming step with that layer as the optimized layer, those "prejudices" should be visualized quite nicely.

It is always tempting to draw parallels between how neural networks function and how human brains work. Since we don't really know a lot about the latter, this is of course rather speculative. Still, in this case, the activation of certain neurons seems close to brain experiments where a researcher artificially activates a bit of the human brain by sticking an electrode in it and the subject experiences a certain image, smell, or memory.

Similarly, humans have an ability to recognize faces and animals in the shapes of clouds. Some mind-altering substances increase this ability. Maybe these substances artificially increase the activation of neural layers in our brains?

12.4 Capturing the Style of an Image

Problem

How do you capture the style of an image?

Solution

Calculate the gram matrix of the convolutional layers of the image.

In the previous recipe we saw how we can visualize what a network has learned by asking it to optimize an image such that it maximizes the activation of a specific neuron. The gram matrix of a layer captures the style of that layer, so if we start with an image filled with random noise and optimize it such that the gram matrices of its layers match the gram matrices of a target image, we'd expect it to start mimicking that target image's style.

The gram matrix is the flattened version of the activations, multiplied by itself transposed.

We can then define a loss function between two sets of activations by subtracting the gram matrices from each, squaring the results, and then summing it all up:

```
def gram_matrix(x):
    if K.image_data_format() != 'channels_first':
        x = K.permute_dimensions(x, (2, 0, 1))
    features = K.batch_flatten(x)
    return K.dot(features, K.transpose(features))

def style_loss(layer_1, layer_2):
    gr1 = gram_matrix(layer_1)
    gr2 = gram_matrix(layer_1)
    return K.sum(K.square(gr1 - gr2))
```

As before, we want a pretrained network to do the work. We'll use it on two images, the image we are generating and the image that we want to capture the style from—in this case Claude Monet's *Water Lilies* from 1912. So, we'll create an input tensor that contains both and load a network without the final layers that takes this tensor as its input. We'll use VGG16 because it is simple, but any pretrained network would do:

```
style_image = K.variable(preprocess_image(style_image_path,
                                          target_size=(1024, 768)))
result_image = K.placeholder(style_image.shape)
input_tensor = K.concatenate([result_image,
                              style_image], axis=0)

model = vgg16.VGG16(input_tensor=input_tensor,
                    weights='imagenet', include_top=False)
```

Once we have the model loaded, we can define our loss variable. We'll go through all layers of the model, and for the ones that have _conv in their name (the convolutional layers), collect the style_loss between the style_image and the result_image:

```
loss = K.variable(0.)
for layer in model.layers:
    if '_conv' in layer.name:
        output = layer.output
        loss += style_loss(output[0, :, :, :], output[1, :, :, :])
```

Now that we have a loss, we can start to optimize. We'll use scipy's fmin_l_bfgs_b optimizer. That method needs a gradient and a loss value to do its job. We can get them with one call, so we need to cache the values. We do this using a handy helper class, Evaluator, that takes a loss and an image:

```
class Evaluator(object):
    def __init__(self, loss_total, result_image):
        grads = K.gradients(loss_total, result_image)
        outputs = [loss_total] + grads
        self.iterate = K.function([result_image], outputs)
        self.shape = result_image.shape

        self.loss_value = None
        self.grads_values = None

    def loss(self, x):
```

```
    outs = self.iterate([x.reshape(self.shape)])
    self.loss_value = outs[0]
    self.grad_values = outs[-1].flatten().astype('float64')
    return self.loss_value

def grads(self, x):
    return np.copy(self.grad_values)
```

We can now optimize an image by calling repeatedly:

```
image, min_val, _ = fmin_l_bfgs_b(evaluator.loss, image.flatten(),
                              fprime=evaluator.grads, maxfun=20)
```

The resulting image starts looking quite reasonable after 50 steps or so.

Discussion

In this recipe we've seen that the gram matrix captures the style of an image effectively. Naively, we might think that the best way to match the style of an image would be to match the activations of all layers directly. But that approach is too literal.

It might not be obvious that the gram matrix approach would work better. The intuition behind it is that by multiplying every activation with every other activation for a given layer, we capture the correlations between the neurons. Those correlations encode the style as it is a measure of the activation distribution, rather than the absolute activations.

With this in mind, there are a couple of things we can experiment with. One thing to consider is zero values. Taking the dot product of a vector with itself transposed will produce a zero if either multiplicand is zero. That makes it impossible to spot correlations with zeros. Since zeros appear quite often, this is rather unwanted. A simple fix is to add a delta to the features before doing the dot operation. A value of -1 works well:

```
    return K.dot(features - 1, K.transpose(features - 1))
```

We can also experiment with adding a constant factor to the expression. This can smooth or exaggerate the results. Again, -1 works well.

A final consideration is that we're taking the gram matrix of all the activations. This might seem odd—shouldn't we do this just for the channels per pixel? What really is happening is that we calculate the gram matrix for the channels for each pixel and then look at how they correlate over the entire image. This allows for a shortcut: we can calculate the mean channels and use that as the gram matrix. This gives us an image that captures the average style and is therefore more regular. It also runs a bit faster:

```
def gram_matrix_mean(x):
    x = K.mean(x, axis=1)
    x = K.mean(x, axis=1)
```

```
features = K.batch_flatten(x)
return K.dot(features - 1,
             K.transpose(features - 1)) / x.shape[0].value
```

The total variation loss we added in this recipe tells the network to keep the difference between neighboring pixels in check. Without this, the result will be more pixelated and more jumpy. In a way this approach is very similar to the regularization we use to keep the weights or output of a network layer in check. The overall effect is comparable to applying a slight blur filter on the output pixel.

12.5 Improving the Loss Function to Increase Image Coherence

Problem

How do you make the resulting image from the captured style less pixelated?

Solution

Add a loss component to control for the local coherence of the image.

The image from the previous recipe already looks quite reasonable. However, if we look closely it seems somewhat pixelated. We can guide the algorithm away from this by adding a loss function that makes sure that the image is locally coherent. We compare each pixel with its neighbor to the left and down. By trying to minimize that difference, we introduce a sort of blurring of the image:

```
def total_variation_loss(x, exp=1.25):
    _, d1, d2, d3 = x.shape
    a = K.square(x[:, :d1 - 1, :d2 - 1, :] - x[:, 1:, :d2 - 1, :])
    b = K.square(x[:, :d1 - 1, :d2 - 1, :] - x[:, :d1 - 1, 1:, :])
    return K.sum(K.pow(a + b, exp))
```

The 1.25 exponent determines how much we punish outliers. Adding this to our loss gives:

```
loss_variation = total_variation_loss(result_image, h, w) / 5000
loss_with_variation = loss_variation + loss_style
evaluator_with_variation = Evaluator(loss_with_variation, result_image)
```

If we run this evaluator for 100 steps we get a pretty convincing-looking picture:

Discussion

In this recipe we added the final component to our loss function that keeps the picture globally looking like the content image. Effectively what we're doing here is optimizing the generated image such that the activations in the upper layers correspond to the content image and the activations of the lower layers to the style image. Since the lower layers correspond to style and the higher layers to content, we can accomplish style transfer this way.

The results can be quite striking, to the point where people new to the field think that computers can now do art. But tuning is still required as some styles are a lot wilder than others, as we'll see in the next recipe.

12.6 Transferring the Style to a Different Image

Problem

How do you apply the captured style from one image to another image?

Solution

Use a loss function that balances the content from one image with the style from another.

It would be easy to run the code from the previous recipe over an existing image, rather than a noise image, but the results aren't that great. At first it seems it is applying the style to the existing image, but with each step the original image dissolves a little. If we keep applying the algorithm the end result will be more or less the same, independent of the starting image.

We can fix this by adding a third component to our loss function, one that takes into account the difference between the generated image and our reference image:

```
def content_loss(base, combination):
    return K.sum(K.square(combination - base))
```

We'll now need to add the reference image to our input tensor:

```
w, h = load_img(base_image_path).size
base_image = K.variable(preprocess_image(base_image_path))
style_image = K.variable(preprocess_image(style2_image_path, target_size=(h, w)))
combination_image = K.placeholder(style_image.shape)
input_tensor = K.concatenate([base_image,
                              style_image,
                              combination_image], axis=0)
```

We load the network as before and define our content loss on the last layer of our network. The last layer contains the best approximation of what the network sees, so this is really what we want to keep the same:

```
loss_content = content_loss(feature_outputs[-1][0, :, :, :],
                            feature_outputs[-1][2, :, :, :])
```

We're going to slightly change the style loss by taking into account the position of the layer in the network. We want lower layers to carry more weight, since the lower layers capture more of the texture/style of an image, while the higher layers are more involved in the content of the image. This makes it easier for the algorithm to balance the content of the image (which uses the last layer) and the style (which uses mostly the lower layers):

```
loss_style = K.variable(0.)
for idx, layer_features in enumerate(feature_outputs):
    loss_style += style_loss(layer_features[1, :, :, :],
                             layer_features[2, :, :, :]) * (0.5 ** idx)
```

Finally, we balance the three components:

```
loss_content /= 40
loss_variation /= 10000
loss_total = loss_content + loss_variation + loss_style
```

Running this on a picture of the Oude Kerk (the Old Church) in Amsterdam with van Gogh's *Starry Skies* as the style input gives us:

12.7 Style Interpolation

Problem

You've captured the styles of two images, and want to apply a style somewhere between the two to another image. How can you blend them?

Solution

Use a loss function that takes an extra float indicating what percentage of each style to apply.

We can easily extend our input tensor to take two style images, say one for summer and one for winter. After we load the model as before, we can now create a loss for each of the styles:

```
loss_style_summer = K.variable(0.)
loss_style_winter = K.variable(0.)
for idx, layer_features in enumerate(feature_outputs):
    loss_style_summer += style_loss(layer_features[1, :, :, :],
                                    layer_features[-1, :, :, :]) * (0.5 ** idx)
    loss_style_winter += style_loss(layer_features[2, :, :, :],
                                    layer_features[-1, :, :, :]) * (0.5 ** idx)
```

We then introduce a placeholder, summerness, that we can feed in to get the desired summerness loss:

```
summerness = K.placeholder()
loss_total = (loss_content + loss_variation +
                loss_style_summer * summerness +
                loss_style_winter * (1 - summerness))
```

Our Evaluator class doesn't have a way of passing in summerness. We could create a new class or subclass the existing one, but in this case we can get away with "monkey patching":

```
combined_evaluator = Evaluator(loss_total, combination_image,
                            loss_content=loss_content,
                            loss_variation=loss_variation,
                            loss_style=loss_style)
iterate = K.function([combination_image, summerness],
                        combined_evaluator.iterate.outputs)
combined_evaluator.iterate = lambda inputs: iterate(inputs + [0.5])
```

This will create an image that is 50% summer, but we can specify any value.

Discussion

Adding yet another component to the loss variable allows us to specify the weights between two different styles. Nothing is stopping us, of course, from adding even more style images and varying their weights. It's also worth exploring varying the relative weights of the style images; van Gogh's *Starry Skies* image is very stark and its style will easily overpower that of more subtle paintings.

CHAPTER 13

Generating Images with Autoencoders

In Chapter 5 we explored how we can generate text in the style of an existing corpus, whether the works of Shakespeare or code from the Python standard library, while in Chapter 12 we looked at generating images by optimizing the activation of channels in a pretrained network. In this chapter we combine those techniques and build on them to generate images based on examples.

Generating images based on examples is an area of active research where new ideas and breakthroughs are reported on a monthly basis. The state-of-the-art algorithms, however, are beyond the scope of this book in terms of model complexity, training time, and data needed. Instead, we'll be working in a somewhat restricted domain: hand-drawn sketches.

We'll start with looking at Google's Quick Draw data set. This is the result of an online drawing game and contains many hand-drawn pictures. The drawings are stored in a vector format, so we'll convert them to bitmaps. We'll pick sketches with one label: cats.

Based on these cat sketches, we'll build an autoencoder model that is capable of learning *catness*—it can convert a cat drawing into an internal representation and then generate something similar-looking from that internal representation. We'll look at visualizing the performance of this network on our cats first.

We'll then switch to a dataset of hand-drawn digits and then move on to *variational autoencoders*. These networks produce dense spaces that are an abstract representation of their inputs from which we can sample. Each sample will result in a realistic looking image. We can even interpolate between points and see how the images gradually change.

Finally, we'll look at *conditional variational autoencoders*, which take into account a label when training and therefore can reproduce images of a certain class in a random fashion.

Code related to this chapter can be found in the following notebooks:

```
13.1 Quick Draw Cat Autoencoder
13.2 Variational Autoencoder
```

13.1 Importing Drawings from Google Quick Draw

Problem

Where can you get a set of everyday hand drawn images?

Solution

Use Google Quick Draw's dataset.

Google Quick Draw (*https://quickdraw.withgoogle.com/*) is an online game where a user is challenged to draw something and see if an AI can guess what they were trying to create. The game is entertaining, and as a side effect a large database of labeled drawings is produced. Google has made this dataset accessible for anybody wanting to play with machine learning.

The data is available in a number of formats (*https://github.com/googlecreativelab/quickdraw-dataset*). We'll work with a binary-encoded version of the simplified vector drawings. Let's start by getting all the cats:

```
BASE_PATH = 'https://storage.googleapis.com/quickdraw_dataset/full/binary/
path = get_file('cat', BASE_PATH + 'cat.bin')
```

We'll collect the images by unpacking them one by one. They are stored in a binary vector format that we'll draw on an empty bitmap. The drawings start with a 15-byte header, so we just keep processing until our file no longer has at least 15 bytes:

```
x = []
with open(path, 'rb') as f:
    while True:
        img = PIL.Image.new('L', (32, 32), 'white')
        draw = ImageDraw.Draw(img)
        header = f.read(15)
        if len(header) != 15:
            break
```

A drawing is a list of strokes, each made up of a series of *x* and *y* coordinates. The *x* and *y* coordinates are stored separately, so we need to zip them into a list to feed into the ImageDraw object we just created:

```
        strokes, = unpack('H', f.read(2))
        for i in range(strokes):
            n_points, = unpack('H', f.read(2))
            fmt = str(n_points) + 'B'
            read_scaled = lambda: (p // 8 for
                                   p in unpack(fmt, f.read(n_points)))
            points = [*zip(read_scaled(), read_scaled())]
            draw.line(points, fill=0, width=2)
        img = img_to_array(img)
        x.append(img)
```

Over a hundred thousand drawings of cats are yours.

Discussion

Harvesting user-generated data using a game is an interesting way to build up a data-set for machine learning. It's not the first time Google has used this technique—a few years ago it ran the Google Image Labeler game (*http://bit.ly/wiki-gil*), where two players that didn't know each other would label images and get points for matching labels. The results of that game were never made available to the public, though.

There are 345 categories in the dataset. In this chapter we're only using cats, but you could take the rest for a spin to build an image classifier. The dataset has drawbacks, chief among them the fact that not all drawings are finished; the game ends when the AI recognizes the drawing, and for a camel drawing two humps might be enough.

 In this recipe we rasterized the images ourselves. Google does make a numpy array version of the data available where the images have been pre-rasterized to 28×28 pixels.

13.2 Creating an Autoencoder for Images

Problem

Is it possible to automatically represent an image as a fixed-sized vector even if it isn't labeled?

Solution

Use an autoencoder.

In Chapter 9 we saw that we can use a convolutional network to classify an image by having consecutive layers go from pixels to local features to more structural features and finally to an abstract representation of the image that we then can use to predict what the image is about. In Chapter 10 we interpreted that abstract representation of the image as a vector in a high-dimensional, semantic space and used the fact that vectors that are close to each other represent similar images as a way to build a reverse image search engine. Finally, in Chapter 12 we saw that we can visualize what the activations of the various neurons on different levels in a convolutional network mean.

To do all this we needed the images to be labeled. Only because the network got to see a large number of dogs, cats, and many other things was it able to learn an abstract representation of these in this high-dimensional space. What if we don't have labels for our images? Or not enough labels to let the network develop an intuition of what is what? In these situations autoencoders can be helpful.

The idea behind an autoencoder is to force the network to represent an image as a vector with a certain size and have a loss function based on how accurately the network is able to reproduce the input image from that representation. The input and the expected output are the same, which means we don't need labeled images. Any set of images will do.

The structure of the network is very similar to what we've seen before; we take the original image and use a series of convolutional layers and pooling layers to reduce the size and increase the depth until we have a one-dimensional vector that is an abstract representation of that image. But instead of calling it a day and using that vector to predict what the image is, we follow this up with the inverse and go from this abstract representation of the image through a set of *upsampling* layers that do the reverse until we are back with an image again. As our loss function we then take the difference between the input and the output image:

```python
def create_autoencoder():
    input_img = Input(shape=(32, 32, 1))

    channels = 2
    x = input_img
    for i in range(4):
        channels *= 2
        left = Conv2D(channels, (3, 3),
                      activation='relu', padding='same')(x)
        right = Conv2D(channels, (2, 2),
                       activation='relu', padding='same')(x)
        conc = Concatenate()([left, right])
        x = MaxPooling2D((2, 2), padding='same')(conc)

    x = Dense(channels)(x)

    for i in range(4):
        x = Conv2D(channels, (3, 3), activation='relu', padding='same')(x)
        x = UpSampling2D((2, 2))(x)
        channels //= 2
    decoded = Conv2D(1, (3, 3), activation='sigmoid', padding='same')(x)
```

```
    autoencoder = Model(input_img, decoded)
    autoencoder.compile(optimizer='adadelta', loss='binary_crossentropy')
    return autoencoder

autoencoder = create_autoencoder()
autoencoder.summary()
```

We can imagine the network architecture as an hourglass. The top and bottom layers represent images. The smallest point in the network is in the middle, and is often referred to as the *latent representation*. We have a latent space with 128 entries here, which means that we force the network to represent each 32×32-pixel image using 128 floats. The only way the network can minimize the difference between the input and the output image is by compressing as much information into the latent representation as possible.

We can train the network as before with:

```
autoencoder.fit(x_train, x_train,
                epochs=100,
                batch_size=128,
                validation_data=(x_test, x_test))
```

This should converge fairly rapidly.

Discussion

Autoencoders are an interesting type of neural network since they are capable of learning a compact, lossy representation of their inputs without any supervision. In this recipe we've used them on images, but they've also successfully been deployed to process text or other data in the form of time series.

There are a number of interesting extensions to the autoencoder idea. One of them is the *denoising* autoencoder. The idea here is to ask the network to predict the target image not from itself, but from a damaged version of itself. For example, we could add some random noise to the input images. The loss function would still compare the output of the network with the original (non-noised) input, so the network would effectively learn how to remove noise from the pictures. In other experiments this technique has proven to be useful when it comes to restoring colors to black and white pictures.

We used the abstract representation of an image in Chapter 10 to create a reverse image search engine, but we needed labels for that. With an autoencoder we don't need those labels; we can measure the distance between images after the model has trained on nothing but a set of images. It turns out that if we use a denoising autoencoder the performance of our image similarity algorithm increases. The intuition here is that the noise tells the network what not to pay attention to, similarly to how data augmentation works (see "Preprocessing of Images" on page 22).

13.3 Visualizing Autoencoder Results

Problem

You'd like to get an idea of how well your autoencoder worked.

Solution

Sample a few random cat pictures from the input and have the model predict those; then render input and output as two rows.

Let's predict some cats:

```
cols = 25
idx = np.random.randint(x_test.shape[0], size=cols)
sample = x_test[idx]
decoded_imgs = autoencoder.predict(sample)
```

And show them in our notebook:

```
def decode_img(tile):
    tile = tile.reshape(tile.shape[:-1])
    tile = np.clip(tile * 400, 0, 255)
    return PIL.Image.fromarray(tile)

overview = PIL.Image.new('RGB', (cols * 32, 64 + 20), (128, 128, 128))
for idx in range(cols):
    overview.paste(decode_img(sample[idx]), (idx * 32, 5))
    overview.paste(decode_img(decoded_imgs[idx]), (idx * 32, 42))
f = BytesIO()
overview.save(f, 'png')
display(Image(data=f.getvalue()))
```

As you can see, the network did pick up on the basic shapes, but doesn't seem to be very sure about itself, which results in vague icon drawings, almost like shadows.

In the next recipe we'll see if we can do better.

Discussion

Since the input and the output of the autoencoder *should* be similar, the best way to check the performance of our network is to just pick some random icons from our validation set and ask the network to reconstruct them. Using PIL to create an image that shows two rows and display it inside of the Jupyter notebook is something we've seen before.

One of the issues with the approach here is that the loss function we are using causes the network to smudge its output. The input drawings contain thin lines, but the output of our model doesn't. Our model has no incentive to predict sharp lines, because it is uncertain of the exact position of the lines, so it would rather spread its bets and draw vague lines. This way there is a high chance that at least some pixels will be a hit. To improve this, we could try to design a loss function that forces the network to limit the number of pixels it draws, or puts a premium on sharp lines.

13.4 Sampling Images from a Correct Distribution

Problem

How do you make sure that every point in the vector represents a reasonable image?

Solution

Use a *variational* autoencoder.

Autoencoders are quite interesting as a way to represent an image as a vector that is much smaller than the image itself. But the space of these vectors is not *dense*; that is, every image has a vector in that space, but not every vector in that space represents a reasonable image. The decoder part of the autoencoder will of course create an image out of any vector, but most of them are just not going to be recognizable. Variational autoencoders do have this property.

In this and the following recipes in the chapter we'll work with the MNIST dataset of handwritten digits, comprised of 60,000 training samples and 10,000 test samples. The approach described here does work on icons, but it complicates the model and for decent performance we'd need more icons than we have. If you are interested, there is a working model in the notebook directory. Let's start by loading the data:

```
def prepare(images, labels):
    images = images.astype('float32') / 255
    n, w, h = images.shape
    return images.reshape((n, w * h)), to_categorical(labels)

train, test = mnist.load_data()
x_train, y_train = prepare(*train)
x_test, y_test = prepare(*test)
img_width, img_height = train[0].shape[1:]
```

The key idea behind a variational autoencoder is to add a term to the loss function that represents the difference in statistical distribution between the images and the abstract representations. For this we'll use the Kullback–Leibler divergence. We can think of this as a distance metric for the space of probability distributions, even though it is technically not a distance metric. The Wikipedia article (*http://bit.ly/k-l-d*) has the details for those who want to read up on the math.

The basic outline of our model is similar to that of the previous recipe. We start out with an input representing our pixels, force this through some hidden layers, and sample it down to a very small representation. We then work our way up again until we have our pixels back:

```
pixels = Input(shape=(num_pixels,))
encoder_hidden = Dense(512, activation='relu')(pixels)
z_mean = Dense(latent_space_depth,
                activation='linear')(encoder_hidden)
z_log_var = Dense(latent_space_depth,
                activation='linear')(encoder_hidden)
z = Lambda(sample_z, output_shape=(latent_space_depth,))(
        [z_mean, z_log_var])
decoder_hidden = Dense(512, activation='relu')
reconstruct_pixels = Dense(num_pixels, activation='sigmoid')
hidden = decoder_hidden(z)
outputs = reconstruct_pixels(hidden)
auto_encoder = Model(pixels, outputs)
```

The interesting part here is the z tensor and the Lambda it gets assigned to. This tensor will hold the latent representation of our image, and the Lambda uses the sample_z method to do the sampling:

```
def sample_z(args):
    z_mean, z_log_var = args
    eps = K.random_normal(shape=(batch_size, latent_space_depth),
                    mean=0., stddev=1.)
    return z_mean + K.exp(z_log_var / 2) * eps
```

This is where we randomly sample points with a normal distribution using the two variables z_mean and z_log_var.

Now on to our loss function. The first component is the reconstruction loss, which measures the difference between the input pixels and the output pixels:

```
def reconstruction_loss(y_true, y_pred):
    return K.sum(K.binary_crossentropy(y_true, y_pred), axis=-1)
```

The second thing we need is a component in our loss function that uses the Kullback–Leibler divergence to steer the distribution in the right direction:

```
def KL_loss(y_true, y_pred):
    return 0.5 * K.sum(K.exp(z_log_var) +
                    K.square(z_mean) - 1 - z_log_var,
                    axis=1)
```

We then simply add this up:

```
def total_loss(y_true, y_pred):
    return (KL_loss(y_true, y_pred) +
            reconstruction_loss(y_true, y_pred))
```

And we can compile our model with:

```
auto_encoder.compile(optimizer=Adam(lr=0.001),
                     loss=total_loss,
                     metrics=[KL_loss, reconstruction_loss])
```

This will handily also keep track of the individual components of the loss during training.

This model is slightly complicated due to the extra loss function and the out-of-band call to `sample_z`; to get a look at the details, it is best viewed in the corresponding notebook. We can now train the model as before:

```
cvae.fit(x_train, x_train, verbose = 1, batch_size=batch_size, epochs=50,
         validation_data = (x_test, x_test))
```

Once the training is finished, we want to use the results by feeding a random point in the latent space and seeing what image rolls out. We can do this by creating a second model that has as an input the middle layer of our `auto_encoder` model and as output our target image:

```
decoder_in = Input(shape=(latent_space_depth,))
decoder_hidden = decoder_hidden(decoder_in)
decoder_out = reconstruct_pixels(decoder_hidden)
decoder = Model(decoder_in, decoder_out)
```

We can now generate a random input and then convert it to a picture:

```
random_number = np.asarray([[np.random.normal()
                             for _ in range(latent_space_depth)]])
def decode_img(a):
    a = np.clip(a * 256, 0, 255).astype('uint8')
    return PIL.Image.fromarray(a)

decode_img(decoder.predict(random_number)
           .reshape(img_width, img_height)).resize((56, 56))
```

Discussion

Variational autoencoders add an important component to autoencoders when it comes to generating images rather than just reproducing images; by making sure that the abstract representations of the images come from a *dense* space where points close to the origin map to likely images, we can now generate images that have the same likelihood distribution as our inputs.

The underlying mathematics are a bit beyond the scope of this book. The intuition here is that some images are more "normal" and some are more unexpected. The latent space has the same characteristics, so points that are drawn from close to the origin correspond to images that are "normal," while more extreme points map to more unlikely images. Sampling from a normal distribution will result in images that have the same mixture of expected and unexpected images as the model saw during training.

Having dense spaces is nice. It allows us to interpolate between points and still get valid outcomes. For example, if we know that one point in the latent space maps to a 6 and another to an 8, we would expect that the points in between would result in images that morph from 6 to 8. If we find the same images but in a different style, we can look for images in between with a mixed style. Or we could even go in the other direction and expect to find a more extreme style.

In Chapter 3 we looked at word embeddings, where each word has a vector that projects it into a semantic space, and the sorts of calculations we can do with those. As interesting as that is, since the space is not dense we typically don't expect to find something between two words that somehow is a compromise between the two—no *mule* between *donkey* and *horse*. Similarly, we can use a pretrained image recognition network to find a vector for a picture of a cat, but the vectors around it don't all represent variations of cats.

13.5 Visualizing a Variational Autoencoder Space

Problem

How can you visualize the diversity of images that you can generate from your latent space?

Solution

Use the two dimensions from the latent space to create a grid of generated images.

Visualizing two dimensions from our latent space is straightforward. For higher dimensions we could first try t-SNE to get back to two dimensions. As luck would have it, we were only using two dimensions in the previous recipe, so we can just go through a plane and map each (x, y) position to a point in the latent space. Since we are using a normal distribution, we'd expect reasonable images to appear in the $[-1.5, 1.5]$ range:

```
num_cells = 10
overview = PIL.Image.new('RGB',
                         (num_cells * (img_width + 4) + 8,
                          num_cells * (img_height + 4) + 8),
                         (128, 128, 128))
vec = np.zeros((1, latent_space_depth))
for x in range(num_cells):
    vec[:, 0] = (x * 3) / (num_cells - 1) - 1.5
    for y in range(num_cells):
        vec[:, 1] = (y * 3) / (num_cells - 1) - 1.5
        decoded = decoder.predict(vec)
        img = decode_img(decoded.reshape(img_width, img_height))
        overview.paste(img, (x * (img_width + 4) + 6,
                             y * (img_height + 4) + 6))
overview
```

This should get us a nice image of the different digits the network learned:

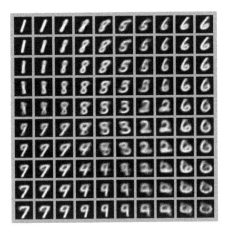

Discussion

By mapping (x, y) to our latent space and decoding the results to images we get a nice overview of what our space contains. As we can see, the space is indeed quite dense. Not all points result in digits per se; some, as expected, represent in-between forms. But the model does find a way to distribute the digits in a natural way on the grid.

The other thing to note here is that our variational autoencoder does a great job of compressing images. Every input image is represented in the latent space by just 2 floats, while their pixel representations use $28 \times 28 = 784$ floats. That's a compression ratio of almost 400, outperforming JPEG by quite a margin. Of course, the compression is rather lossy—a handwritten 5 will after encoding and decoding still look like a handwritten 5 and still be in the same style, but at a pixel level there is no real correspondence. Also, this form of compression is extremely domain-specific. It only works for handwritten digits, while JPEG can be used to compress all sorts of images and photos.

13.6 Conditional Variational Autoencoders

Problem

How do we generate images of a certain type rather than completely random ones?

Solution

Use a conditional variational autoencoder.

The autoencoder from the previous two recipes does a great job generating random digits and is also capable of taking in a digit and encoding it in a nice, dense, latent space. But it doesn't know a 5 from a 3, and so the only way we can get it to generate a random 3 is to first find all the 3s in the latent space and then sample from that sub-space. Conditional variational autoencoders help here by taking in the label as an input and then concatenating the label to the latent space vector z in the model.

This does two things. First, it lets the model take the actual label into account when learning the encoding. Second, since it adds the label to the latent space, our decoder will now take both a point in the latent space and a label, which allows us to explicitly ask for a specific digit to be generated. The model now looks like this:

```
pixels = Input(shape=(num_pixels,))
label = Input(shape=(num_labels,), name='label')
inputs = concat([pixels, label], name='inputs')

encoder_hidden = Dense(512, activation='relu',
                       name='encoder_hidden')(inputs)
z_mean = Dense(latent_space_depth,
               activation='linear')(encoder_hidden)
z_log_var = Dense(latent_space_depth,
                  activation='linear')(encoder_hidden)
z = Lambda(sample_z,
           output_shape=(latent_space_depth, ))([z_mean, z_log_var])
zc = concat([z, label])

decoder_hidden = Dense(512, activation='relu')
reconstruct_pixels = Dense(num_pixels, activation='sigmoid')
decoder_in = Input(shape=(latent_space_depth + num_labels,))
hidden = decoder_hidden(decoder_in)
decoder_out = reconstruct_pixels(hidden)
decoder = Model(decoder_in, decoder_out)

hidden = decoder_hidden(zc)
outputs = reconstruct_pixels(hidden)
cond_auto_encoder = Model([pixels, label], outputs)
```

We train the model by providing it with both the images and the labels:

```
cond_auto_encoder.fit([x_train, y_train], x_train, verbose=1,
                      batch_size=batch_size, epochs=50,
                      validation_data = ([x_test, y_test], x_test))
```

We can now generate an explicit number 4:

```
number_4 = np.zeros((1, latent_space_depth + y_train.shape[1]))
number_4[:, 4 + latent_space_depth] = 1
decode_img(cond_decoder.predict(number_4).reshape(img_width, img_height))
```

Since we specify which digit to generate in a one-hot encoding, we can also ask for something in between two numbers:

```
number_8_3 = np.zeros((1, latent_space_depth + y_train.shape[1]))
number_8_3[:, 8 + latent_space_depth] = 0.5
number_8_3[:, 3 + latent_space_depth] = 0.5
decode_img(cond_decoder.predict(number_8_3).reshape(
    img_width, img_height))
```

Which produces indeed something in between:

Another interesting thing to try is to put the digits on the *y*-axis and use the *x*-axis to pick values for one of our latent dimensions:

```
num_cells = 10
overview = PIL.Image.new('RGB',
                         (num_cells * (img_width + 4) + 8,
                          num_cells * (img_height + 4) + 8),
                         (128, 128, 128))
img_it = 0
vec = np.zeros((1, latent_space_depth + y_train.shape[1]))
for x in range(num_cells):
    vec = np.zeros((1, latent_space_depth + y_train.shape[1]))
    vec[:, x + latent_space_depth] = 1
    for y in range(num_cells):
        vec[:, 1] = 3 * y / (num_cells - 1) - 1.5
        decoded = cond_decoder.predict(vec)
        img = decode_img(decoded.reshape(img_width, img_height))
        overview.paste(img, (x * (img_width + 4) + 6,
                             y * (img_height + 4) + 6))
overview
```

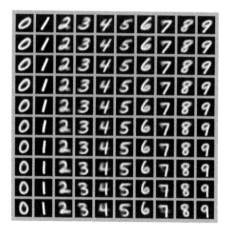

As you can see, the latent space expresses the style of the digit and the style is consistent across digits. In this case it seems that it controls how much the digit is slanted.

Discussion

The conditional variational autoencoder marks the final stop on our journey through the various autoencoders. This type of network enables us to map our digits to a dense latent space that is also labeled, allowing us to sample random images while specifying what type they should be.

A side effect of providing the labels to the network is that it now no longer has to learn the numbers, but can focus on the style of the numbers.

CHAPTER 14

Generating Icons Using Deep Nets

In the previous chapter we looked at generating hand-drawn sketches from the Quick Draw project and digits from the MNIST dataset. In this chapter we'll try three types of networks on a slightly more challenging task: generating icons.

Before we can do any generating we need to get our hands on a set of icons. Searching online for "free icons" results in a lot of hits. None of these are "free as in speech" and most of them struggle where it comes to "free as in beer." Also, you can't freely reuse the icons, and usually the sites strongly suggest you pay for them after all. So, we'll start with how to download, extract, and process icons into a standard format that we can use in the rest of the chapter.

The first thing we'll try is to train a conditional variational autoencoder on our set of icons. We'll use the network we ended up with in the previous chapter as a basis, but we'll add some convolutional layers to it to make it perform better since the icon space is so much more complex than that of hand-drawn digits.

The second type of network we'll try is a generative adversarial network. Here we'll train two networks, one to generate icons and another to distinguish between generated icons and real icons. The competition between the two leads to better results.

The third and final type of network we'll try is an RNN. In Chapter 5 we used this to generate texts in a certain style. By reinterpreting icons as a set of drawing instructions, we can use the same technique to generate images.

Code related to this chapter can be found in the following notebooks:

14.1 Acquiring Icons for Training

Problem

How do you get a large set of icons in a standard format?

Solution

Extract them from the Mac application *Icons8*.

Icons8 distributes a large set of icons—over 63,000. This is partly because icons of different formats are counted double, but still, it is a nice set. Unfortunately the icons are distributed inside applications for Mac and Windows. The good news is that a Mac *.dmg* archive is really just a p7zip archive containing an application, which itself is also a p7zip archive. Let's start by downloading the app. Navigate to *https:// icons8.com/app* and make sure to download the Mac version (even if you are on Linux or Windows). Now install the command-line version of p7zip for your favorite operating system and extract the contents of the *.dmg* file to its own folder:

```
7z x Icons8App_for_Mac_OS.dmg
```

The *.dmg* contains some metainformation and the Mac application. Let's unpack the app too:

```
cd Icons8\ v5.6.3
7z x Icons8.app
```

Like an onion, this thing has many layers. You should now see a *.tar* file that also needs unpacking:

```
tar xvf icons.tar
```

This gives us a directory called *icons* that contains an *.ldb* file, which suggests that the directory represents a LevelDB database. Switching to Python, we can take a look inside:

```python
# Adjust to your local path:
path = '/some/path/Downloads/Icons8 v5.6.3/icons'
db = plyvel.DB(path)

for key, value in db:
    print(key)
    print(value[:400])
    break

> b'icon_1'
b'TSAF\x03\x00\x02\x00\x07\x00\x00\x00\x00\x00\x00\x00$\x00\x00\x00
\x18\x00\x00\x00\r\x00\x00\x00-\x08id\x00\x08Messaging\x00\x08categ
ory\x00\x19\x00\x03\x00\x00\x00\x08Business\x00\x05\x01\x08User
Interface\x00\x08categories\x00\x18\x00\x00\x00\x03\x00\x00\x00\x08
Basic Elements\x00\x05\x04\x01\x05\x01\x08Business
```

```
Communication\x00\x05\x03\x08subcategories\x00\x19\x00\r\x00\x00\x00
\x08contacts\x00\x08phone book\x00\x08contacts
book\x00\x08directory\x00\x08mail\x00\x08profile\x00\x08online\x00
\x08email\x00\x08records\x00\x08alphabetical\x00\x08sim\x00\x08phone
numbers\x00\x08categorization\x00\x08tags\x00\x0f9\x08popularity\x00
\x18\x00\x00\x02\x00\x00\x00\x1c\x00\x00\x00\xe8\x0f\x00\x00<?xml
version="1.0" encoding="utf-8"?>\n<!-- Generato'
```

Bingo. We have found our icons, and they seem to be encoded using the *.svg* vector format. It looks like they are contained in yet another format, with the header TSAF. Reading online, it seems to be some IBM-related format, but a Python library to extract data from this is not easy to find. Then again, this simple dump suggests that we are dealing with key/value pairs separated by a \x00 with the key and value separated by a \x08. It doesn't quite pan out, but it is good enough to build a hacky parser:

```
splitter = re.compile(b'[\x00-\x09]')

def parse_value(value):
    res = {}
    prev = ''
    for elem in splitter.split(value):
        if not elem:
            continue
        try:
            elem = elem.decode('utf8')
        except UnicodeDecodeError:
            continue
        if elem in ('category', 'name', 'platform',
                    'canonical_name', 'svg', 'svg.simplified'):
            res[elem] = prev
        prev = elem
    return res
```

This extracts the SVGs and some basic properties that might come in handy later. The various platforms contain more or less the same icons, so we need to pick one platform. iOS seems to have the most icons, so let's go with that:

```
icons = {}
for _, value in db:
    res = parse_value(value)
    if res.get('platform') == 'ios':
        name = res.get('name')
        if not name:
            name = res.get('canonical_name')
            if not name:
                continue
        name = name.lower().replace(' ', '_')
        icons[name] = res
```

Now let's write this all to disk for later processing. We'll keep the SVGs but also write out bitmaps as PNGs:

```
saved = []
for icon in icons.values():
    icon = dict(icon)
    if not 'svg' in icon:
        continue
    svg = icon.pop('svg')
    try:
        drawing = svg2rlg(BytesIO(svg.encode('utf8')))
    except ValueError:
        continue
    except AttributeError:
        continue
    open('icons/svg/%s.svg' % icon['name'], 'w').write(svg)
    p = renderPM.drawToPIL(drawing)
    for size in SIZES:
        resized = p.resize((size, size), Image.ANTIALIAS)
        resized.save('icons/png%s/%s.png' % (size, icon['name']))
    saved.append(icon)
json.dump(saved, open('icons/index.json', 'w'), indent=2)
```

Discussion

Even though there are many sites online advertising free icons, in practice getting a good training set is rather involved. In this case we found the icons as SVGs inside a mysterious TSAF store inside a LevelDB database inside a Mac app inside of the *.dmg* file that we downloaded. On the one hand, this seems more involved than it should be. On the other hand, it goes to show that with a little detective work we can uncover some very interesting datasets.

14.2 Converting the Icons to a Tensor Representation

Problem

How do you convert the saved icons into a format suitable for training a network?

Solution

Concatenate them and normalize them.

This is similar to how we handled images for the pretrained network, except that now we will train our own network. We know all images will be 32×32 pixels, and we'll keep track of the mean and standard deviation so we can normalize and denormalize the images correctly. We'll also split the data up into a training set and a test set:

```
def load_icons(train_size=0.85):
    icon_index = json.load(open('icons/index.json'))
    x = []
    img_rows, img_cols = 32, 32
    for icon in icon_index:
```

```
        if icon['name'].endswith('_filled'):
            continue
        img_path = 'icons/png32/%s.png' % icon['name']
        img = load_img(img_path, grayscale=True,
                    target_size=(img_rows, img_cols))
        img = img_to_array(img)
        x.append(img)
    x = np.asarray(x) / 255
    x_train, x_val = train_test_split(x, train_size=train_size)
    return x_train, x_val
```

Discussion

The processing is fairly standard. We read in the images, append them all to one array, normalize the array, and then split the resulting set into a training set and test set. We normalize by just dividing the grayscale pixels by 255. The activation we'll use later on is a sigmoid, which will only produce positive numbers, so no need to subtract the mean.

14.3 Using a Variational Autoencoder to Generate Icons

Problem

You'd like to generate icons in a certain style.

Solution

Add convolutional layers to the MNIST solution of Chapter 13.

The variational autoencoder we used to generate digits had a latent space of only two dimensions. We can get away with such a small space because ultimately there isn't that much variation between handwritten digits. By their nature, there are only 10 different ones that all look fairly similar. Moreover, we used a fully connected layer to go to and from the latent space. Our icons are much more diverse, so we'll use a few convolutional layers to reduce the size of the image before we apply a fully connected layer and end up with our latent state:

```
input_img = Input(shape=(32, 32, 1))
channels = 4
x = input_img
for i in range(5):
    left = Conv2D(channels, (3, 3),
                activation='relu', padding='same')(x)
    right = Conv2D(channels, (2, 2),
                activation='relu', padding='same')(x)
    conc = Concatenate()([left, right])
    x = MaxPooling2D((2, 2), padding='same')(conc)
    channels *= 2
```

```
    x = Dense(channels)(x)
    encoder_hidden = Flatten()(x)
```

We handle the loss function and distribution as before. The weight for the KL_loss is important. Set it too low and the resulting space won't be dense. Set it too high and the network will quickly learn that predicting empty bitmaps gets it a decent reconstruction_loss and a great KL_loss:

```
z_mean = Dense(latent_space_depth,
               activation='linear')(encoder_hidden)
z_log_var = Dense(latent_space_depth,
                  activation='linear')(encoder_hidden)

def KL_loss(y_true, y_pred):
    return (0.001 * K.sum(K.exp(z_log_var)
           + K.square(z_mean) - 1 - z_log_var, axis=1))

def reconstruction_loss(y_true, y_pred):
    y_true = K.batch_flatten(y_true)
    y_pred = K.batch_flatten(y_pred)
    return binary_crossentropy(y_true, y_pred)

    def total_loss(y_true, y_pred):
        return (reconstruction_loss(y_true, y_pred)
               + KL_loss(y_true, y_pred))
```

Now we'll upscale the latent state back into an icon. As before, we do this in parallel for the encoder and the autoencoder:

```
z = Lambda(sample_z,
           output_shape=(latent_space_depth, ))([z_mean, z_log_var])
decoder_in = Input(shape=(latent_space_depth,))

d_x = Reshape((1, 1, latent_space_depth))(decoder_in)
e_x = Reshape((1, 1, latent_space_depth))(z)
for i in range(5):
    conv = Conv2D(channels, (3, 3), activation='relu', padding='same')
    upsampling = UpSampling2D((2, 2))
    d_x = conv(d_x)
    d_x = upsampling(d_x)
    e_x = conv(e_x)
    e_x = upsampling(e_x)
    channels //= 2

final_conv = Conv2D(1, (3, 3), activation='sigmoid', padding='same')
auto_decoded = final_conv(e_x)
decoder_out = final_conv(d_x)
```

To train the network, we need to make sure the training and test sets have a size that is divisible by the batch_size, as otherwise the KL_loss function will fail:

```
def truncate_to_batch(x):
    l = x.shape[0]
    return x[:l - l % batch_size, :, :, :]

x_train_trunc = truncate_to_batch(x_train)
x_test_trunc = truncate_to_batch(x_test)
x_train_trunc.shape, x_test_trunc.shape
```

We can sample some random icons from the space as before:

As you can see, the network definitely learned something about icons. They tend to have some sort of box that is filled in somewhat and usually don't touch the outsides of the 32×32 container. But it is still rather vague!

Discussion

To apply the variational autoencoder we developed in the previous chapter on the more heterogeneous space of icons we need to use convolutional layers that step by step reduce the dimensions of the bitmap and increase the abstraction level until we are in the latent space. This is very similar to how image recognition networks function. Once we have our icons projected in a 128-dimensional space, we use the upsampling layers for both the generator and the autoencoder.

The result is more interesting than a slam dunk. Part of the issue is that icons, like the cats in the previous chapter, contain a lot of line drawings, which makes it hard for the network to get them exactly right. When in doubt, the network will opt for vague lines instead. Worse, icons often contain regions that are dithered like a checkerboard. These patterns are certainly learnable, but an off-by-one pixel error would mean that the entire answer is now completely wrong!

Another reason why the performance of our network is relatively poor is that we have relatively few icons. The next recipe shows a trick to get around that.

14.4 Using Data Augmentation to Improve the Autoencoder's Performance

Problem

How can you improve on the performance of your network without getting more data?

Solution

Use data augmentation.

Our autoencoder in the previous recipe learned the vague outlines of our icon set, but nothing more than that. The results suggested that it was picking up on something, but not enough to do a stellar job. Throwing more data at the problem could help, but it would require us to find more icons, and those icons would have to be sufficiently similar to our original set to help. Instead we're going to generate more data.

The idea behind data augmentation, as discussed in Chapter 1, is to generate variations of the input data that shouldn't matter to the network. In this case we want our network to learn the notion of *iconness* by feeding it icons. But if we flip or rotate our icons, does that make them less *icony*? Not really. Doing this will increase our input by a factor of 16. Our network will learn from these new training examples that rotations and flipping don't matter and hopefully perform better. Augmentation would look like this:

```
def augment(icons):
    aug_icons = []
    for icon in icons:
        for flip in range(4):
            for rotation in range(4):
                aug_icons.append(icon)
                icon = np.rot90(icon)
            icon = np.fliplr(icon)
    return np.asarray(aug_icons)
```

Let's apply that to our training and test data:

```
x_train_aug = augment(x_train)
x_test_aug = augment(x_test)
```

Training the network will now obviously take a bit longer. But the results are better, too:

Discussion

Data augmentation is a technique widely used when it comes to computer images. Rotations and flips are sort of obvious ways of doing this, but given the fact that we actually started out with the *.svg* representation of the icons there are a number of other things we could do. SVG is a vector format, so we could easily create icons that have a slight rotation or magnification without getting the sort of artifacts that we'd get if our baseline data comprised just bitmaps.

The icon space that we ended up with is better than the one from the previous recipe and it seems to capture some form of iconness.

14.5 Building a Generative Adversarial Network

Problem

You'd like to construct a network that can generate images and another that can learn to distinguish generated images from the originals.

Solution

Create an image generator and an image discriminator that can work together.

The key insight behind generative adversarial networks is that if you have two networks, one generating images and one judging the generated images, and train them in tandem, they keep each other on their toes as they learn. Let's start with a generator network. This is similar to what we did with the decoder bit of an autoencoder:

```
inp = Input(shape=(latent_size,))
x = Reshape((1, 1, latent_size))(inp)

channels = latent_size
padding = 'valid'
strides = 1
for i in range(4):
    x = Conv2DTranspose(channels, kernel_size=4,
                        strides=strides, padding=padding)(x)
    x = BatchNormalization()(x)
    x = LeakyReLU(.2)(x)

    channels //= 2
    padding = 'same'
    strides = 2

x = Conv2DTranspose(1, kernel_size=4, strides=1, padding='same')(x)
image_out = Activation('tanh')(x)

model = Model(inputs=inp, outputs=image_out)
```

The other network, the discriminator, will take in an image and output whether it thinks it is generated or one of the originals. In that sense it looks like a classic convolutional network that has just a binary output:

```
inp = Input(shape=(32, 32, 1))
x = inp

channels = 16

for i in range(4):
```

```
        layers = []
        conv = Conv2D(channels, 3, strides=2, padding='same')(x)
        if i:
            conv = BatchNormalization()(conv)
        conv = LeakyReLU(.2)(conv)
        layers.append(conv)
        bv = Lambda(lambda x: K.mean(K.abs(x[:] - K.mean(x, axis=0)),
                            axis=-1,
                            keepdims=True))(conv)
        layers.append(bv)
        channels *= 2
        x = Concatenate()(layers)

    x = Conv2D(128, 2, padding='valid')(x)
    x = Flatten(name='flatten')(x)

    fake = Dense(1, activation='sigmoid', name='generation')(x)

    m = Model(inputs=inp, outputs=fake)
```

In the next recipe we'll look at how to train these two networks together.

Discussion

Generative adversarial networks or GANs are a fairly recent innovation for generating images. One way to look at them is to see the two component networks, the generator and the discriminator, as learning together, becoming better in competition.

The other way to look at them is to see the discriminator as a dynamic loss function for the generator. A straightforward loss function works well when a network is learning to distinguish between cats and dogs; something is a cat, or it isn't and we can use as a loss function the difference between the answer and the truth.

When generating images, this is trickier. How do you compare two images? Earlier in this chapter, when we were generating images using autoencoders, we ran into this problem. There, we just compared images pixel by pixel; that works when seeing if two images are the same, but it doesn't work so well for similarity. Two icons that are exactly the same but offset by one pixel won't necessarily have many pixels in the same position. As a result, the autoencoder often opted to generate fuzzy images.

Having a second network do the judging allows the overall system to develop a sense of image similarity that is more fluid. Moreover, it can become stricter as the images become better, while with the autoencoder if we start with too much emphasis on the dense space the network will never learn.

14.6 Training Generative Adversarial Networks

Problem

How do you train the two components of a GAN together?

Solution

Fall back on the underlying TensorFlow framework to run both networks together.

Normally we just let Keras do the heavy lifting when it comes to talking to the underlying TensorFlow framework. But the best we can do using Keras directly is alternate between training the generator and the discriminator network, which is suboptimal. Qin Yongliang has written a blog post (*http://bit.ly/2ILx7Te*) that describes how to get around this.

We'll start by generating some noise and feeding that into the generator to get a generated image, and then feed a real image and a generated image into the discriminator:

```
noise = Input(shape=g.input_shape[1:])
real_data = Input(shape=d.input_shape[1:])

generated = g(noise)
gscore = d(generated)
rscore = d(real_data)
```

Now we can construct two loss functions. The generator is scored against how likely to be real the discriminator thought the image was. The discriminator is scored on a combination of how well it did with fake and real images:

```
dloss = (- K.mean(K.log((1 - gscore) + .1 * K.log((1 - rscore)
        + .9 * K.log((rscore)))
gloss = - K.mean(K.log((gscore))
```

Now we'll calculate the gradients to optimize these two loss functions for the trainable weights of the two networks:

```
optimizer = tf.train.AdamOptimizer(1e-4, beta1=0.2)
grad_loss_wd = optimizer.compute_gradients(dloss, d.trainable_weights)
update_wd = optimizer.apply_gradients(grad_loss_wd)
grad_loss_wg = optimizer.compute_gradients(gloss, g.trainable_weights)
update_wg = optimizer.apply_gradients(grad_loss_wg)
```

We collect the various steps and tensors:

```
other_parameter_updates = [get_internal_updates(m) for m in [d, g]]
train_step = [update_wd, update_wg, other_parameter_updates]
losses = [dloss, gloss]
learning_phase = K.learning_phase()
```

And we're ready to set up the trainer. Keras needs the `learning_phase` set:

```
def gan_feed(sess,batch_image, z_input):
    feed_dict = {
        noise: z_input,
        real_data: batch_image,
        learning_phase: True,
    }
    loss_values, = sess.run([losses], feed_dict=feed_dict)
```

The variables of which we can provide by generating our own batches:

```
sess = K.get_session()
l = x_train.shape[0]
l -= l % BATCH_SIZE
for i in range(epochs):
    np.random.shuffle(x_train)
    for batch_start in range(0, l, BATCH_SIZE):
        batch = x_train[batch_start: batch_start + BATCH_SIZE]
        z_input = np.random.normal(loc=0.,
                                   scale=1.,
                                   size=(BATCH_SIZE, LATENT_SIZE))
        losses = gan_feed(sess, batch, z_input)
```

Discussion

Updating the weights for both networks in one go took us down to the level of TensorFlow itself. While this is a bit hairy, it is also good to get to know the underlying systems from time to time and not always rely on the "magic" that Keras provides.

There are a number of implementations on the web that use the easy way out and just run both networks step by step, but not at the same time.

14.7 Showing the Icons the GAN Produces

Problem

How do you show the progress that the GAN is making while it learns?

Solution

Add an icon renderer after each epoch.

Since we're running our own batch processing, we might as well take advantage of this and update the notebook with the intermediate result at the end of each epoch. Let's start with rendering a set of icons using the generator:

```
def generate_images(count):
    noise = np.random.normal(loc=0.,
                             scale=1.,
                             size=(count, LATENT_SIZE))
    for tile in gm.predict([noise]).reshape((count, 32, 32)):
        tile = (tile * 300).clip(0, 255).astype('uint8')
        yield PIL.Image.fromarray(tile)
```

Next, let's put them on a poster overview:

```
def poster(w_count, h_count):
    overview = PIL.Image.new('RGB',
                             (w_count * 34 + 2, h_count * 34 + 2),
                             (128, 128, 128))
    for idx, img in enumerate(generate_images(w_count * h_count)):
        x = idx % w_count
        y = idx // w_count
        overview.paste(img, (x * 34 + 2, y * 34 + 2))
    return overview
```

We can now add the following code to our epoch loop:

```
clear_output(wait=True)
f = BytesIO()
poster(8, 5).save(f, 'png')
display(Image(data=f.getvalue()))
```

After one epoch some vague icons start to appear already:

Another 25 epochs and we are really starting to see some iconness:

Discussion

The final results for generating icons using GANs are better than what we got out of the autoencoders. Mostly, the drawings are a lot sharper, which can be attributed to having the discriminator network decide whether an icon is any good, rather than comparing icons on a pixel-by-pixel basis.

 There has been an explosion of applications for GANs and their derivatives, ranging from reconstructing 3D models from pictures to coloring of old pictures and super-resolution, where the network increases the resolution of a small image without making it look blurred or blocky.

14.8 Encoding Icons as Drawing Instructions

Problem

You'd like to convert icons into a format that is suitable to train an RNN.

Solution

Encode the icons as drawing instructions.

RNNs can learn sequences, as we saw in Chapter 5. But what if we wanted to generate icons using an RNN? We could simply encode each icon as a sequence of pixels. One way to do this would be to view an icon as a sequence of pixels that have been "turned on." There are 32 * 32 = 1,024 different pixels, so that would be our vocabulary. This does work, but we can do a little better by using actual drawing instructions.

If we treat an icon as a series of scanlines, we need only 32 different tokens for the pixels in a scanline. Add one token to move to the next scanline and a final token to mark the end of an icon and we have a nice sequential representation. Or, in code:

```
def encode_icon(img, icon_size):
    size_last_x = 0
    encoded = []
    for y in range(icon_size):
        for x in range(icon_size):
            p = img.getpixel((x, y))
            if img.getpixel((x, y)) < 192:
                encoded.append(x)
                size_last_x = len(encoded)
        encoded.append(icon_size)
    return encoded[:size_last_x]
```

We can then decode an image by going through the pixels:

```
def decode_icon(encoded, icon_size):
    y = 0
    for idx in encoded:
        if idx == icon_size:
            y += 1
        elif idx == icon_size + 1:
            break
        else:
            x = idx
            yield x, y

icon = PIL.Image.new('L', (32, 32), 'white')
for x, y in decode_icon(sofar, 32):
    if y < 32:
        icon.putpixel((x, y), 0)
```

Discussion

Encoding icons as a set of drawing instructions is just another way of preprocessing the data such that a network will have an easier job learning what we want it to learn, similar to other approaches we saw in Chapter 1. By having explicit drawing instructions we make sure, for example, that the network doesn't learn to draw vague lines, as our autoencoder was prone to do—it won't be able to.

14.9 Training an RNN to Draw Icons

Problem

You'd like to train an RNN to generate icons.

Solution

Train a network based on the drawing instructions.

Now that we can encode single icons as drawing instructions, the next step is to encode a whole set. Since we're going to feed chunks into the RNN, asking it to predict the next instruction, we actually construct one big "document":

```
def make_array(icons):
    res = []
    for icon in icons:
        res.extend(icon)
        res.append(33)
    return np.asarray(res)

def load_icons(train_size=0.90):
    icon_index = json.load(open('icons/index.json'))
```

```
    x = []
    img_rows, img_cols = 32, 32
    for icon in icon_index:
        if icon['name'].endswith('_filled'):
            continue
        img_path = 'icons/png32/%s.png' % icon['name']
        x.append(encode_icon(PIL.Image.open(img_path), 32))
    x_train, x_val = train_test_split(x, train_size=train_size)
    x_train = make_array(x_train)
    x_val = make_array(x_val)
    return x_train, x_val

x_train, x_test = load_icons()
```

We'll run with the same model that helped us generate our Shakespearean text:

```
def icon_rnn_model(num_chars, num_layers, num_nodes=512, dropout=0.1):
    input = Input(shape=(None, num_chars), name='input')
    prev = input
    for i in range(num_layers):
        lstm = LSTM(num_nodes, return_sequences=True,
                    name='lstm_layer_%d' % (i + 1))(prev)
        if dropout:
            prev = Dropout(dropout)(lstm)
        else:
            prev = lstm
    dense = TimeDistributed(Dense(num_chars,
                                  name='dense',
                                  activation='softmax'))(prev)
    model = Model(inputs=[input], outputs=[dense])
    optimizer = RMSprop(lr=0.01)
    model.compile(loss='categorical_crossentropy',
                  optimizer=optimizer,
                  metrics=['accuracy'])
    return model

model = icon_rnn_model(34, num_layers=2, num_nodes=256, dropout=0)
```

Discussion

To see in more detail how the network we use here is trained and the data is generated, it might be a good idea to look back at Chapter 5.

You can experiment with different numbers of layers and nodes or try different values for dropout. Different RNN layers also have an effect. The model is somewhat fragile; it is easy to get into a state where it doesn't learn anything or, when it does, gets stuck on a local maximum.

14.10 Generating Icons Using an RNN

Problem

You've trained the network; now how do you get it to produce icons?

Solution

Feed the network some random bits of your test set and interpret the predictions as drawing instructions.

The basic approach here is again the same as when we were generating Shakespearean text or Python code; the only difference is that we need to feed the predictions into the icon decoder to get icons out. Let's first run some predictions:

```
def generate_icons(model, num=2, diversity=1.0):
    start_index = random.randint(0, len(x_test) - CHUNK_SIZE - 1)
    generated = x_test[start_index: start_index + CHUNK_SIZE]
    while num > 0:
        x = np.zeros((1, len(generated), 34))
        for t, char in enumerate(generated):
            x[0, t, char] = 1.
        preds = model.predict(x, verbose=0)[0]
        preds = np.asarray(preds[len(generated) - 1]).astype('float64')
        exp_preds = np.exp(np.log(preds) / diversity)
```

The `diversity` parameter controls how far the predictions are from deterministic (which the model will turn into if `diversity` is 0). We need this to generate diverse icons, but also to avoid getting stuck in a loop.

We'll collect each prediction in a variable, `so_far`, which we flush every time we encounter the value 33 (end of icon). We also check whether the y value is in range—the model learns more or less the size of the icons, but will sometimes try to color outside of the lines:

```
        if next_index == 33:
            icon = PIL.Image.new('L', (32, 32), 'white')
            for x, y in decode_icon(sofar, 32):
                if y < 32:
                    icon.putpixel((x, y), 0)
            yield icon
            num -= 1
        else:
            sofar.append(next_index)
```

With this, we can now draw a "poster" of icons:

```
cols = 10
rows = 10
overview = PIL.Image.new('RGB',
```

```
                    (cols * 36 + 4, rows * 36 + 4),
                    (128, 128, 128))
for idx, icon in enumerate(generate_icons(model, num=cols * rows)):
    x = idx % cols
    y = idx // cols
    overview.paste(icon, (x * 36 + 4, y * 36 + 4))
overview
```

Discussion

The icons generated using the RNN are the boldest of the three attempts we under-
took in this chapter and arguably capture the nature of iconness best. The model
learns symmetry and the basic shapes found in icons and even occasionally dithers to
get a notion of halftones across.

We could try to combine the different approaches in this chapter. For example,
instead of trying to predict the next drawing instruction, we could have an RNN that
takes in the drawing instructions, capture the latent state at that point, and then have
a second RNN based on that state reconstruct the drawing instructions. This way we
would have an RNN-based autoencoder. In the text world there have been some suc-
cesses in this area.

RNNs can also be combined with GANs. Instead of having a generator network that
takes a latent variable and upscales it into an icon, we'd use an RNN to generate drawing instructions and then have the discriminator network decide whether these are
real or fake.

CHAPTER 15

Music and Deep Learning

The other chapters in this book are all about processing of images or texts. Those chapters represent the balance of media in deep learning research, but that is not to say that sound processing isn't interesting and that we haven't seen some great developments in this area in the last few years. Speech recognition and speech synthesis are what made home assistants like Amazon Alexa and Google Home a possibility. The old sitcom joke where the phone dials the wrong number hasn't really been current since Siri came out.

It is easy to start experimenting with these systems; there are APIs out there that let you get a simple voice app up and running in a few hours. The voice processing, however, is done in Amazon, Google, or Apple's data center, so we can't really count these as deep learning experiments. Building state-of-the-art voice recognition systems is hard, although Mozilla's Deep Speech is making some impressive progress.

This chapter focuses on music. We'll start out with training a music classification model that can tell us what music we're listening to. We'll then use the results of this model to index local MP3s, making it possible to find songs similar in style. After that we'll use the Spotify API to create a corpus of public playlists that we'll use to train a music recommender.

The notebooks for this chapter are:

    15.1 Song Classification
    15.2 Index Local MP3s
    15.3 Spotify Playlists
    15.4 Train a Music Recommender

15.1 Creating a Training Set for Music Classification

Problem

How do you get and prepare a set of music for classification?

Solution

Create spectrograms from the test set provided by the University of Victoria in Canada.

You could try to do this by plugging in that dusty external drive with your MP3 collection on it and relying on the tags on those songs. But a lot of those tags may be somewhat random or missing, so it's best to get started with a training set from a scientific institution that is nicely labeled:

```
wget http://opihi.cs.uvic.ca/sound/genres.tar.gz
tar xzf genres.tar.gz
```

This should get us a directory, *genres*, with subdirectories containing music of different genres:

```
>ls ~/genres
blues  classical  country  disco  hiphop  jazz  metal  pop  reggae  rock
```

Those directories contain sound files (*.au*), 100 clips per genre, each 29 seconds long. We could try to feed the raw sound frames directly into the network and maybe an LSTM would pick up something, but there are better ways of preprocessing sounds. Sound is really sound waves, but we don't hear waves. Instead, we hear tones of a certain frequency.

So a good way to make our network behave more like our hearing works is to convert sound into blocks of spectrograms; each sample will be represented by a series of audio freqencies and their respective intensities. The librosa library for Python has some standard functions for this and also provides what's called a *melspectrogram*, a type of spectrogram that is meant to closely emulate how human hearing works. So let's load up the music and convert the fragments to melspectrograms:

```
def load_songs(song_folder):
    song_specs = []
    idx_to_genre = []
    genre_to_idx = {}
    genres = []
    for genre in os.listdir(song_folder):
        genre_to_idx[genre] = len(genre_to_idx)
        idx_to_genre.append(genre)
        genre_folder = os.path.join(song_folder, genre)
        for song in os.listdir(genre_folder):
            if song.endswith('.au'):
```

```
                signal, sr = librosa.load(
                    os.path.join(genre_folder, song))
                melspec = librosa.feature.melspectrogram(
                    signal, sr=sr).T[:1280,]
                song_specs.append(melspec)
                genres.append(genre_to_idx[genre])
    return song_specs, genres, genre_to_idx, idx_to_genre
```

Let's also have a quick look at some of the genres as spectrograms. Since those spectrograms are now just matrices, we can treat them as bitmaps. They are really quite sparse, so we are going to overexpose them to see more details:

```
def show_spectogram(show_genre):
    show_genre = genre_to_idx[show_genre]
    specs = []
    for spec, genre in zip(song_specs, genres):
        if show_genre == genre:
            specs.append(spec)
            if len(specs) == 25:
                break
    if not specs:
        return 'not found!'
    x = np.concatenate(specs, axis=1)
    x = (x - x.min()) / (x.max() - x.min())
    plt.imshow((x *20).clip(0, 1.0))

show_spectogram('classical')
```

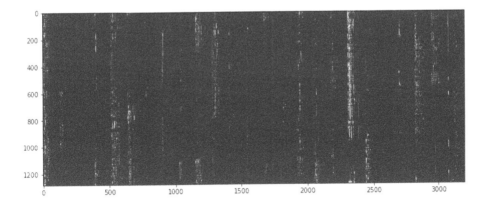

```
show_spectogram('metal')
```

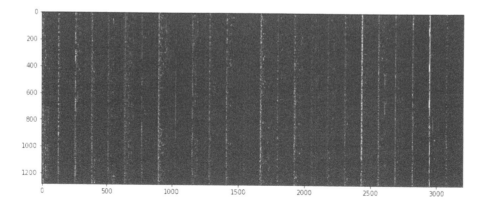

Even though it is hard to say what exactly the pictures mean, there is some suggestion that metal has more of a rigid structure than classical music, which is maybe not completely unexpected.

Discussion

As we've seen throughout this book, preprocessing data before letting networks do their thing increases our chances of success significantly. When it comes to sound processing, librosa has functions for almost anything you could wish for, from loading sound files and playing them inside notebooks to visualizing them and doing any kind of preprocessing.

Visually inspecting spectrograms doesn't tell us much, but it does give us a hint that they are different for different genres of music. We'll see in the next recipe whether a network can learn to distinguish between them too.

15.2 Training a Music Genre Detector

Problem

How do you set up and train a deep network to detect music genres?

Solution

Use a one-dimensional convolutional network.

We've used convolutional networks in this book for image detection (see Chapter 9) and for text (see Chapter 7). It might seem that treating our spectrograms as images would be the more logical way to proceed, but we are actually going to go with a one-dimensional convolutional network. Each frame in our spectrogram represents a frame of music. Using a convolutional net to convert stretches of time into a more abstract representation makes sense when we try to classify genres; reducing the "height" of the frames is less intuitively sensible.

We'll start by stacking some layers on top of each other. This will reduce the size of our input from 128 dimensions wide to 25. The GlobalMaxPooling layer will then make this into a 128-float vector:

```
inputs = Input(input_shape)
x = inputs
for layers in range(3):
x = Conv1D(128, 3, activation='relu')(x)
x = BatchNormalization()(x)
x = MaxPooling1D(pool_size=6, strides=2)(x)
x = GlobalMaxPooling1D()(x)
```

This is followed by a few fully connected layers to get to the labels:

```
for fc in range(2):
x = Dense(256, activation='relu')(x)
    x = Dropout(0.5)(x)

    outputs = Dense(10, activation='softmax')(x)
```

Before we feed our data into the model, we'll split each song into 10 fragments of 3 seconds each. We do this to increase the amount of data, since 1,000 songs isn't really that much:

```
def split_10(x, y):
    s = x.shape
    s = (s[0] * 10, s[1] // 10, s[2])
    return x.reshape(s), np.repeat(y, 10, axis=0)

genres_one_hot = keras.utils.to_categorical(
    genres, num_classes=len(genre_to_idx))

x_train, x_test, y_train, y_test = train_test_split(
    np.array(song_specs), np.array(genres_one_hot),
    test_size=0.1, stratify=genres)

x_test, y_test = split_10(x_test, y_test)
x_train, y_train = split_10(x_train, y_train)
```

Training this model gives us accuracy of around 60% after 100 epochs, which is not bad, but certainly not superhuman. We can improve upon this result by taking advantage of the fact that we split each song into 10 fragments and use the information across the chunks to get to a result. Majority voting would be one strategy, but it turns out that going with whatever chunk the model is most sure of works even better. We can do this by splitting the data back into 100 chunks and applying argmax on each of them. This will get us for each one the index in the entire chunk. By applying modulo 10 we get the index into our label set:

```
def unsplit(values):
    chunks = np.split(values, 100)
    return np.array([np.argmax(chunk) % 10 for chunk in chunks])

predictions = unsplit(model.predict(x_test))
truth = unsplit(y_test)
accuracy_score(predictions, truth)
```

This gets us up to 75% accuracy.

Discussion

With 100 songs for each of our 10 genres, we don't have a lot of training data. Splitting our songs up into 10 chunks of 3 seconds each gets us to somewhere half decent, although our model still ends up overfitting a bit.

One thing to explore would be to apply some data augmentation techniques. We could try adding noise to the music, speeding it up a bit, or slowing it down though the spectrogram itself might not really change that much. It would be better to get our hands on a larger set of music.

15.3 Visualizing Confusion

Problem

How do you show the mistakes that the network makes in a clear way?

Solution

Graphically display a confusion matrix.

A confusion matrix has columns for each of the genres representing the truth and rows for the genres the model predicted. The cells contain the counts for each (truth, prediction) pair. sklearn comes with a handy method to calculate it:

```
cm = confusion_matrix(pred_values, np.argmax(y_test, axis=1))
print(cm)

[[65 13  0  6  5  1  4  5  2  1]
 [13 54  1  3  4  0 20  1  0  9]
 [ 5  2 99  0  0  0 12 33  0  2]
 [ 0  0  0 74 29  1  8  0 18 10]
 [ 0  0  0  2 55  0  0  1  2  0]
 [ 1  0  0  1  0 95  0  0  0  6]
 [ 8 17  0  2  5  2 45  0  1  4]
 [ 4  4  0  1  2  0 10 60  1  4]
 [ 0  1  0  1  0  1  0  0 64  5]
 [ 4  9  0 10  0  0  1  0 12 59]]
```

We can visualize this a bit more clearly by shading the matrix. Transposing the matrix so we can see the confusion per row also makes things a bit easier to process:

```
plt.imshow(cm.T, interpolation='nearest', cmap='gray')
plt.xticks(np.arange(0, len(idx_to_genre)), idx_to_genre)
plt.yticks(np.arange(0, len(idx_to_genre)), idx_to_genre)

plt.show()
```

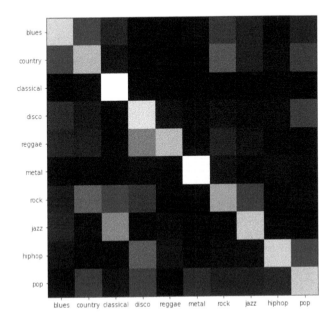

Discussion

Confusion matrices are a neat way to display the performance of a network, but they also give you an idea of where it goes wrong, which might hint at how to improve things. In the example in this recipe we can see that the network does very well at distinguishing classical music and metal from other types of music, but it does less well at distinguishing rock from country. None of this is unexpected, of course.

15.4 Indexing Existing Music

Problem

You'd like to build an index over pieces of music that captures their style.

Solution

Treat the last fully connected layer of the model as an embedding layer.

In Chapter 10 we built a reverse search engine for images by interpreting the last fully connected layer of an image recognition network as image embeddings. We can do something similar with music. Let's start by collecting some MP3s—you probably have a collection of them lying around somewhere:

```
MUSIC_ROOT = _</path/to/music>_
mp3s = []
for root, subdirs, files in os.walk(MUSIC_ROOT):
    for fn in files:
        if fn.endswith('.mp3'):
            mp3s.append(os.path.join(root, fn))
```

Then we'll index them. As before, we extract a melspectrogram. We also fetch the MP3 tags:

```
def process_mp3(path):
    tag = TinyTag.get(path)
    signal, sr = librosa.load(path,
                              res_type='kaiser_fast',
                              offset=30,
                              duration=30)
    melspec = librosa.feature.melspectrogram(signal, sr=sr).T[:1280,]
        if len(melspec) != 1280:
            return None
    return {'path': path,
            'melspecs': np.asarray(np.split(melspec, 10)),
            'tag': tag}

songs = [process_mp3(path) for path in tqdm(mp3s)]
songs = [song for song in songs if song]
```

We want to index every spectrogram of all MP3s—we can do that in one batch if we concatenate all of them together:

```
inputs = []
for song in songs:
    inputs.extend(song['melspecs'])
inputs = np.array(inputs)
```

To get to the vector representation, we'll construct a model that returns the fourth-to-last layer from our previous model and run it over the collected spectra:

```
cnn_model = load_model('zoo/15/song_classify.h5')
vectorize_model = Model(inputs=cnn_model.input,
                        outputs=cnn_model.layers[-4].output)
vectors = vectorize_model.predict(inputs)
```

A simple nearest neighbor model lets us now find similar songs. Given a song, we'll look up for each of its vectors what the other nearest vectors are. The very first result we can skip, since it is the vector itself:

```
nbrs = NearestNeighbors(n_neighbors=10, algorithm='ball_tree').fit(vectors)
def most_similar_songs(song_idx):
    distances, indices = nbrs.kneighbors(
        vectors[song_idx * 10: song_idx * 10 + 10])
    c = Counter()
    for row in indices:
        for idx in row[1:]:
            c[idx // 10] += 1
    return c.most_common()
```

Trying this out on a random song seems to work:

```
song_idx = 7
print(songs[song_idx]['path'])

print('---')
for idx, score in most_similar_songs(song_idx)[:5]:
    print(songs[idx]['path'], score)
print('')

00 shocking blue - Venus (yes the.mp3
---
00 shocking blue - Venus (yes the.mp3 20
The Shocking Blue/Have A Nice Day_ Vol 1/00 Venus.mp3 12
The Byrds/00 Eve of Destruction.mp3 12
Goldfinger _ Weezer _ NoFx _ L/00 AWESOME.mp3 6
```

Indexing songs using the last fully connected layer of our model works reasonably well. In this example it not only finds the original song, but also a slightly different version of that song that happens to be in the MP3 collection. Whether the other two songs returned are really similar in style is a judgment call, but they are not completely different.

The code here could be used as a basis to build something like Shazam; record a bit of music, run that through our vectorizer, and see which indexed song it matches most closely. Shazam's algorithm is different and predates the popularity of deep learning.

By taking a short bit of music and finding other music that sounds similar, we have the basics for a music recommender system. The fact that it only works for music we already have access to does limit its usefulness a bit, though. In the rest of this chapter we'll look at another approach to building a music recommender system.

15.5 Setting Up Spotify API Access

Problem

How can you get access to a large set of music data?

Solution

Use the Spotify API.

The system we created in the previous recipe is a sort of music recommender, but it only recommends songs it has already seen. By harvesting playlists and songs from the Spotify API we can build up a much larger training set. Let's start by registering a new app at Spotify. Head over to *https://beta.developer.spotify.com/dashboard/applica tions*, and create a new application.

 The URL mentioned here starts with beta. By the time you are reading this, the new application interface on Spotify might have come out of beta and the URL might have changed.

You'll need to log in first and possibly register before that. Once you've created an app, go to the app page and note the Client ID and the Client Secret. Since the secret is, well, secret, you'll need to press the button to show it.

Enter your various details in three constants:

```
CLIENT_ID = '<your client id>'
CLIENT_SECRET = '<your secret>'
USER_ID = '<your user id>'
```

You can now access the Spotify API:

```
uri = 'http://127.0.0.1:8000/callback'
token = util.prompt_for_user_token(USER_ID, '',
                            client_id=CLIENT_ID,
                            client_secret=CLIENT_SECRET,
                            redirect_uri=uri)
session = spotipy.Spotify(auth=token)
```

The first time you run this code, the API will ask you to enter a URL into a browser. This works somewhat awkwardly when run from a notebook; the URL to redirect to will be printed in the window where your notebook server runs. However, if you press the Stop button in the browser, it will show you the URL to redirect to. Click on that URL. It will redirect to something starting with *http://127.0.0.1* that won't resolve, but that doesn't matter. Enter that URL back into the box that now shows up in the notebook page and press Enter. This should authorize you.

You only need to do this once; the token gets stored locally in a file named *.cache-<username>*. If something goes wrong, delete this file and try again.

Discussion

The Spotify API is a remarkably great source for musical data. The API is accessible through a nicely designed REST API with well-defined endpoints that return self-describing JSON documents.

The API documentation (*https://developer.spotify.com/web-api/*) has information on how to access songs, artists, and playlists, including rich metainformation like album covers.

15.6 Collecting Playlists and Songs from Spotify

Problem

You need to create a training set for your music recommender.

Solution

Search for common words to find playlists and fetch the songs that belong to them.

As rich as the Spotify API is, there is no easy way to get a set of public playlists. You can search for them by word, though. In this recipe we'll use that as a way to get access to a nice body of playlists. Let's start by implementing a function to fetch all playlists matching a search term. The only complication in the code is due to the fact that we need to recover from timeouts and other errors:

```
def find_playlists(session, w, max_count=5000):
    try:
        res = session.search(w, limit=50, type='playlist')
        while res:
            for playlist in res['playlists']['items']:
                yield playlist
                max_count -= 1
                if max_count == 0:
                    raise StopIteration
            tries = 3
            while tries > 0:
                try:
                    res = session.next(res['playlists'])
                    tries = 0
                except SpotifyException as e:
                    tries -= 1
                    time.sleep(0.2)
                    if tries == 0:
                        raise
```

```
except SpotifyException as e:
    status = e.http_status
    if status == 404:
        raise StopIteration
    raise
```

We'll start with one word, "a," and fetch 5,000 playlists that contain that word. We'll keep track of all those playlists, but also count the words that occur in the titles of those playlists. That way when we're done with the word "a," we can do the same with the word that occurs most. We can keep doing this until we have enough playlists:

```
while len(playlists) < 100000:
    for word, _ in word_counts.most_common():
        if not word in words_seen:
            words_seen.add(word)
            print('word>', word)
            for playlist in find_playlists(session, word):
                if playlist['id'] in playlists:
                    dupes += 1
                elif playlist['name'] and playlist['owner']:
                    playlists[playlist['id']] = {
                        'owner': playlist['owner']['id'],
                        'name': playlist['name'],
                        'id': playlist['id'],
                    }
                    count += 1
                    for token in tokenize(playlist['name'],
                                          lowercase=True):
                        word_counts[token] += 1
            break
```

The playlists we fetched don't actually contain the songs; for this we need to do a separate call. To get all the tracks of a playlist, use:

```
def track_yielder(session, playlist):
    res = session.user_playlist_tracks(playlist['owner'], playlist['id'],
        fields='items(track(id, name, artists(name, id), duration_ms)),next')
    while res:
        for track in res['items']:
            yield track['track']['id']
        res = session.next(res)
        if not res or  not res.get('items'):
            raise StopIteration
```

Getting a large set of songs and playlists can take a significant amount of time. To get some decent results, we need at least 100,000 playlists, but something closer to a million would be better. Getting 100,000 playlists and their songs takes about 15 hours on a decent connection—it's doable, but not something you'd want to do over and over again, so we'd better save the results.

We are going to store three datasets. The first contains the playlist information itself —we don't actually need this for the next recipe, but it is useful to check things.

Secondly, we'll store the IDs of the songs in the playlists in a big text file. And finally, we'll store the per-song information. We'll want to be able to look up these details in a dynamic fashion, so we're going to use a SQLite database for this. We'll write out the results as we collect song information to keep memory usage under control:

```
conn = sqlite3.connect('data/songs.db')
c = conn.cursor()
c.execute('CREATE TABLE songs '
          '(id text primary key, name text, artist text)')
c.execute('CREATE INDEX name_idx on songs(name)')

tracks_seen = set()
with open('data/playlists.ndjson', 'w') as fout_playlists:
    with open('data/songs_ids.txt', 'w') as fout_song_ids:
        for playlist in tqdm.tqdm(playlists.values()):
            fout_playlists.write(json.dumps(playlist) + '\n')
            track_ids = []
            for track in track_yielder(session, playlist):
                track_id = track['id']
                if not track_id:
                    continue
                if not track_id in tracks_seen:
                    c.execute("INSERT INTO songs VALUES (?, ?, ?)",
                              (track['id'], track['name'],
                               track['artists'][0]['name']))
                track_ids.append(track_id)
            fout_song_ids.write(' '.join(track_ids) + '\n')
            conn.commit()
conn.commit()
```

Discussion

In this recipe we looked at building up a database of playlists and their songs. Since there is no clear way to get a balanced sample of public playlists from Spotify, we took the approach of using the search interface and trying popular keywords. While this works, the set we've acquired is hardly unbiased.

For one thing, we get the popular keywords from the playlists that we fetched. This does give us words that are relevant for music, but can easily increase the skewing we already have. If we end up with playlists that are disproportionately about country music then our word lists will also start to fill up with country-related words, which in turn will have us fetch more country music.

The other bias risk is that fetching playlists that contain popular words will get us popular songs. Terms like "greatest" and "hits" will occur often and cause us to get a lot of greatest hits; niche albums have less of a chance to be picked up.

15.7 Training a Music Recommender

Problem

You've fetched a large set of playlists, but how do you use them to train your music recommender system?

Solution

Use an off-the-shelf Word2vec model and treat song IDs as words.

In Chapter 3 we explored how a Word2vec model projects words into a semantic space with nice properties; similar words end up in the same neighborhood and relations between words are somewhat consistent. In Chapter 4 we used an embedding technique to build a movie recommender. In this recipe we combine both approaches. Rather than training our own model, we'll use an off-the-shelf model for Word2vec, but we'll use the results to build a recommender for music.

The gensim module we used in Chapter 3 also comes with the possibility to train a model. All it needs is an iterator that produces series of tokens. This isn't too hard since we have our playlists stored as lines in a file, with each line containing the IDs of the songs separated by spaces:

```
class WordSplitter(object):
    def __init__(self, filename):
        self.filename = filename

    def __iter__(self):
        with open(self.filename) as fin:
            for line in fin:
                yield line.split()
```

After that training the model is a single-line operation:

```
model = gensim.models.Word2Vec(model_input, min_count=4)
```

Depending on how many songs/playlists the previous recipe resulted in, this could take a while. Let's save the model for future use:

```
with open('zoo/15/songs.word2vec', 'wb') as fout:
    model.save(fout)
```

15.8 Recommending Songs Using a Word2vec Model

Problem

How do you use your model to predict songs based on an example?

Solution

Use the Word2vec distances and your SQLite3 database of songs.

The first step is to get a set of `song_ids` given a song name or part of it. The `LIKE` operator will get us a selection of songs that match the searched-for pattern. Song names, though, are hardly unique these days. Even for the same artists there are different versions around. So we need some way of scoring them. Luckily, we can use the vocab property of our model—the records in it have a *count* property. The more often a song appears in our playlists, the more likely it is that it is the song we are after (or at least the song we know most about):

```
conn = sqlite3.connect('data/songs.db')
def find_song(song_name, limit=10):
    c = conn.cursor()
    c.execute("SELECT * FROM songs WHERE UPPER(name) LIKE '%"
              + song_name + "%'")
    res = sorted((x + (model.wv.vocab[x[0]].count,)
                    for x in c.fetchall() if x[0] in model.wv.vocab),
                  key=itemgetter(-1), reverse=True)
    return [*res][:limit]

for t in find_song('the eye of the tiger'):
    print(*t)

2ZqGzZWWZXEyPxJy6N9QhG The eye of the tiger Chiara Mastroianni 39
4rrOol3zvLiEBmep7HaHtx The Eye Of The Tiger Survivor 37
0R85QWa6KRzB8p44XXE7ky The Eye of the Tiger Gloria Gaynor 29
3GxdO4rTwVfRvLRIZFXJVu The Eye of the Tiger Gloria Gaynor 19
1W602jfZkdAsbabmJEYfFi The Eye of the Tiger Gloria Gaynor 5
6g197iis9V2HP7gvc5ZpGy I Got the Eye of the Tiger Circus Roar 5
00VQxzTLqwqBBE0BuCVeer The Eye Of The Tiger Gloria Gaynor 5
28FwycRDU81YOiGgIcxcPq The Eye of the Tiger Gloria Gaynor 5
62UagxK6LuPbqUmlygGjcU It's the Eye of the Tiger Be Cult 4
6lUHKc9qrIHvkknXIrBq6d The Eye Of The Tiger Survivor 4
```

Now we can pick the song we really are after, in this case possibly the one by Survivor. Now on to suggesting songs. We let our model do the heavy lifting:

```
similar = dict(model.most_similar([song_id]))
```

Now we have a lookup table from song ID to score, which we can easily expand to a list of actual songs:

```
song_ids = ', '.join(("'%s'" % x) for x in similar.keys())
c.execute("SELECT * FROM songs WHERE id in (%s)" % song_ids)
res = sorted((rec + (similar[rec[0]],) for rec in c.fetchall()),
             key=itemgetter(-1),
             reverse=True)
```

The output for "The Eye of the Tiger" is:

```
Girls Just Wanna Have Fun Cyndi Lauper 0.9735351204872131
Enola Gay - Orchestral Manoeuvres In The Dark 0.9719518423080444
You're My Heart, You're My Soul Modern Talking 0.9589041471481323
Gold - 2003 Remastered Version Spandau Ballet 0.9566971659660339
Dolce Vita Ryan Paris 0.9553133249282837
Karma Chameleon - 2002 Remastered Version Culture Club 0.9531201720237732
Bette Davis Eyes Kim Carnes 0.9499865770339966
Walking On Sunshine Katrina & The Waves 0.9481900930404663
Maneater Daryl Hall & John Oates 0.9481032490730286
Don't You Want Me The Human League 0.9471924901008606
```

This looks like a decent mix of upbeat '80s-ish music.

Discussion

Using Word2vec is an effective way to create a song recommender. Rather than training our own model as we did in Chapter 4, we used an off-the-shelf model here from gensim. There is less tuning, but it works well since the words in a sentence and songs in a playlist are fairly comparable.

Word2vec works by trying to predict a word from its context. This prediction leads to an embedding that causes words that are similar to each other to appear near each other. Running the same process over songs in a playlist means trying to predict a song based on the context of the song in the playlist. Similar songs end up near each other in the song space.

With Word2vec it turns out that relations between words also have meaning. The vector separating the words "queen" and "princess" is similar to the vector separating "king" and "prince." It would be interesting to see if something similar can be done with songs—what is the Beatles version of "Paint It Black" by the Rolling Stones? This would, however, require us to somehow project artists into the same space.

CHAPTER 16

Productionizing Machine Learning Systems

Building and training a model is one thing; deploying your model in a production system is a different and often overlooked story. Running code in a Python notebook is nice, but not a great way to serve web clients. In this chapter we'll look at how to get up and running for real.

We'll start with embeddings. Embeddings have played a role in many of the recipes in this book. In Chapter 3, we looked at the interesting things we can do with word embeddings, like finding similar words by looking at their nearest neighbors or finding analogues by adding and subtracting embedding vectors. In Chapter 4, we used embeddings of Wikipedia articles to build a simple movie recommender system. In Chapter 10, we saw how we can treat the output of the final layer of a pretrained image classification network as embeddings for the input image and use this to build a reverse image search service.

Just as with these examples, we find that real-world cases often end with embeddings for certain entities that we then want to query from a production-quality application. In other words, we have a set of images, texts, or words and an algorithm that for each produces a vector in a high-dimensional space. For a concrete application, we want to be able to query this space.

We'll start with a simple approach: we'll build a nearest neighbor model and save it to disk, so we can load it when we need it. We'll then look at using Postgres for the same purpose.

We'll also explore using microservices as a way to expose machine learning models using Flask as a web server and Keras's ability to save and load models.

The following notebooks are available for this chapter:

```
16.1 Simple Text Generation
16.2 Prepare Keras Model for TensorFlow Serving
16.3 Prepare Model for iOS
```

16.1 Using Scikit-Learn's Nearest Neighbors for Embeddings

Problem

How do you quickly serve up the closest matches from an embedding model?

Solution

Use scikit-learn's nearest neighbor's algorithm and save the model into a file. We'll continue the code from Chapter 4, where we created a movie prediction model. After we've run everything, we normalize the values and fit a nearest neighbor model:

```
movie = model.get_layer('movie_embedding')
movie_weights = movie.get_weights()[0]
movie_lengths = np.linalg.norm(movie_weights, axis=1)
normalized_movies = (movie_weights.T / movie_lengths).T
nbrs = NearestNeighbors(n_neighbors=10, algorithm='ball_tree').fit(
    normalized_movies)
with open('data/movie_model.pkl', 'wb') as fout:
    pickle.dump({
        'nbrs': nbrs,
        'normalized_movies': normalized_movies,
        'movie_to_idx': movie_to_idx
    }, fout)
```

We can then later load the model again with:

```
with open('data/movie_model.pkl', 'rb') as fin:
    m = pickle.load(fin)
movie_names = [x[0] for x in sorted(movie_to_idx.items(),
            key=lambda t:t[1])]
distances, indices = m['nbrs'].kneighbors(
    [m['normalized_movies'][m['movie_to_idx']['Rogue One']]])
for idx in indices[0]:
    print(movie_names[idx])

Rogue One
Prometheus (2012 film)
Star Wars: The Force Awakens
Rise of the Planet of the Apes
Star Wars sequel trilogy
Man of Steel (film)
Interstellar (film)
Superman Returns
```

```
The Dark Knight Trilogy
Jurassic World
```

Discussion

The simplest way to productionize a machine learning model is to save it to disk after the training is done and then to load it up when it is needed. All major machine learning frameworks support this, including the ones we've used throughout this book, Keras and scikit-learn.

This solution is great if you are in control of memory management. In a production web server this is often not the case, however, and when you have to load a large model into memory when a web request comes in, latency obviously suffers.

16.2 Use Postgres to Store Embeddings

Problem

You'd like to use Postgres to store embeddings.

Solution

Use the Postgres Cube extension.

The Cube extension allows for the handling of high-dimensional data, but it needs to be enabled first:

```
CREATE EXTENSION cube;
```

Once that is done, we can create a table and corresponding index. To make it also possible to search on movie names, we'll create a text index on the movie_name field, too:

```
DROP TABLE IF EXISTS movie;
CREATE TABLE movie (
            movie_name TEXT PRIMARY KEY,
            embedding FLOAT[] NOT NULL DEFAULT '{}'
);
CREATE INDEX movie_embedding ON movie USING gin(embedding);
CREATE INDEX movie_movie_name_pattern
    ON movie USING btree(lower(movie_name) text_pattern_ops);
```

Discussion

Postgres is a free database that is remarkably powerful, not least because of the large number of extensions that are available. One of those modules is the cube module. As the name suggests, it was originally meant to make 3-dimensional coordinates available as a primitive, but it has since been extended to index arrays up to 100 dimensions.

Postgres has many extensions that are well worth exploring for anybody handling sizeable amounts of data. In particular, the ability to store less-structured data in the form of arrays and JSON documents inside of classical SQL tables comes in handy when prototyping.

16.3 Populating and Querying Embeddings Stored in Postgres

Problem

Can you store our model and query results in Postgres?

Solution

Use `psycopg2` to connect to Postgres from Python.

Given a username/password/database/host combination we can easily connect to Postgres using Python:

```
connection_str = "dbname='%s' user='%s' password='%s' host='%s'"
conn = psycopg2.connect(connection_str % (DB_NAME, USER, PWD, HOST))
```

Inserting our previously built model works like any other SQL operation in Python, except that we need to cast our numpy array to a Python list:

```
with conn.cursor() as cursor:
    for movie, embedding in zip(movies, normalized_movies):
        cursor.execute('INSERT INTO movie (movie_name, embedding)'
                       ' VALUES (%s, %s)',
                (movie[0], embedding.tolist()))
conn.commit()
```

Once this is done, we can query the values. In this case we take (part of) a title of a movie, find the best match for that movie, and return the most similar movies:

```
def recommend_movies(conn, q):
    with conn.cursor() as cursor:
        cursor.execute('SELECT movie_name, embedding FROM movie'
                       '     WHERE lower(movie_name) LIKE %s'
                       '     LIMIT 1',
                       ('%' + q.lower() + '%',))
        if cursor.rowcount == 0:
            return []
        movie_name, embedding = cursor.fetchone()
        cursor.execute('SELECT movie_name, '
                       '          cube_distance(cube(embedding), '
                       '                    cube(%s)) as distance '
```

```
             '    FROM movie'
             '    ORDER BY distance'
             '    LIMIT 5',
            (embedding,))
        return list(cursor.fetchall())
```

Discussion

Storing an embedding model in a Postgres database allows us to query it directly, without having to load the model up on every request, and is therefore a good solution when we want to use such a model from a web server—especially when our web setup was Postgres-based to begin with, of course.

Running a model or the results of a model on the database server that is powering your website has the added advantage that you can seamlessly mix ranking components. We could easily extend the code of this recipe to include the Rotten Tomatoes ratings in our movies table, from which point on we could use this information to help sort the returned movies. However, if the ratings and similarity distance come from a different source, we would either have to do an in-memory join by hand or return incomplete results.

16.4 Storing High-Dimensional Models in Postgres

Problem

How do you store a model with more than 100 dimensions in Postgres?

Solution

Use a dimension reduction technique.

Let's say we wanted to load Google's pretrained Word2vec model that we used in Chapter 3 into Postgres. Since the Postgres cube extension (see Recipe 16.2) limits the number of dimensions it will index to 100, we need to do something to make this fit. Reducing the dimensionality using singular value decomposition (SVD)—a technique we met in Recipe 10.4—is a good option. Let's load up the Word2vec model as before:

```
model = gensim.models.KeyedVectors.load_word2vec_format(
    MODEL, binary=True)
```

The normalized vectors per word are stored in the syn0norm property, so we can run the SVD over that. This does take a little while:

```
svd = TruncatedSVD(n_components=100, random_state=42,
                   n_iter=40)
reduced = svd.fit_transform(model.syn0norm)
```

We need to renormalize the vectors:

```
reduced_lengths = np.linalg.norm(reduced, axis=1)
normalized_reduced = reduced.T / reduced_lengths).T
```

Now we can look at the similarity:

```
def most_similar(norm, positive):
    vec = norm[model.vocab[positive].index]
    dists = np.dot(norm, vec)
    most_extreme = np.argpartition(-dists, 10)[:10]
    res = ((model.index2word[idx], dists[idx]) for idx in most_extreme)
    return list(sorted(res, key=lambda t:t[1], reverse=True))
for word, score in most_similar(normalized_reduced, 'espresso'):
    print(word, score)

espresso 1.0
cappuccino 0.856463080029
chai_latte 0.835657488972
latte 0.800340435865
macchiato 0.798796776324
espresso_machine 0.791469456128
Lavazza_coffee 0.790783985201
mocha 0.788645681469
espressos 0.78424218748
martini 0.784037414689
```

The results still look reasonable, but they are not exactly the same. The last entry, martini, is somewhat unexpected in a list of caffeinated pick-me-ups.

Discussion

The Postgres cube extension is great, but comes with the caveat that it only works for vectors that have 100 or fewer elements. The documentation helpfully explains this limitation with: "To make it harder for people to break things, there is a limit of 100 on the number of dimensions of cubes." One way around this restriction is to recompile Postgres, but that's only an option if you directly control your setup. Also, it requires you to keep doing this as new versions of the database come out.

Reducing the dimensionality before inserting our vectors into the database can easily be done using the TruncatedSVD class. In this recipe we used the entire set of words from the Word2vec dataset, which led to the loss of some precision. If we not only reduce the dimensionality of the output but also cut down the number of terms, we can do better. SVD can then find the most important dimensions for the data that we provide, rather than for all the data. This can even help by generalizing a bit and papering over a lack of data in our original input.

16.5 Writing Microservices in Python

Problem

You'd like to write and deploy a simple Python microservice.

Solution

Build a minimal web app using Flask, returning a JSON document based on a REST request.

First we need a Flask web server:

```
app = Flask(__name__)
```

We then define the service we want to offer. As an example, we'll take in an image and return the size of the image. We expect the image to be part of a POST request. If we don't get a POST request, we'll return a simple HTML form so we can test the service without a client. The @app.route decoration specifies that the return_size handles any requests at the root, supporting both GET and POST:

```
@app.route('/', methods=['GET', 'POST'])
def return_size():
  if request.method == 'POST':
    file = request.files['file']
    if file:
      image = Image.open(file)
      width, height = image.size
      return jsonify(results={'width': width, 'height': height})
  return '''
  <h1>Upload new File</h1>
  <form action="" method=post enctype=multipart/form-data>
    <p><input type=file name=file>
      <input type=submit value=Upload>
  </form>
  '''
```

Now all we have to do is run the server at a port:

```
app.run(port=5050, host='0.0.0.0')
```

Discussion

REST was originally meant as a full-blown resource management framework that assigns URLs to all resources in a system and then lets clients interact with the whole spectrum of HTTP verbs, from PUT to DELETE. Like many APIs out there, we forego all that in this example and just have a GET method defined on one handler that triggers our API and returns a JSON document.

The service we developed here is of course rather trivial; having a microservice for just getting the size of an image is probably taking the concept a little too far. In the next recipe we'll explore how we can use this approach to serve up the results of a previously developed machine learning model.

16.6 Deploying a Keras Model Using a Microservice

Problem

You want to deploy a Keras model as a standalone service.

Solution

Expand your Flask server to forward requests to a pretrained Keras model.

This recipe builds on the recipes in Chapter 10, where we downloaded thousands of images from Wikipedia and fed them into a pretrained image recognition network, getting back a 2,048-dimensional vector describing each image. We'll fit a nearest neighbor model on these vectors so that we can quickly find the most similar image, given a vector.

The first step is to load the pickled image names and nearest neighbor model and instantiate the pretrained model for image recognition:

```
with open('data/image_similarity.pck', 'rb') as fin:
    p = pickle.load(fin)
    image_names = p['image_names']
    nbrs = p['nbrs']
base_model = InceptionV3(weights='imagenet', include_top=True)
model = Model(inputs=base_model.input,
              outputs=base_model.get_layer('avg_pool').output)
```

We can now modify how we handle the incoming image by changing the bit of code after if file:. We'll resize the image to the target size of the model, normalize the data, run the prediction, and find the nearest neighbors:

```
img = Image.open(file)
target_size = int(max(model.input.shape[1:]))
img = img.resize((target_size, target_size), Image.ANTIALIAS)
pre_processed = preprocess_input(
    np.asarray([image.img_to_array(img)]))
vec = model.predict(pre_processed)
distances, indices = nbrs.kneighbors(vec)
res = [{'distance': dist,
        'image_name': image_names[idx]}
       for dist, idx in zip(distances[0], indices[0])]
return jsonify(results=res)
```

Feed it an image of a cat, and you should see a large number of cats sampled from the Wikipedia images—with one photo of kids playing with a home computer thrown in.

Discussion

By loading the model on startup and then feeding in the images as they come in, we can cut down on the latency that we would get if we followed the approach of the first recipe in this section. We're effectively chaining two models here, the pretrained image recognition network and the nearest neighbor classifier, and exporting the combination as one service.

16.7 Calling a Microservice from a Web Framework

Problem

You want to call a microservice from Django.

Solution

Use `requests` to call the microservice while handling the Django request. We can do this along the lines of the following example:

```
def simple_view(request):
    d = {}
    update_date(request, d)
    if request.FILES.get('painting'):
        data = request.FILES['painting'].read()
        files = {'file': data}
        reply = requests.post('http://localhost:5050',
                              files=files).json()
        res = reply['results']
        if res:
            d['most_similar'] = res[0]['image_name']
    return render(request, 'template_path/template.html', d)
```

Discussion

The code here is from a Django request handler, but things should look really similar in other web frameworks, even ones based on a different language than Python.

The key thing here is that we separate the session management of the web framework from the session management of our microservice. This way we know that at any given time there is exactly one instance of our model, which makes latency and memory use predictable.

`Requests` is a straightforward module for making HTTP calls. It doesn't support making async calls, though. In the code for this recipe that isn't important, but if we need to call multiple services, we'd want to do that in parallel. There are a number of options for this, but they all fall into the pattern where we fire off calls to the backends at the beginning of our request, do the processing we need to, and then, when we need the results, wait on the outstanding requests. This is a good setup for building high-performance systems using Python.

16.8 TensorFlow seq2seq models

Problem

How do you productionize a seq2seq chat model?

Solution

Run a TensorFlow session with an output-capturing hook.

The seq2seq model that Google published is a very nice way to quickly develop sequence-to-sequence models, but out of the box the inference phase can only be run using stdin and stdout. It's entirely possible to call out from our microservice this way, but that means we'll incur the latency cost of loading the model up on every call.

A better way is to instantiate the model manually and capture the output using a hook. The first step is to reinstate the model from the checkpoint directory. We need to load both the model and the model configuration. The model feeds in the source_tokens (i.e., the chat prompt) and we'll use a batch size of 1, since we'll do this in an interactive fashion:

```
checkpoint_path = tf.train.latest_checkpoint(model_path)
train_options = training_utils.TrainOptions.load(model_path)
model_cls = locate(train_options.model_class) or \
  getattr(models, train_options.model_class)
model_params = train_options.model_params
model = model_cls(
    params=model_params,
    mode=tf.contrib.learn.ModeKeys.INFER)
source_tokens_ph = tf.placeholder(dtype=tf.string, shape=(1, None))
source_len_ph = tf.placeholder(dtype=tf.int32, shape=(1,))
model(
  features={
    "source_tokens": source_tokens_ph,
    "source_len": source_len_ph
  },
  labels=None,
  params={
  }
)
```

The next step is to set up the TensorFlow session that allows us to feed data into the model. This is all fairly boilerplate stuff (and should make us appreciate frameworks like Keras even more):

```
saver = tf.train.Saver()
def _session_init_op(_scaffold, sess):
    saver.restore(sess, checkpoint_path)
    tf.logging.info("Restored model from %s", checkpoint_path)
scaffold = tf.train.Scaffold(init_fn=_session_init_op)
session_creator = tf.train.ChiefSessionCreator(scaffold=scaffold)
sess = tf.train.MonitoredSession(
    session_creator=session_creator,
    hooks=[DecodeOnce({}, callback_func=_save_prediction_to_dict)])
return sess, source_tokens_ph, source_len_pht
```

We've now configured a TensorFlow session with a hook to DecodeOnce, which is a class that implements the basic functionality of the inference task but then, when it is done, calls the provided callback function to return the actual results.

In the code for *seq2seq_server.py* we can then use this to handle an HTTP request as follows:

```
@app.route('/', methods=['GET'])
def handle_request():
  input = request.args.get('input', '')
  if input:
    tf.reset_default_graph()
    source_tokens = input.split() + ["SEQUENCE_END"]
    session.run([], {
        source_tokens_ph: [source_tokens],
        source_len_ph: [len(source_tokens)]
      })
    return prediction_dict.pop(_tokens_to_str(source_tokens))
```

This will let us handle seq2seq calls from a simple web server.

Discussion

The way we feed data into the seq2seq TensorFlow model in this recipe is not very pretty, but it is effective and in terms of performance a much better option than using stdin and stdout. Hopefully an upcoming version of this library will provide us with a nicer way to use these models in production, but for now this will have to do.

16.9 Running Deep Learning Models in the Browser

Problem

How do you run a deep learning web app without a server?

Solution

Use Keras.js to run the model in the browser.

Running a deep learning model in the browser sounds crazy. Deep learning needs lots of processing power, and we all know that JavaScript is slow. But it turns out that you can run models in the browser at a decent speed with GPU acceleration. Keras.js (*https://transcranial.github.io/keras-js/#*) has a tool to convert Keras models to something that the JavaScript runtime can work with, and it uses WebGL to get the GPU to help with this. It's an amazing bit of engineering and it comes with some impressive demos. Let's try this on one of our own models.

The notebook `16.1 Simple Text Generation` is taken from the Keras example directory and trains a simple text generation model based on the writings of Nietzsche. After training we save the model with:

```
model.save('keras_js/nietzsche.h5')
with open('keras_js/chars.js', 'w') as fout:
    fout.write('maxlen = ' + str(maxlen) + '\n')
    fout.write('num_chars = ' + str(len(chars)) + '\n')
    fout.write('char_indices = ' + json.dumps(char_indices, indent=2) + '\n')
    fout.write('indices_char = ' + json.dumps(indices_char, indent=2) + '\n')
```

Now we need to convert the Keras model to the Keras.js format. First get the conversion code using:

```
git clone https://github.com/transcranial/keras-js.git
```

Now open a shell and, in the directory where you saved the model, execute:

```
python <git-root>/keras-js/python/encoder.py nietzsche.h5
```

This should give you a *nietzsche.bin* file.

The next step is to use this file from a web page.

We'll do this in the file *nietzsche.html*, which you'll find in the *keras_js* directory of the *deep_learning_cookbook* repository. Let's take a look. It starts with code to load the Keras.js library and the variables we saved from Python:

```
<script src="https://unpkg.com/keras-js"></script>
<script src="chars.js"></script>
```

At the bottom we have a very simple bit of HTML that lets the user enter some text and then press a button to run the model to extend the text in a Nietzschean way:

```
<textarea cols="60" rows="4" id="textArea">
    i am all for progress, it is
</textarea><br/>
<button onclick="runModel(250)" disabled id="buttonGo">Go!</button>
```

Now let's load the model and, when it's done, enable the currently disabled button `buttonGo`:

```
const model = new KerasJS.Model({
    filepath: 'sayings.bin',
    gpu: true
})

model.ready().then(() => {
    document.getElementById("buttonGo").disabled = false
})
```

In `runModel` we first need to one-hot encode the text data using the `char_indices` we imported before:

```
function encode(st) {
    var x = new Float32Array(num_chars * st.length);
    for(var i = 0; i < st.length; i++) {
        idx = char_indices[ch = st[i]];
        x[idx + i * num_chars] = 1;
    }
    return x;
};
```

We can now run the model with:

```
return model.predict(inputData).then(outputData => {
    ...
    ...
})
```

The `outputData` variable will contain a probability distribution for each of the characters in our vocabulary. The easiest way to make sense of that is to pick just the character with the highest probability:

```
var maxIdx = -1;
var maxVal = 0.0;
for (var idx = 0; idx < output.length; idx ++) {
    if (output[idx] > maxVal) {
        maxVal = output[idx];
        maxIdx = idx;
    }
}
```

Now we just add that character to what we had so far and do the same thing again:

```
var nextChar = indices_char["" + maxIdx];
document.getElementById("textArea").value += nextChar;
if (steps > 0) {
    runModel(steps - 1);
}
```

Discussion

Being able to run models straight in the browser creates entirely new possibilities for productionalizing. It means you don't need a server to do the actual calculations, and with WebGL you even get GPU acceleration for free. Check out the fun demos at *https://transcranial.github.io/keras-js*.

There are limitations to this approach. To use the GPU, Keras.js uses WebGL 2.0. Unfortunately, not all browsers support this at the moment. Moreover, tensors are encoded as WebGL textures, which are limited in size. The actual limit depends on your browser and hardware. You can of course fall back to CPU only, but that means running in pure JavaScript.

A second limitation is the size of the models. Production-quality models often have sizes of tens of megabytes, which isn't a problem at all when they are loaded up once on the server but might create issues when they need to be sent to a client.

 The *encoder.py* script has a flag called `--quantize` that will encode the weights of the model as 8-bit integers. This reduces the size of the model by 75%, but it means the weights will be less precise, which might hurt prediction accuracy.

16.10 Running a Keras Model Using TensorFlow Serving

Problem

How do you run a Keras model using Google's state-of-the art server?

Solution

Convert the model and invoke the TensorFlow Serving toolkit to write out the model spec so you can run it using TensorFlow Serving.

TensorFlow Serving is part of the TensorFlow platform; according to Google it's a flexible, high-performance serving system for machine learning models, designed for production environments.

Writing out a TensorFlow model in a way that TensorFlow Serving will work with is somewhat involved. Keras models need even more massaging in order for this to work. In principle, any model can be used as long as the model has only one input and only one output—a restriction that comes with TensorFlow Serving. Another is that TensorFlow Serving only supports Python 2.7.

The first thing to do is recreate the model as a testing-only model. Models behave differently during training and testing. For example, the `Dropout` layer only randomly drops neurons while training—during testing everything is used. Keras hides this from the user, passing the learning phase in as an extra variable. If you see errors stating that something is missing from your input, this is probably it. We'll set the learning phase to 0 (false) and extract the config and the weights from our character CNN model:

```
K.set_learning_phase(0)
char_cnn = load_model('zoo/07.2 char_cnn_model.h5')
config = char_cnn.get_config()
if not 'config' in config:
    config = {'config': config,
              'class_name': 'Model'}

weights = char_cnn.get_weights()
```

At this point it might be useful to run a prediction on the model so we can later see that it still works:

```
tweet = ("There's a house centipede in my closet and "
         "since Ryan isn't here I have to kill it....")
encoded = np.zeros((1, max_sequence_len, len(char_to_idx)))
for idx, ch in enumerate(tweet):
    encoded[0, idx, char_to_idx[ch]] = 1

res = char_cnn.predict(encoded)
emojis[np.argmax(res)]

u'\ude03'
```

We can then rebuild the model with:

```
new_model = model_from_config(config)
new_model.set_weights(weights)
```

In order for the model to run, we need to provide TensorFlow Serving with the input and output spec:

```
input_info = utils.build_tensor_info(new_model.inputs[0])
output_info = utils.build_tensor_info(new_model.outputs[0])
prediction_signature = signature_def_utils.build_signature_def(
        inputs={'input': input_info},
        outputs={'output': output_info},
        method_name=signature_constants.PREDICT_METHOD_NAME)
```

We can then construct the `builder` object to define our handler and write out the definition:

```
outpath = 'zoo/07.2 char_cnn_model.tf_model/1'
shutil.rmtree(outpath)

legacy_init_op = tf.group(tf.tables_initializer(), name='legacy_init_op')
builder = tf.saved_model.builder.SavedModelBuilder(outpath)
builder.add_meta_graph_and_variables(
        sess, [tf.saved_model.tag_constants.SERVING],
        signature_def_map={
            'emoji_suggest': prediction_signature,
        },
```

```
        legacy_init_op=legacy_init_op)
    builder.save()
```

Now we run the server with:

```
tensorflow_model_server \
    --model_base_path="char_cnn_model.tf_model/" \
    --model_name="char_cnn_model"
```

You can either get the binaries directly from Google or build them from source—see the installation instructions (*https://www.tensorflow.org/serving/setup*) for details.

Let's see if we can call the model from Python. We'll instantiate a prediction request and use grpc to make a call:

```
request = predict_pb2.PredictRequest()
request.model_spec.name = 'char_cnn_model'
request.model_spec.signature_name = 'emoji_suggest'
request.inputs['input'].CopyFrom(tf.contrib.util.make_tensor_proto(
    encoded.astype('float32'), shape=[1, max_sequence_len, len(char_to_idx)]))

channel = implementations.insecure_channel('localhost', 8500)
stub = prediction_service_pb2.beta_create_PredictionService_stub(channel)
result = stub.Predict(request, 5)
```

Get the actual predicted emojis:

```
response = np.array(result.outputs['output'].float_val)
prediction = np.argmax(response)
emojis[prediction]
```

Discussion

TensorFlow Serving is the way to productionize models blessed by Google but using it with a Keras model is somewhat involved compared to bringing up a custom Flask server and handling the input and output ourselves.

It does have advantages, though. For one thing, since is not custom, these servers all behave the same. Furthermore, it is an industrial-strength server that supports versioning and can load models straight from a number of cloud providers.

16.11 Using a Keras Model from iOS

Problem

You'd like to use a model trained on the desktop from a mobile app on iOS.

Solution

Use CoreML to convert your model and talk to it directly from Swift.

This recipe describes how to build an app for iOS, so you'll need a Mac with Xcode installed to run the example. Moreover, since the example uses the camera for detection, you'll also need an iOS device with a camera to try it out.

The first thing to do is to convert the model. Unfortunately Apple's code only supports Python 2.7 and also seems to lag a bit when it comes to supporting the latest versions of `tensorflow` and `keras`, so we'll set specific versions. Open a shell to set up Python 2.7 with the right requirements and type in:

```
virtualenv venv2
source venv2/bin/activate
pip install coremltools
pip install h5py
pip install keras==2.0.6
pip install tensorflow==1.2.1
```

Then start Python and enter:

```
from keras.models import load_model
import coremltools
```

Load the previously saved model and the labels:

```
keras_model = load_model('zoo/09.3 retrained pet recognizer.h5')
class_labels = json.load(open('zoo/09.3 pet_labels.json'))
```

Then convert the model:

```
coreml_model = coremltools.converters.keras.convert(
    keras_model,
    image_input_names="input_1",
    class_labels=class_labels,
    image_scale=1/255.)
coreml_model.save('zoo/PetRecognizer.mlmodel')
```

You could also skip this and work with the *.mlmodel* file in the *zoo* directory.

Now start Xcode, create a new project, and drag the *PetRecognizer.mlmodel* file to the project. Xcode automatically imports the model and makes it callable. Let's recognize some pets!

Apple has an example project on its website (*https://apple.co/2HPUHOW*) that uses a standard image recognition network. Download this project, unzip it, and then open it with Xcode.

In the project overview, you should see a file called *MobileNet.mlmodel*. Delete that and then drag the *PetRecognizer.mlmodel* file to where *MobileNet.mlmodel* used to be. Now open *ImageClassificationViewController.swift* and replace any occurences of `MobileNet` with `PetRecognizer`.

You should now be able to run the app as before, but with the new model and output classes.

Discussion

Using a Keras model from an iOS app is surprisingly simple, at least if we stick to the examples that Apple's SDK ships with. The technology is quite recent though, and there are not a lot of working examples out there that are radically different from Apple's examples. Moreover, CoreML only works on Apple operating systems, and then only on iOS 11 or higher or macOS 10.13 or higher.

Index

datasets, exploring with Pandas, 75
deep dreaming, 149-152
deep learning, brief history of, vii
denoising autoencoder, 165
dialogue, extracting from texts, 105
dimension reduction, 213
discriminator network, 10, 183
Django, calling microservice from, 217
Dropout layer, 222
dropout technique
    correcting overfitting with, 31, 93
    improving emoji suggester performance
        with, 92-94

E

embeddings
    defined, 22
    populating/querying, 212
    storing with Postgres, 211
    using scikit-learn nearest neighbor algo-
        rithm for, 210
    Word2vec model, 35
emojis, suggesting, 83-102
    collecting Twitter data for model training,
        89-91
    combining models, 101-102
    constructing your own embeddings, 96-97
    increasing performance with dropout/
        multiple windows, 92-94
    sentiment classifier for, 83-87
    simple emoji predictor, 91
    using a convolutional network for sentiment
        analysis, 87-89
    using an RNN for classification, 97-99
    visualizing comparisons of different models,
        99
    word-level model for, 94
ensemble model, 101-102
entity classes, 41-45
exploding gradient problem, 65

F

Facebook API, as data source, 17
Faster RCNN
    finding multiple objects in image, 137-139
    training a pretrained model, 139-141
feature vectors, 76
filter, defined, 5
Firehose API, 13

fit method (Keras), 19
Flask, 215
Flickr API, 14
    collecting a set of labeled images with, 117
    improving image search results from, 120
fully connected layer, defined, 2
fully connected networks, 2-5
function method (Keras), 69

G

generative adversarial networks (GANs)
    building, 183-184
    showing icons produced by, 186-188
    training, 185
generator network, 10, 183
gensim package, 36, 96, 206
GeoPandas, 47
getting unstuck, 25-33
Google Quick Draw, 162
government websites, as data source, 17
GPU (graphics processing units), viii
    tensorflow-gpu and, x
    training and batch size, 33
    WebGL and, 220
gram matrix
    calculating for convolutional layers of an
        image, 152-155
    for capturing image styles, 152-155

H

hidden layers, defined, 4
high-dimensional models, storing in Postgres,
    213
high-dimensional space, finding nearest neigh-
    bors in, 129
hyperbolic tangent (tanh) function, 2, 30
hyperparameter, 28
hyperparameter tuning, 93

I

icon generation
    acquiring icons for training, 176-178
    building a GAN for, 183-184
    converting icons to tensor representation,
        178
    deep nets for, 175-192
    encoding icons as drawing instructions, 188

showing the icons produced by GAN, 186-188

training a GAN for, 185

training an RNN for, 189-190

using data augmentation to improve autoencoders performance, 181

variational autoencoder for, 179-181

with an RNN, 191

Icons8, 176-178

image coherence, 155

image generation

    autoencoder creation for, 163-165

    autoencoders for, 161-174

    conditional variational autoencoders for, 172-174

    importing drawings from Google Quick Draw, 162

    sampling images from a correct distribution, 167-170

    visualizing a variational autoencoder space, 170

    visualizing autoencoder results, 166

image processing

    and activation function, 30

    building an inverse image search service, 125-132

    detecting multiple images, 133-141

        (see also multiple images, detecting)

    Flickr as data source, 14

    generating icons with deep nets, 175-192

    generating images with autoencoders, 161-174

    image style, 143-159

    multiple image classes in single image, 133-141

    preprocessing, 22

    projecting into an n-dimensional space, 128

    reusing a pretrained image recognition network, 113-124

image recognition network

    building a classifier that can tell cats from dogs, 118-120

    improving search results, 120

    loading a pretrained network, 114

    preprocessing images, 114-116

    removing outliers from set of images, 120

    retraining for specialized images, 122-124

    reusing of pretrained network, 113-124

    running inference on images, 116

using Flickr API to collect a set of labeled images, 117

image style, 143-159

    applying captured style, 156

    capturing, 152-155

    exaggeration of what a network sees, 149-152

    improving loss function to increase image coherence, 155

    interpolation, 158

    octaves and scaling, 147

    visualizing CNN activations, 144-147

ImageDataGenerator class, 23

inference, running, 116

Internet Archive, 15

interpolation of image style, 158

inverse image search service, 125-132

    acquiring images from Wikipedia, 125-127

    exploring local neighborhoods in embeddings, 130-132

    finding nearest neighbors in high-dimensional spaces, 129

    projecting images into an n-dimensional space, 128

iOS, using a Keras model from, 224-226

K

k-nearest neighbors algorithm, 129, 210

Keras

    creating data batches with fit method, 19

    creating feature vectors from text, 76

    deploying model using a microservice, 216

    function method, 69

    ImageDataGenerator class, 23

    loading pretrained image recognition network with, 114

    predicting values for question matching, 80-82

    running a model using TensorFlow Serving toolkit, 222-224

    solving runtime errors, 27

    using a model trained on the desktop from a mobile app on iOS, 224-226

Keras.js, 220-222

kernel, defined, 5

Kullback-Leibler divergence, 167

L

latent representation, 165

latent space, visualizing diversity of images generated from, 170
layers, 1, 4
learning rate, optimizing, 33
linear activation function, 30
linear regression model, 57-59
long short-term memory network (LSTM), 8, 98
loss function
    applying captured style, 156
    image style interpolation, 158
    improving to increase image coherence, 155
    network troubleshooting and, 26
    question/answer model and, 78
LSTM (long short-term memory network), 8, 98

M
machine learning systems, productionizing (see productionizing of machine learning systems)
maps, visualizing country data on, 47
max pooling, 6, 89
mean squared error, 78
melspectrograms, 194
microservices
    calling from a web framework, 217
    for deploying a Keras model, 216
    writing/deploying in Python, 215
Minsky, Marvin, vii
MLP (multilayer perceptron) model, vii
model training
    chatbot based on seq2seq framework, 108-111
    for GANs, 185
    for movie embeddings, 53-56
    for music genre detector, 196-198
    for music recommender system, 206
    for word embeddings, 96-97
    of pretrained Faster RCNN model, 139-141
    of RNN to draw icons, 189-190
    to reverse engineer a transformation, 103-105
    with Pandas, 79
models
    networks vs., 2
    pretrained (see pretrained models)
movie recommender system
    based on outgoing Wikipedia links, 49-59

building a system based on embeddings, 56
predicting simple movie properties, 57-59
training data collection, 49-52
training movie embeddings, 53-56
multilayer perceptron (MLP) model, vii
multiple images, detecting, 133-141
    pretrained classifier for, 133-137
    training a pretrained Faster RCNN model, 139-141
    using Faster RCNN for object detection, 137-139
music, 193-208
music classification
    graphic display of confusion matrix, 198
    indexing existing music, 199-201
    training a music genre detector, 196-198
    training set creation for, 194-196
music recommender system, 202-208
    collecting playlists and songs from Spotify, 203-205
    recommending songs with Word2vec model, 206-208
    setting up Spotify API access, 202
    training from playlists, 206

N
n-dimensional space, projecting images into, 128
naive Bayes classification, 84-86
nearest neighbors, 129
    (see also k-nearest neighbors algorithm)
    for music classification, 201
network
    defined, 1
    model vs., 2
network structure, optimizing, 32
neural networks (generally)
    origins, vii
    types of, 1-11
        (see also specific types, e.g., convolutional neural networks)
neurons
    extracting activations from, 69-71
    maximizing activation of, 144-147
    visualizing recurrent network activations, 69-71
nodes, map, 13
normalization, 23, 30

About the Author

Douwe Osinga is an experienced software engineer, formerly with Google, and founder of three startups. He maintains a popular software project website, partly focused on machine learning (*https://douweosinga.com/projects/machine_learning*).

Colophon

The animal on the cover of *Deep Learning Cookbook* is a common loon or great northern diver (*Gavia immer*). It can be found near remote freshwater lakes of the northern US and Canada, as well as in southern parts of Greenland, Iceland, Norway, and Alaska.

During the summer breeding season, the adult's plumage has an aristocratic flair; its head and neck are black with an iridescent sheen, its back is spotted black and white, and its breast is white. In winter and during migration, its plumage changes to plain gray on the back and head with a white throat. The common loon is seasonally monogamous; pairs form and stay together for the breeding season and separate when they migrate in winter. The female lays two eggs once a year. The young leave the nest within 1–2 days after hatching and are capable of flight within 10–11 weeks.

The loon is built to be a powerhouse swimmer because its webbed feet are set far back on its body—yet this inherited variation hampers its mobility on land. With barely a splash it slips beneath the water's surface to forage for food. Its diet mainly consists of small fish, with an occasional crustacean or frog. It is solitary during feeding but gathers in flocks at night.

The loon symbolizes the wilderness of the north; its yodeling call is a characteristic sound of early summer in the north woods.

Many of the animals on O'Reilly covers are endangered; all of them are important to the world. To learn more about how you can help, go to *animals.oreilly.com*.

The cover image is from *British Birds*. The cover fonts are URW Typewriter and Guardian Sans. The text font is Adobe Minion Pro; the heading font is Adobe Myriad Condensed; and the code font is Dalton Maag's Ubuntu Mono.

Milton Keynes UK
Ingram Content Group UK Ltd.
UKHW051822120924
448259UK00007B/99

9 781491 995846